PRAISE FOR
The Vertical Veg Guide to Container Gardening

'Food deserts and the associated human health concerns that exist in urban environments belie the costs of a failing food system. Growing fresh and nutritious produce in the city is a most important aspect of any food quality discussion. *Vertical Veg* provides ideas and guidance for the individual to create "a green oasis in a concrete space". A simple pot of soil can support tasty herbs, salad greens and more. Mark Ridsdill Smith shows us how to take these ideas to the limits of available space, both his and his neighbors. These actions are infectious and inclusive – nourishing the body, nurturing the soul and connecting the community.'

Nigel Palmer, author of *The Regenerative Grower's Guide to Garden Amendments*

'I love the image of many small urban gardens growing in containers – so useful and beautiful where water is available. There is a lot of good information in this book, whether you intend to make a container garden or sow plants in the ground. I know it will be a good guide for this (non-urban) gardener for years to come.'

Deborah Madison, author of *An Onion in My Pocket* and *Vegetable Literacy*

'Mark has eliminated every excuse – you can garden wherever you live, without exception. He goes further than just salad greens by outlining a plan for most vegetables known to gardening. Despite the dedication, I contend that it will be as beneficial to those who want to container garden in the suburbs and the countryside as well as in the concrete jungle! We all are better off with this book. This book is detailed with many creative pointers gleaned from his years of experience container gardening. Fun to read.'

Peter Burke, author of *Year-Round Indoor Salad Gardening*

'Mark's enthusiasm is infectious and together with his attention to often-overlooked details, will give you confidence and knowledge to grow an impressive amount of food in seriously small spaces, where you probably thought you could not! He has been practising what he preaches for a long time and continually refines his methods, to be able to share with you many effective ways to harvest fresh vegetables throughout the year.'

Charles Dowding, author of *Skills for Growing* and *No Dig Gardening*

'The impression that the fine art of gardening can be achieved only by those with large amounts of space is slowly and surely becoming disproved. Mark's container gardening book deals another major blow to that myth with a comprehensive guide, both practical and scientific, to growing edibles without the need for open ground. With many people in urban areas now living in flats, whose outdoor access is limited to balconies or small community areas, this book lays out with thorough advice how to garden in container conditions and how to enjoy the social, physical, and mental benefits of gardening with the massive bonus of having access to fresh food. What I most love about this book is that it is entirely based around Mark's practical experiences – he is a container gardener to his soul, and whether you are an experienced gardener or just starting out, it is the perfect launch to your endeavours.'

Chris Collins, TV presenter and head of horticulture at Garden Organic

'If you want bumper harvests from brick walls and block paving, this book shows you how. A cornucopia of sage advice and cunning tips, it's verbal fertiliser for your growing plans. But small space gardening is also about people, and Mark's considerate humanity blooms in every chapter.'

Tom Heap, BBC *Countryfile*

'Mark has filled this book with so many insights from years of first-hand trial-and-error and building a real green community around growing food in challenging situations. I hope it inspires an army of urban vegetable growers to make the most of their outside spaces – I couldn't put this down.'

Sian Berry, Green Party member of the London Assembly

'Like all the best educators Mark is an excellent storyteller, and his enthusiasm and personal commitment shine from every page....

'On a practical level this book details every important aspect of how to succeed growing in containers. From composting to watering, propagation to plant choices, there are detailed investigations and recommendations....

'Don't be fooled by the "good for beginners" intro. The depth of research and recording and the factual guidance is as good as it gets. This is a masterwork for all gardeners to enjoy – even the most experienced.'

Graham Bell, author, practicing gardener, teacher of permaculture

The Vertical Veg
Guide to Container Gardening

The Vertical Veg

Guide to Container Gardening

How to grow an abundance of

herbs, vegetables and fruit in small spaces

MARK RIDSDILL SMITH

Chelsea Green Publishing

White River Junction, Vermont

London, UK

Commissioning Editor: Jonathan Rae
Project Manager: Patricia Stone
Developmental Editor: Muna Reyal
Copy Editor: Caroline West
Proofreader: Anne Sheasby
Indexer: Nancy Crompton
Designer: Melissa Jacobson

Printed in the United States of America.
First printing March 2022.
10 9 8 7 6 5 4 3 2 1   22 23 24 25 26

Our Commitment to Green Publishing

Chelsea Green sees publishing as a tool for cultural change and ecological stewardship. We strive to align our book
manufacturing practices with our editorial mission and to reduce the impact of our business enterprise in the
environment. We print our books and catalogs on chlorine-free recycled paper, using vegetable-based inks
whenever possible. This book may cost slightly more because it was printed on paper that contains recycled fiber,
and we hope you'll agree that it's worth it. *The Vertical Veg Guide to Container Gardening* was printed on paper
supplied by Versa that is made of recycled materials and other controlled sources.

Library of Congress Cataloging-in-Publication Data
Names: Ridsdill Smith, Mark, 1965– author.
Title: The Vertical Veg guide to container gardening : how to grow an abundance of herbs, vegetables
   and fruit in small spaces / Mark Ridsdill Smith
Other titles: How to grow an abundance of herbs, vegetables and fruit in small spaces
Description: White River Junction, Vermont : Chelsea Green Publishing, 2022. | Includes index.
Identifiers: LCCN 2021056131 | ISBN 9781645021506 (paperback) | ISBN 9781645020790 (hardcover)
   | ISBN 9781645020806 (ebook)
Subjects: LCSH: Container gardening. | Balcony gardening. | Patio gardening. | Handbooks and manuals.
Classification: LCC SB324.4 .R53 2022 | DDC 635.9/86—dc23/eng/20211201
LC record available at https://lccn.loc.gov/2021056131

Chelsea Green Publishing
85 North Main Street, Suite 120
White River Junction, Vermont USA

Somerset House
London, UK

www.chelseagreen.com

*This book is dedicated
to all the people growing
food in unpromising,
concrete urban spaces
around the world.*

Contents

Introduction

When I started growing food on my balcony in 2009, I had little idea of what I was doing, what was possible or where it would lead.

Discovering that we could pick fresh, delicious food nearly every day from such a small space felt like a miracle. I never imagined that my family could live in a city without a garden and still be nearly self-sufficient in homegrown fruit and vegetables for eight months of the year.

Growing changed our life in other ways, too, some quite unexpected. After ten years of living in the same home, I got to meet and chat to neighbours intrigued by the vegetables growing outside the front door – and started to feel part of the local community for the first time. Our meals tasted more delicious using freshly picked, homegrown vegetables and herbs, and we started to eat more healthily without even thinking about it. Unlike most kids in the city, my three-year-old son could forage for fresh alpine strawberries and tomatoes from the windowsill, and watch spiders spin and woodlice scuttle on the balcony. Instead of throwing coffee grounds and banana skins in the bin, we recycled them in a wormery.

My northwest-facing balcony, measuring 3 × 2m (9 × 6ft). I didn't have high hopes for its growing potential but thought it would be fun to try.

By my second year of 'serious' growing, we were picking something for most meals for much of the year.

Our leftovers became a precious resource to make compost instead of waste. The plants and flowers brought invigorating scents, buzzing bees and beauty into our everyday life. Without making a conscious decision, we started calling our small, concrete balcony 'the garden'. Getting our hands in the soil, watching seeds emerge and harvesting supper from pots proved to be creative, relaxing and fulfilling – and a perfect foil to our busy city life.

My growing story started in around 2004 when, recalling happy childhood memories of a family allotment and podding broad beans together, I put my name down for an allotment in Camden, London. In 2009, after five years on the waiting list, I discovered I still had over 20 years to wait! With nothing to lose, I decided to see what I could grow on my balcony. My previous container-growing attempts had been half-hearted and fairly unsuccessful (I kept forgetting to water and even the rocket died), but this time I decided I was going to go for it.

I was completely untrained as a gardener, but I quickly discovered that with just a little knowledge I could grow quite a lot of food, and soon we had fresh herbs, salad and vegetables to hand whenever we wanted them. This was exciting and encouraged me to find space for more containers. Growing quickly became a central part of our lives.

In around 2009, there was also a mini 'grow your own' revolution in the UK. Many urban folk were frustrated gardeners, without a garden and unable to get an allotment. Few people at that time were aware of the potential of container growing. One day, cycling around London, I noticed many empty balconies, rooftops and other bare concrete spaces. I imagined how

Tending the plants outside the front door proved a wonderful way to meet and chat to people who lived in the area – and feel more connected to our local community.

I have written this book to try to address the specific needs and challenges of growing lots of food at home in containers as well as to draw more attention to the wide variety of ways that growing at home can improve lives, communities and cities.

My growing – and this book – is informed by several different and equally important sources. Running workshops for new growers, and learning about the challenges they were facing, helped shape the 'How To' sections. Over the years, specialists and professional growers have generously shared their knowledge with me on everything from chillies and herbs to wormeries and compost. I have applied their learning to my own growing in containers and now draw on it extensively to add depth and quality to the information given here. I have also chatted online with other enthusiasts who grow food at home in containers all over the world, sharing tips, ideas, successes and failures. We have enjoyed an exciting journey of discovery together and our conversations have helped shape a lot of the ideas and information in this book.

wonderful it would be if more of them were filled with pots of edible plants – and the joy it could give to people tending them and to those walking by. This is when I had the idea to devote my working life to inspiring and supporting small-space food growing. My friend, Martin, came up with the name 'Vertical Veg' for my blog and I started running workshops and stalls locally. There has been no turning back.

At the start of my 'serious' growing, I found it hard to get good-quality information tailored to growing food in containers in the city. Inevitably, most experienced and professional growers and writers grew in fields, large gardens, allotments or 'small' holdings of several acres. There was much to learn from their knowledge and experience, but many of the challenges (and benefits) of growing in containers on a few feet of concrete were quite different.

Last but not least, I have learned much from my own growing successes and the many failures. I started growing on my balcony in London, and this soon spread to the windowsills, then to the space at the front of the house, which belonged to my downstairs neighbour, and also to the space in front of my next-door neighbour's house. When we moved north to Newcastle upon Tyne, I grew in the concrete backyards of two rented homes before moving six years ago to the home we currently live in. I now have a container garden in the concrete front yard that is large enough to experiment with different fruit trees and bushes, as well as more vegetables and herbs, and a small paved and sunnier patio at the back of the house where I grow herbs and tomatoes. And, finally, I now have that long-awaited

With a few plants, the front yard becomes a warmer, more welcoming space – and gives us a good supply of fruit, herbs and vegetables.

allotment, which has given me a fascinating opportunity to learn about growing in the ground and to compare this with containers.

My aim for this book is threefold. First, if you've never grown before, I hope to demystify growing and make it accessible, so you can achieve success in a short space of time. Second, if you want to create an abundant and productive edible garden in containers, I hope this will be a springboard as well as a comprehensive manual to support you.

Finally, I want to offer practical ideas on how growing in containers in the city can help you become more involved in your local community, support and observe nature, recycle food waste and live more sustainably, as well as to eat healthier food with far more flavour than any you buy. Above all, I want to share the joy and fulfilment that creating a green oasis in a concrete space has brought me – and thousands of others – in the hope it will give you the same joy, too.

Part I
First Steps

I love being able to pop outside to pick what we need just before eating.

Chapter 1

Growing in the City

– allotment, community project
or container garden?

For those with itchy growing fingers in flats in the middle of the city, there are often three options: to get an allotment, help out at a community growing project, or grow in containers at home. All three are excellent in their own way and one often leads to another. It comes down to individual preferences, how much time you have, what community projects or allotments are available near you, and what, if any, growing space you have at home, so it's worth quickly looking at the main differences.

Allotments are ideal for growing space-hungry vegetables, such as parsnips, Brussels sprouts, potatoes, broad beans, and larger fruit trees. They're often lovely, quiet spaces to escape to at the weekend and on long summer evenings. Travel there and back can eat into growing time (mine is just a 10-minute walk away, but that's still a 20-minute round trip) and, with busy lives, many people find it hard to get there regularly enough. Most sites are friendly and welcoming, but check first as stories of allotment feuds aren't uncommon.

Community growing projects vary hugely in character, resources and how they are run. The choice of what to grow and pick is usually made by the community, and this may differ from what you'd choose to grow at home. They can be wonderful places to help out, enjoy the community vibe, meet others and pick up local growing tips. If there are any near you, do check them out.

The biggest benefit of growing at home in containers is that the plants are on your doorstep. You can enjoy them every day, pop out and tend to them when you have ten minutes to spare, and pick what you want as you need it (it's hard to overstate the value of this). Although the community benefits of growing at home are less obvious, they are still significant, as we will see. The potential for growing at home will depend on the size and suitability of the growing space. Many small spaces can be highly productive, but please bear in mind that container gardens are less suitable for space-hungry crops like parsnips and Brussels sprouts and they do need more regular attention than allotments.

With container growing, you are also in complete control of how many pots you have and can therefore avoid the stress that a large allotment or garden often creates.

I grow in and love all three of these options. However, if I could only have one, I would grow in containers at home. Simply because I like having plants (and nature) on my doorstep where I can enjoy them and pick from them every day. I also enjoy the opportunity it gives me to meet other people in the immediate vicinity of where I live.

How much food can be grown in a small space?

It's possible to grow more food in many small spaces than is often realised. For example, in 2010, on my northwest-facing balcony in

A harvest from the sunny, south-facing windowsills at the front of my London flat.

London, south-facing windowsills and a growing ladder outside the front door, I was able to grow 83.4kg (184lb) of food, worth approximately £899 in one year. This value was calculated using premium supermarket prices but justifiably, I think, on account of the quality of homegrown produce. See 'Table 1.1 Harvests from My Balcony and Windowsills in 2010', page 9, to get a better idea of what we actually managed to produce and the equivalent number of supermarket packs – a lot of salad and herbs as you can see!

Of course, the amount that can be grown in a space varies hugely, depending on both its size and suitability for growing. Some spaces are sunny and sheltered, and ideal for plants to thrive; others present a challenge such as wind or shade that needs to be overcome first (see *Chapter 11 Solutions to*

A container garden does not have to be large to be rewarding. These pots of mint, chives and parsley on a shady windowsill still provided me with fresh herbs nearly every day.

TABLE 1.1. Harvests from My Balcony and Windowsills in 2010

2010 harvests	Weight	Supermarket equivalents
Tomatoes	28.4kg (63lb)	113 punnets @ 250g (9oz) each
Salad leaves and microgreens	16.3kg (36lb)	163 packs @ 100g (3½oz) each
Squash and marrow	9.6kg (21lb)	4 BIG squashes
Runner and French beans	9.4kg (21lb)	47 packs @ 200g (7oz) each
Asian greens (pak choi, mustards and choy sum)	4.4kg (10lb)	22 packs @ 200g (7oz) each
Herbs	3.3kg (7lb)	165 packs @ 20g (¾oz) each
Courgettes	2.8kg (6lb)	14 packs @ 200g (7oz) each
New potatoes	1.2kg (3lb)	2 bags @ 500g (18oz) each
Peas	800g (28oz)	4 packs @ 200g (7oz) each
Other (rhubarb, radishes, aubergines, chillies)	7kg (15lb)	Not applicable
Grand total	83.4kg (184lb)	

Common Challenges). The shape and design of the space will also affect how many containers can be squeezed in and the weight of soil that can be supported. And size, of course, is very relative. I often talk about my 'small', 1.8 × 2.4m (6 × 8ft) balcony, but many flats have less outdoor space and some have none at all.

It often comes down to luck as to whether your space is good for growing or not. But, even in the least promising of spaces, it's often still possible to create a worthwhile and rewarding garden, after a bit of trial and error. Container gardens do not need to be expensive, large or highly productive to give joy and change lives. Even just a few pots of herbs can be rewarding, add flavour and nutritional value to almost every meal, look pretty and smell wonderful, attract bees and other pollinators, and offer new opportunities to meet neighbours. For example, I once created a small kitchen herb garden with just three pots on a shady windowsill.

Chapter 2

New to Growing?

If you are new to growing or still mastering the basics, the next few pages will give you some ideas on when and how to make a successful start.

A paradox of growing is that while there is *always* more to learn, the underlying basics are simple and can be mastered quickly. With just a little information and practise, you should be able to have many successes.

You do not need *all* the information in this book when you first start, so please don't feel that you do. The guidance provided in this chapter, *Chapter 4 Eight Steps to Success* (particularly the 'Keeping It Simple' summaries), and *Chapter 9 Your First Growing Projects* are all you need to get growing. I also recommend reading *Chapter 3 How to Design Your Container Garden* early on, too.

You can then dip into *Chapter 5 Useful Growing Skills* as needed, refer to *Part III: What to Grow* for inspiration, and turn to the 'Troubleshooting' section that starts on page 150 in *Chapter 8 Growing in Harmony with Life* or to *Chapter 11 Solutions to Common Challenges* if you have a problem. I suggest you skim through the content of these sections so you know what they cover.

To discover more about how you can get the most out of growing in small spaces, see *Chapter 12 More Reasons to Grow at Home*.

Growing can be made to sound overcomplicated. Plants really only have five basic requirements: plenty of light; air in the soil for the roots to breathe; water; food; and not to be too hot or cold. If you can provide them with these, they will usually be happy.

Getting started

Lack of time is a common obstacle to getting started. The good news is that you have a lot of control over how much time and attention a container garden needs. You can choose the number of pots and what you grow, and make the garden easy to look after (see, for example, *Chapter 11 Solutions to Common Challenges*, 'Making watering easier', page 231).

The trick is to start small. Look at the ideas in *Chapter 9 Your First Growing Projects* for inspiration. You don't need much to grow a few trays of microgreens or herbs,

and they are quick and easy to set up. And, once you are up and running, remember that you don't need a large container garden to get a lot out of it – if time is limited, a few low-maintenance herbs or fruit trees can still provide a lot of pleasure.

Learning to grow

There are no right or wrong ways to learn how to grow edible plants, but I recommend that you try the following early on:

1. Start growing something sooner rather than later. It's easy to put this off due to lack of time or feeling that you need more information first, but there are quick, easy ways to start. You can find some ideas in *Chapter 9 Your First Growing Projects*.
2. Pick up a little basic information – it goes a long way – but don't feel that you need to know everything. You'll learn more by having a go with an open mind

Perennial herbs such as bay and sage are less work to grow than annual vegetables like tomatoes.

Growing in the Ground versus Containers

How is growing in the ground different to growing in containers? Vegetables in the ground are more self-sufficient than those grown in containers. They can put down deeper roots, draw on water and food reserves from deep in the soil, and form more beneficial associations with fungi and other microbial life. In favourable weather, they can survive for weeks without any attention.

Vegetables in containers, on the other hand, have more limited supplies of water and food available to them. Just as a pet cat relies on its owner for regular water and food, so plants in containers rely on you for watering and feeding. Regular attention is key to successful container gardening.

and not worrying if anything goes wrong. If we regard these attempts as a learning opportunity, we can learn as much from our failures as successes.

3. Observe. Try to get into the habit of keeping an eye on your plants and their progress. Spotting any problems early makes it easier to put them right. And by watching how plants grow, you will learn a lot, too.

Navigating learning and online information

There are lots of ways to learn about growing, including from books, videos and online forums as well as through courses and workshops. Community growing projects also provide practical experience and the opportunity to learn from others. The choice is yours.

The internet is an excellent source of inspiration but, as with any other area, the quality of information varies considerably, advice is often confusing or contradictory, and it's not always easy to work out what is important or accurate (plus many articles are written for search engine optimisation and not based on practical experience). It's a good place for ideas but try to use one or two trusted sites or books for most of your growing advice (see *Further Reading*, page 285, for suggestions).

Local online gardening forums can also be useful for advice and information on plant swaps, community growing projects and gardening suppliers that are specific to your area.

Collect the tools you need

In container gardening, most jobs can be done with your bare hands or with things you may already have at home, like kitchen scissors. Apart from pots, some seeds and compost, you don't really need much to get started with the growing ideas outlined in *Chapter 9 Your First Growing Projects* (for example, you can use a plastic milk bottle with holes in the top instead of a watering can).

But, as your growing evolves, a few tools can help. The most useful basic tools are listed opposite, although even these can often be found or improvised if you wish (see *Chapter 11 Solutions to Common Challenges*, 'The cost of growing', page 227).

Pea shoots are quick and easy to grow, and they also taste delicious. They can be grown in all manner of recycled containers and are a great way to get started.

A watering can with a fine 'rose' for watering seedlings (the 'rose' attaches to the spout and has small holes to convert the flow into a fine spray).

A trowel

Seed labels and an indelible pen

Seed trays or modules

Secateurs

A spray bottle for foliar feeding – an old cleaning spray bottle, thoroughly washed, works well.

Plant supports like canes or bean poles

Garden twine to tie plants to canes.

A wormery and/or Bokashi bin

You might choose to invest in one or two good-quality tools that will last a lifetime. The two I prize most are a copper trowel with a blade sharp enough to cut through stems and roots and a good-quality watering can with a fine brass rose.

Keen growers will also find some of these additional tools useful:

A garden sieve – for sieving worm compost.

A heated propagator – useful for starting off chillies or aubergines and for growing cuttings.

A grow light – LED grow lights are cheaper, more efficient and make it easier to raise healthy seedlings inside in early spring.

For watering larger container gardens: a water butt, garden hose or compact hose reel.

You will also need containers, fertilisers, seeds and plants, and compost or growing media of some sort. These are all dealt with in more detail in *Chapter 4 Eight Steps to Success.*

A garden sieve is useful for sifting large twigs and bits of plastic out of worm compost or compost made from green waste.

A rose with a fine spray is useful for watering seedlings without damaging them.

This copper trowel is my favourite garden tool – and is as good today as it was ten years ago.

Contradictory Gardening Advice and Garden Myths

One of the most confusing aspects of learning to grow is the fact that advice is often contradictory. Sometimes this is because ideas about growing have been handed down without proper testing (these are the 'gardening myths'). Examples of myths include the importance of adding crocks to improve drainage and that water drops scorch leaves on hot days. Research has found that neither is true.

At other times you'll receive conflicting advice because there are many variables in growing, including climate, soil and seed variety. What works in one situation may not work in another. This is also why you may struggle with a plant that has been described as 'easy to grow' by someone else: a frustrating experience!

In truth, gardening is a constant quest for understanding. There is still so much we don't fully understand. Our knowledge will continue to evolve, and I have no doubt that people will look at some of the advice in this book in years to come and ask: 'How could he have thought that?'

When to start growing?

Traditionally, the growing season kicks off in early spring. If you're new to growing, it's easy to feel under pressure to sow seeds straightaway. But when the weather is cold, the days are short and light levels are low, it's harder to coax seeds into life and raise healthy plants. It's much easier in the warm, brighter days of late spring and early summer. Even mid-summer or early autumn is not too late to start. There is, of course, nothing wrong with starting seeds in early spring; just bear in mind that it does get easier later in the year. Ideas for easy seasonal projects can be found in 'Table 2.1 Easy First Growing Projects for Different Months of the Year'.

TABLE 2.1. Easy First Growing Projects for Different Months of the Year

When	What to sow or plant
Late March–April	Sow pea shoots, fava shoots, radishes or rocket microgreens outside, to harvest two to four weeks after sowing (depending on temperature). Sow tomatoes inside.
May	As above, plus plant potatoes and sow chard, rocket, kale, peas, spring onions and radishes. Plant out supermarket mint or parsley.
June–early July	Sow runner beans, French beans or courgette seeds outside or buy tomato and chilli plants. Buy and plant herbs such as rosemary, sage, thyme and other common herbs. Sow microgreens like pea shoots.
Late July–early August	Sow kale, chard, spinach and salads outside for late-autumn and winter harvests. Buy tomato or courgette plants or herbs (as above).
September	Sow rocket, mustards, pea shoots and most other microgreens for autumn harvests.
October	Sow pea shoots and fava shoots for late-autumn harvests.

Keeping Records

It's helpful to keep a record of the dates you sow different crops, when they were ready to harvest, and how well they did. This will be really useful information to help inform future years.

There are many ways to keep records, so choose whatever works best for you. It might be a simple table (see 'A Plan for the Year' box, page 18), with added notes detailing actual sowing dates and other learnings, or it could be a growing diary. I've just started a five-year diary to make it easy to compare different years. Alternatively, simply taking photos on your phone as you progress through the season can provide a useful visual record of what you did when.

A Plan for the Year

January
Make a plan for the year.
Plant new fruit trees.
Order seeds.

February
Prune and repot fruit trees.
Sow inside: Chillies, peppers and aubergines later in the month (until mid-March).

March
Sow inside: Tomatoes (best from late March until the end of April).
Sow outside in early March: Pea and fava shoots, peas (until April) and Jerusalem artichokes.
Sow outside in late March: Rocket, mustards, radishes, spring onions and coriander.

April
Sow inside from mid-April: French and runner beans, nasturtiums, courgettes, squash, cucumbers and New Zealand spinach (all until the end of May).
Sow outside: Potatoes, beetroot, lettuce, parsley, sorrel, chard, kale, spinach, more salad leaves (such as rocket) and Asian leaves like pak choi.
Divide and repot mint plants. Repot other herbs in larger pots as needed (or next month).
A good time to start a wormery (any time until July).

May
Sow inside: Basil.
Sow outside: More salads and leafy vegetables like chard if needed. A good month to sow most root vegetables, including beetroot, carrots, leeks and radishes.
Pot up supermarket herbs and stock up on other herb plants (any time until August).
Harden off indoor sowings for a week or two.

June
Sow outside: French and runner beans, cucumbers, courgettes and squash (if not already sown inside); plus, summer salads like New Zealand spinach, summer purslane, nasturtiums and lettuce.
Transplant all indoor sowings outside after the last frost (look this up for your area).
Support climbing plants like tomatoes and squash as they grow and start pinching out the side shoots on vine tomatoes.
Start liquid feeding fruiting crops once flowering starts (and keep feeding until fruiting stops).

July
Sow outside: Bulbing fennel for autumn; mustards, rocket and other salad leaves for early autumn; chard and kale for winter.
A good month to take herb cuttings.

August
Sow outside: Mooli, Asian greens like choy sum, mustards and pak choi, and salads such as land cress and lamb's lettuce for autumn and winter. The best month to sow coriander.
Mulch hungry crops like courgettes and tomatoes with worm compost if you have it.

September

Sow outside: Rocket, mustards and other fast-growing leaves in the first half of the month (see *Chapter 7 How to Grow More Food in a Small Space*, 'Table 7.3 Winter Sowing Timetable', page 139).

October

Sow outside: Last sowing of pea and fava shoots.

Order bare-root fruit trees for planting over winter.

Prepare a wormery for winter.

November

Reflect on the year: What grew well and what you learned, ready for next year.

Protect winter crops with cloches or horticultural fleece if needed.

December

Pick the occasional winter salad treat.

Sleep and dream.

French beans are normally sown inside in April or outside later in May or early June.

What to do when

Once you've made a start, you will probably begin thinking about what else you want to grow. If you're not sure what to grow yet, I hope you'll find lots of ideas in *Part III: What to Grow* and other parts of the book.

A common hurdle for new growers is knowing what to sow/plant – and do – when. Even more experienced growers find it easy to forget – myself included. However, this problem is easily addressed by making a simple plan for the year to help remind you. Pin it on your fridge, add it to your electronic diary or wherever it will most easily jog your memory – it's quick and straightforward to do:

> ▶ Make a list of what you want to grow, which is a fun job for an evening. Make sure you've checked out how much sun your space gets first – see *Chapter 4 Eight Steps to Success*, 'Step 1: Match the crops to how much sun your space has', page 36.
> ▶ Look up the recommended sowing dates for each crop. See 'A Plan for the Year' box, page 18, for an example of how best to plan the year ahead, or use a seed-sowing calendar for your region. Or just check the sowing times suggested on the backs of seed packets.
> ▶ Make a list of what you want to sow/plant and do each month.

Each crop needs to be sown at the right time of year to do well (normally there is a window of a few weeks or months, depending on the crop). Too early, and the crop might be killed by frost; too late, and it may not have enough time to grow and mature. To give you an idea of timings, the planner on page 18 is a sample of a typical month-by-month plan for the year for quite a substantial container garden (you will

probably want to start with something smaller). These are the approximate timings I use in Newcastle upon Tyne, which is in the north of the UK – timings for different parts of the UK and other Northern Hemisphere temperate regions will be similar. But in warmer regions, like London, most seeds can be sown a week or two earlier than here in Newcastle (though it won't do any harm to use the timings recommended in the planner – it is normally easier to sow things a bit later in any case). Outdoor sowings will also be influenced by the weather – in a cold year, push them back a week or two. If you are unsure, it can make sense to sow two batches of your favourite crops a few weeks apart – so if one is damaged by frost (or eaten by slugs or pigeons), you have a backup. It can also be interesting to compare which does best (later sowings often catch up).

Why are different crops sown at different times?

The sowing time for each crop is influenced by the time it takes to mature and how hardy (frost tolerant) it is. Understanding this can help you work out how much leeway there is to sow each crop. For example, pea shoots, which are hardy and ready to eat in two to four weeks, can be sown almost any time from March through to October. By contrast, aubergines, which are tender (killed by frost) and take several months to mature, need to be sown in a shorter window – between February and early April. If they are sown after April, they will not have time to fruit before the autumn frosts arrive. The average times that different vegetables take to mature can be seen in *Chapter 10 The Best Herbs, Fruit and Veg for Containers*, 'Table 10.2 Guide to the Best Vegetables for Containers', page 200.

Chapter 3

How to Design Your Container Garden

When starting a new container garden, the first thing is to get to know your growing space, particularly how much sun it gets, and then to start growing in a few pots. As well as gaining valuable experience, this will help you to learn what grows well in your space – and to plan how you might develop your container garden in the future. Some people then like to design their container garden slowly as they go, adding a few more pots every now and then. Others prefer to plan more major redesigns as and when they feel ready.

This chapter starts by discussing how sun and wind affect growing and considers what you can hope to achieve from a container garden. It then looks at some practical questions that are helpful to ask when you are designing one, including the safety considerations, which it's wise to think about early on, particularly if you are growing high up on windowsills, a balcony or rooftop, or right next to a heavily congested road.

Sun, wind and the 'microclimate'

Each urban space has its own unique microclimate, which is determined by how much sun it receives, how sheltered it is, and how much heat is reflected from surrounding bricks. Different growing spaces in the same street – even in the same home – can have quite different microclimates.

The microclimate will affect how easy it is to grow in a space and what will grow well. Many urban spaces have excellent microclimates for growing, while others are trickier. Learning about yours will help you choose the most suitable crops and then to grow them more successfully.

The first and most important task is to observe how much sun your space gets, as this will have the most impact on what you can grow. To do this, I highly recommend that you explore the easy 'Photo Exercise' in *Chapter 4 Eight Steps to Success*, page 38.

Once you start growing, you will continue to learn as the seasons roll round. Try to observe how the sun and wind patterns shift. Which areas get the most and least sun in spring, summer, autumn and winter? Does wind usually come from the same direction or does it change through the year? How often do different areas get frost in winter?

It can take a while to learn about these details, even in a small space. I was still discovering new things about the sun and wind after three years growing on my balcony. Now, when I move to a new home, I always start by growing in just a few pots for the first year. This helps me to learn about the sun and wind before investing time in designing and building a larger container garden. The key factors that affect growing are:

Sun and light levels: These are critical and looked at in detail in the next chapter. As well as direct sun, reflected light also makes a difference. If your space doesn't get much sun, there are ideas on what you can do in *Chapter 11 Solutions to Common Challenges*, 'Too little sun: shady spaces', page 241.

My London balcony was exposed to northeasterly winds in spring and early summer, and I had to protect tender plants like courgettes under improvised cloches. However, it was more sheltered from southwesterly winds in summer.

Wind: Most plants don't grow well in strong or persistent winds. Some rooftops and balconies are exposed, and even patios and front yards can sit in wind tunnels created by surrounding buildings. If you find that wind is an issue, there are often ways to minimise it and grow successfully. For further advice, see *Chapter 11 Solutions to Common Challenges*, 'Wind', page 239.

Temperature: In general, while the sun is good for growing, excessive heat can cause stress to plants and make pots dry out faster. This will be a familiar issue for anyone growing in hot or tropical climates, but small spaces surrounded by concrete can become heat traps in summer even in temperate climates. For tips on how to deal with excessive heat, see *Chapter 11 Solutions to Common Challenges*, 'Too hot: suntraps, hot climates and heatwaves', page 242.

Some plants offer multiple benefits. Lavender is pretty, attracts bees, smells wonderful and can be used in cooking.

Design questions

In addition to the microclimate, here are some questions and practicalities to consider when designing a larger container garden.

What do you want to get out of your container garden?

Every container garden is unique and each of us has a different set of motivations for wanting to start one. The simple pleasure of growing is as good a reason as any. Here, to offer a few ideas, are some of the possibilities. None of them are mutually exclusive – a container garden can help you realise all of these:

Beauty: There are many pretty edibles such as nasturtiums, lavender, runner beans and 'Cavolo Nero' kale.

Salad self-sufficiency: Homegrown salad tastes so much better than supermarket leaves, and it's possible to be self-sufficient in salad with just a few containers.

Food with more flavour: You can eat fresh herbs with every meal, expand your larder with exotic edibles and enjoy the unsurpassed flavour of freshly picked, homegrown chillies and tomatoes.

Good health: Choose nutritious foods like kale, blueberries and microgreens.

Attract wildlife: Grow flowers to support pollinators, create birdbaths and basin ponds, and provide homes for solitary bees.

Enjoy scent: This is often overlooked but our sense of smell is one of our most evocative senses. Lavender, mint and roses are among the fragrant plants suitable for containers.

Grow speciality foods: If you like a particular cuisine or style of cooking, you can grow the fresh ingredients, whether these are Jamaican vegetables, Asian herbs, or vegetables and sprouts to support a raw-food or plant-based diet.

Save money: By choosing what you grow and caring for it carefully, you can cultivate many ingredients at home for a fraction of the price of shop-bought produce.

Be more sustainable: If you build using recycled materials, collect rainwater, recycle food waste to make compost, and save seed, you'll be creating a garden with greater sustainability.

A birdbath provides a valuable drinking and bathing place for birds – and good theatre, too!

What else do you need the space for?

Before you fill every bit of your balcony or patio with pots, think about how else the space will be used, whether for sunbathing, eating or drying the washing. When I started growing, I was so caught up with enthusiasm that I didn't leave any space to sit on the balcony!

Where is the nearest water source?

Watering is the most time-consuming part of container growing. For larger container gardens, it will save a lot of time if you have a water source close to the plants. Where possible, an outside tap or a water butt is ideal. If this isn't feasible, neat and compact mini hose reels, run from an indoor tap, can offer a good alternative.

In London, my small balcony had an outside tap and water butt, and I could water it in less than ten minutes. But it took half an hour to water the same number of containers

A container garden can be built almost entirely with recycled materials. These mushroom trays are ideal for growing microgreens.

at the front of the house because I had to carry watering cans from the kitchen up and down the stairs.

What about storage space?

Where will you store tools, fertiliser and compost? Sometimes, it's possible to squeeze in new storage areas when you design a space. For example, the space under a shelf for pots can be used for storage or a large box can double up as a bench and storage space.

Will water drip on the neighbour's washing?

After watering containers, water may drip out of them. If you live in a flat that is above others, you won't want this dripping on your neighbour's balcony or washing.

Containers with water reservoirs (discussed in the next chapter) make it easier to reduce the amount of water runoff (just add water until the reservoir is full). And because the water doesn't pass through the soil, any drips will have less soil in them.

Alternatively, you can use large plastic trays to catch the drips. But if you try this, make sure your plants don't sit in puddles of water for long periods or they will drown (plant roots need air).

Another option is to water early in the morning or late at night – after checking there is no washing on the balconies below.

Where possible, talk to your neighbours about your growing. Good communication will help address and resolve any issues that do arise. Gifting produce or easy-to-care-for plants such as mint can also be an invaluable way of creating and sharing an appreciation for growing at home.

How many pots?

One of the unwritten rules of container gardening is that there is always (or nearly always) space to squeeze in another pot. This is all part of the creative fun. But sometimes it's possible to end up with more pots than you can easily look after.

There are no rules about the ideal number of pots, and often the size of your

A shelf or box for plant pots can double up as useful storage space for compost bags and tools. This is my front yard – I used the same principle, on a smaller scale, on my balcony.

My front yard a few years ago. I am constantly moving containers around, adding to them and sometimes taking them away. This flexibility is one of the benefits of container growing.

space and the amount of time you have will be the limiting factors. As a guide, though, aim for enough pots to make your container gardening and the effort feel worthwhile. It's common to find that the more you invest in a container garden, the more rewarding growing becomes (and the easier it is to remember to water – there is less incentive with just one or two pots).

At the same time, it slightly defeats the point if you get stressed by having too many pots to look after. Luckily, container gardens can easily be made smaller as well as larger. I've often rationalised a container garden after an over-ambitious season.

If you are starting your first container garden, I recommend adding a few containers each year, gradually increasing the number as you learn. However, if you have an urge to create a container empire straight-

away, don't let me hold you back: it can be fun! Just be aware that there is more risk of buying pots or plants that you discover aren't ideal later.

I've enjoyed discovering how much I can grow in a small space, cramming almost every inch available with pots. One consequence is that I can spend 30 minutes a day watering in summer, the odd hour here and there sowing seeds, plus full half days' gardening on several weekends of the year. I appreciate that's too big a time commitment for many people. However, a very worthwhile container garden can still be looked after in much less time. For example, eight pots of herbs, four trays of salad, two chillies, two tomatoes, a pot of runner beans and a couple of fruit trees can normally be watered in just five minutes a day – and would still give you plenty of fresh food to eat.

Temporary or long-term?

How long you plan to stay in your home will influence your approach to container gardening. You can think longer term in more permanent homes – planting fruit trees that take several years to be productive, for example. Container gardens can be equally rewarding in short-term accommodation, but you'll want to design them with the likely length of your stay in mind. You'll find ideas for this scenario in *Chapter 11 Solutions to Common Challenges*, 'Growing in rented or temporary accommodation', page 248.

How often and how long will you be away?

Plants in containers need regular attention. If you go away regularly or for long periods, you can plan for this. You might have a neighbour or a friend who will be happy to water for you in exchange for picking rights. Or you can look at ways to reduce the amount of manual watering needed – as I discuss in *Chapter 11 Solutions to Common Challenges*, 'Making watering easier', page 231 – or just opt for fast crops such as microgreens during the periods you are at home.

Any special requirements?

Container gardens can be designed to meet specific needs such as wheelchair access. Heights can be adjusted by fixing containers to a wall at the required level or putting them on pallets or strong plastic boxes.

A quick word on 'beauty'

Gardening programmes and magazines often focus on perfection. But, from working with hundreds of container gardeners, I've learnt that you don't need an aesthetically pleasing or aspirational 'lifestyle' garden to get a lot out of growing.

Still, even if you don't aspire to the perfection of lifestyle magazines or Instagram, you'll probably want your growing space to look as attractive as you can and it's still possible to create a beautiful container garden even when using recycled materials.

If your container garden is in a publicly visible space, a pretty collection of pots and planters will also inspire others and be an asset to the community. You'll find practical tips on creating a beautiful container garden in *Chapter 12 More Reasons to Grow at Home*, 'Grow for beauty and fragrance', page 268.

Organic growing?

There are several approaches to growing, such as organic, biodynamic and permaculture, that can provide useful ideas and principles for container growing in the city. If you choose to follow one, bear in mind that it may not be easy to apply *all* its principles.

You do not need an 'aspirational' or sophisticated garden to be able to experience the beauty of plants like this pot marigold.

Not all the plants in my container garden are edible. I also grow some *Verbena bonariensis* as they add height and colour and because butterflies and bees like the flowers. They also cast very little shade over other plants.

For example, it may not be practical to make large volumes of compost or weed teas in a small space.

Rather than rigidly following the rules of any particular system, I find it more helpful to draw on a wide range of ideas while focusing on principles that nurture all life. It's also important to acknowledge that many 'modern' organic growing methods – and most permaculture design principles – have their roots in ideas pioneered over thousands of years by indigenous peoples in Africa, Asia and around the world. And there is much to relearn from our farming ancestors (see, for example, Bruce Pascoe's book, *Dark Emu: Aboriginal Australia and the Birth of Agriculture*). Here are some of the principles I follow:

▶ I completely avoid the use of pesticides, including 'natural' pesticides that contain ingredients like chilli or garlic (any mixture that kills one insect will kill others, too).

▶ I use homemade fertiliser as much as possible and supplement with purchased fertiliser based on natural ingredients (like seaweed or chicken manure) when needed.

▶ I recycle and compost as much garden and food waste as I can.

▶ I'm happy to share a proportion of my harvests with other animals – birds and caterpillars, etc – so my growing efforts help to feed the wider ecosystem.

▶ I grow a diverse range of plants, including flowering plants, to support pollinators.

▶ I try to grow open-pollinated plants as much as possible and limit the number of F1 hybrids (see *Chapter 5 Useful Growing Skills*, 'The Difference Between F1, GMO and Open-pollinated Seeds' box, page 89).

You'll need to consider what is important to you and work out your own principles, bearing in mind what is realistic given the space, time and budget you have. But you can be confident that if you avoid using poisonous chemicals in pesticides, you will create more life and biodiversity in the city, however you grow and whichever approach or principles you adopt.

Draw a plan

Once you've observed the sun in your space, worked out what you want to grow and thought through the practical considerations, you may find it helpful to draw a plan. A plan will help you work out how to arrange your growing space aesthetically and practically. It can be a rough sketch to help you think through ideas or a neat plan drawn to scale.

On your plan, first mark the sunniest and least sunny places. Put crops like tomatoes in the sunniest places. Wormeries, water butts and storage boxes can go in shady areas. If you draw and cut out scaled pictures of your pots, wormery and furniture, you can move these around on your plan like a jigsaw to find the best arrangement.

When working out what to put where, try to think of your space in three dimensions – as a cube rather than a flat space. How can you make best use of all the space in the cube? Where can you grow climbers, add hanging baskets or put shelves? Can you attach strings anywhere to support climbers?

If you make copies of your plan, you can mark on what you grow in the different containers each season. This will provide a record that you can look back on (and will probably be more useful than you think).

Safety considerations

Overall, the potential benefits of urban growing far outweigh the risks. But it's still useful to be aware of the risks, so you can assess them carefully.

Weight of pots

Pots and soil, particularly when waterlogged, can be very heavy to lift and move. Their combined weight and where they are placed is also critical. This is particularly important on balconies and rooftops. A collapsing roof is a real and serious risk.

The number and size of pots you can safely have will depend on the design and construction of the building. *The only way to be certain is to consult the architectural plans for the weight-bearing load or to hire a structural engineer to advise you.*

If this is not viable, err on the side of caution. Use small, lightweight plastic pots and lightweight soil mixes. You should also avoid large pots completely or place them on top of a load-supporting wall. Try to attach some planters directly to walls, where possible, to reduce the load on the floor.

Moving heavy bags of compost and pots is also an issue to consider for those with back problems or mobility issues. Choosing lightweight materials and using a trolley or a dolly to shift heavy pots can help.

Pots falling off

Check that any pot on a windowsill or ledge is secured so that it can't fall or be blown off. Falling pots are potentially lethal and can also damage property.

Specialist gardening suppliers sell brackets and attachments for fixing containers in place. A DIY solution on windowsills is to screw strong metal eyes into the wall on each side of the window (you'll need a drill and wall plugs), an inch or two below the top of the window box. You can then secure the window box by tying a strong metal wire between the two eyes and tightening it

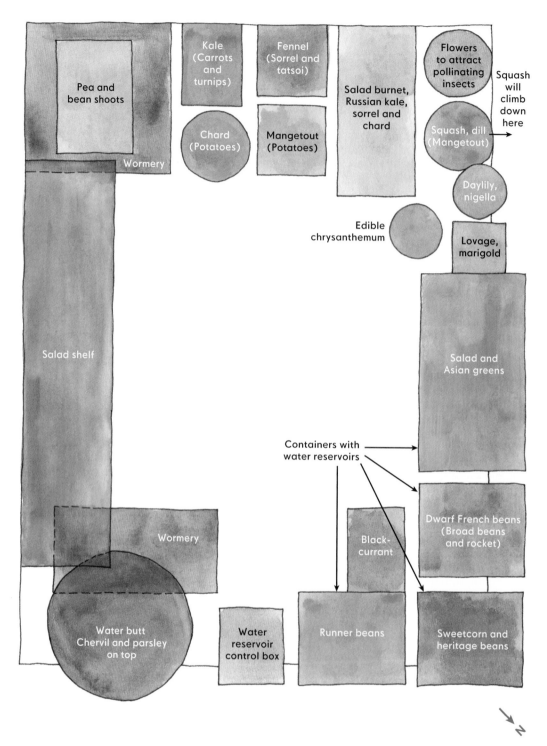

Plan for my northwest facing, 9 feet by 6 feet, balcony garden. My growing started off much simpler than this and evolved slowly over several years. Plants in (brackets) already harvested from these containers earlier in the year.

It's vital to be sure that your balcony or rooftop can support the weight of pots. All the heavy pots on my balcony were placed directly on top of the supporting wall that ran round the edge.

around the window box until it is firmly secured (see the photograph of the EarthBox on my windowsill in *Chapter 4 Eight Steps to Success*, page 47).

Air pollution

Rising air pollution is a concern in many urban areas. However, unless you live right next to a very busy road, the available evidence suggests that the risk to food growing is low to negligible. An unpublished study of the effect of air pollution on edible plants by Dr Claire Walsh at Newcastle University in 2017 found there was no significant accumulation of heavy metals or other pollutants in the soil over five months on urban roads with both light and moderate traffic. Similarly, a 2018 study in Barcelona found that even in high-traffic areas concentrations of lead in lettuce were below the EU legislated limit. On the other hand, a 2012 study in Berlin, Germany, did find that vegetables grown close to heavy traffic had lead concentrations slightly above the EU limit. This study also found that barriers between the traffic and the food growing, such as a hedge or wall, significantly reduced the amount of contamination. In other words, if your home faces onto roads with very heavy traffic, try and grow at the back of the house or behind a wall or hedge, if possible.

It's also important to balance the potential risks from air pollution with the health and well-being benefits of growing your own produce (see *Chapter 12 More*

Reasons to Grow at Home, 'Grow for health', page 258. And, if you do live next to a very busy road, bear in mind that the degree of risk posed to health depends on the amount eaten. For example, consuming a large portion of potatoes grown by a busy roadside every day (perhaps accounting for 20 per cent of a diet) would pose a more significant risk than eating herbs, which might account for just 1 per cent or less of a diet.

Giving food a thorough wash before eating to remove dirt and any pollution that may have settled on the outside is always recommended.

Soil pollution

If you buy compost from a reputable company, it should have been tested for any pollutants. Green compost, made from garden and food waste (and sometimes called municipal compost), should have been tested, but check with your local supplier. If you are based in the UK, look for green compost with the PAS 100 specification, which will have been tested for heavy metals and other toxins as well as weed seeds.

Soil pollution becomes more of an issue if you dig up garden soil to add to a potting mix. The soil in urban areas is often contaminated by past industrial activity. Even if it isn't toxic, it is often of poor quality and can be mixed with builders' rubble. You can sometimes get maps from the local environment agency that show areas with known polluted soil or you can pay to get soil tested.

Part II

How to Grow

Woodland fruits like these blueberries will grow well and ripen in just three or four hours of sun.

Chapter 4

Eight Steps to Success

This chapter outlines my eight steps to container-growing success. Follow these and you'll be successful most of the time which, as a gardener, is all you can hope for!

All the essential information you need to know for each step when you start growing is summarised in the 'Keeping It Simple' boxes. Then, for each step, I have also included more detailed information that will be useful as your growing evolves. I also try to explain *why* some of the steps are important as I think this can help to demystify the growing process which, in turn, can increase confidence. In summary, the eight steps are:

Step 1: Match the crops to how much sun your space has. For example, subtropical crops like tomatoes and chillies need more sun to grow well than leafy crops like salads or herbs.

Step 2: Choose the right container, as size is important.

Step 3: Use a good-quality compost – this is like the foundations of a house, invisible but essential for long-term success.

Step 4: Check drainage – good drainage is vital because plant roots need air to breathe, or they will drown.

Step 5: Space your plants for optimum growth and harvests – it's easy to overcrowd them in containers, but plants need space to grow large.

Step 6: Create a watering routine – work out a daily routine that works for you and your plants.

Step 7: Feed your crops – in containers, plants need feeding for optimal harvests.

Step 8: Observe and keep learning – and try not to worry if things don't work out.

Step 1: Match the crops to how much sun your space has

The amount of sun your space gets will determine what you can grow. Urban spaces are often overshadowed by buildings, trees and fences. This can result in a complex, changing pattern of sunlight across the space – and sometimes very little sun at all.

Most vegetables and fruits grow best in full sun (gardeners define 'full sun' as six hours or more a day at mid-summer), but some will grow fine in less. Knowing the minimum sun requirements that different crops need will help you to select those that match the sun available in your growing space.

When I started growing, I couldn't understand why the minimum sun requirements weren't mentioned on seed packets. But, after trial and error, I worked out some general rules that are surprisingly reliable (though, as with all general rules, there are a few exceptions).

As you can see from the 'Infographic showing the sun requirements of different crops', see opposite, if your space only gets three hours of sun, there is still a wide choice of edible crops to grow. You just need to edit

your selection carefully. There are more tips on growing in less sunny spaces in *Chapter 11 Solutions to Common Challenges*, 'Too little sun: shady spaces', page 241.

Choosing what and where to grow

It is not uncommon for small growing spaces to have a complex and changing pattern of sun. This is caused by the variation in the height and position of the sun through the day (and also through the year) and by the shadows cast by surrounding trees and buildings.

In the Northern Hemisphere, the sun rises in the east, travels in an arc round to the south and then sets in the west. In winter, it climbs substantially lower in the sky and travels on a shorter arc. A north-facing balcony that gets a few hours of sun in summer may get no sun at all in winter, while a southwest-facing balcony will, unless overshadowed by other buildings, get sun for most of the day in summer and winter. Knowing which direction your growing spaces face will help you anticipate how the sun will vary and which parts will get the most sun. There are also apps and online tools that will help you map out how the path of the sun will vary in your area from month to month.

As a typical example of how the sun can vary in a small space, I have included a sketch of my London balcony (see 'Balcony Plan: How the Sun Varied on My Balcony and What I Grew', page 38). It had patches of full sun (six hours-plus), part sun (five to six hours' sun) and part shade (three to four hours' sun). This information enabled me to work out what to grow in each place.

Three ways to map the sun in your space

You may already have a rough idea of how much sun your space gets. However, as the

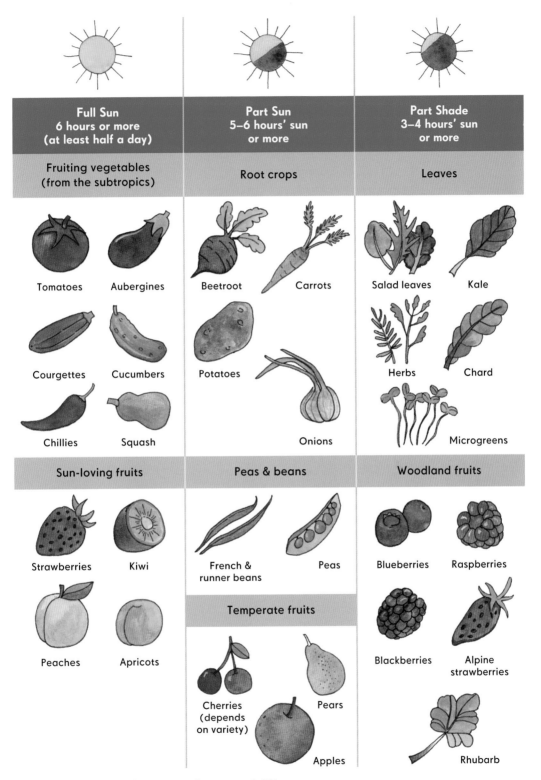

Full Sun 6 hours or more (at least half a day)	Part Sun 5–6 hours' sun or more	Part Shade 3–4 hours' sun or more
Fruiting vegetables **(from the subtropics)**	**Root crops**	**Leaves**

Fruiting vegetables (from the subtropics)

Tomatoes Aubergines

Courgettes Cucumbers

Chillies Squash

Root crops

Beetroot Carrots

Potatoes

Onions

Leaves

Salad leaves Kale

Herbs Chard

Microgreens

Sun-loving fruits

Strawberries Kiwi

Peaches Apricots

Peas & beans

French & Peas
runner beans

Temperate fruits

Cherries Pears
(depends
on variety)

Apples

Woodland fruits

Blueberries Raspberries

Blackberries Alpine
strawberries

Rhubarb

Infographic showing the sun requirements of different crops.

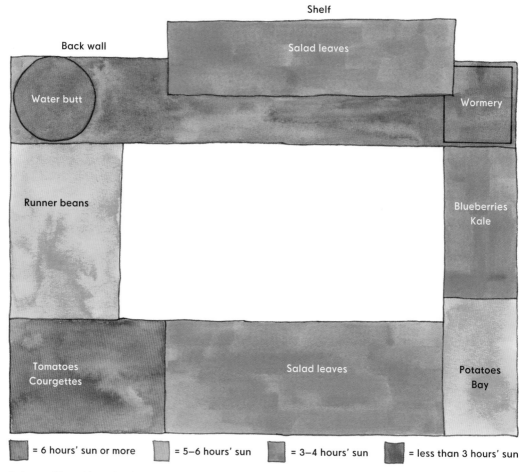

Shelf

Back wall

Salad leaves

Water butt

Wormery

Runner beans

Blueberries
Kale

Tomatoes
Courgettes

Salad leaves

Potatoes
Bay

■ = 6 hours' sun or more ▢ = 5–6 hours' sun ■ = 3–4 hours' sun ■ = less than 3 hours' sun

Balcony Plan: How the Sun Varied on My Balcony and What I Grew.

sun is so important to growing success, I recommend getting as clear a picture as you can over the coming months and years. Here are three ways to learn about how the sun varies across a space:

1. Observation

Make a conscious effort to observe your space at different times of day. This can be a lovely, mindful way to relax and connect with the space, as you develop a feel for which areas get the most and the least sun.

When observing a space, remember to look up, as higher areas often get more sun. Sometimes it is possible to take advantage

of these with hanging baskets or shelves on the walls.

2. Photo exercise

This is an easy and useful exercise that I highly recommend because it will quickly give you an accurate snapshot of how the sun varies across a space.

Choose a sunny day when you'll be at home and, with your phone or camera, take photos of the space from the same position every hour or two throughout the day. You can set a repeating alarm to remind you.

At the end of the day, it's fascinating to look through and compare the photos. You'll

Move pots around to find areas with the most sun. When we rented a home with a backyard, no sun reached the floor on one side of the yard. By improvising this shelf near the top of the wall, the salads received enough sun to grow quite well.

see how the sun patterns change, where the sunniest spots are and, crucially, how many hours of sun each area gets.

3. Grow and learn

If you are someone who just likes to get on with things, you can also learn about the sun in a space as you grow in it. Observe and grow – and move your pots around to find the best places for your plants.

What happens in too little sun?

If a sun-loving plant like a tomato is grown in a space which receives just four hours of sun, the chances are that it will grow reasonably well to begin with, and then it will probably:

▸ Show increased pest problems as it will become weaker and less able to fight off pests.
▸ Produce few or no fruits – or the fruits won't ripen properly.

Similarly, a leafy crop that is given less than three hours of sun a day will usually grow spindly and weak and be more likely to have pest problems.

Can plants have too much sun?

While most crops grow best in plenty of sun, excessive heat can stress plants. For tips on growing in hot climates and hot spaces, see *Chapter 11 Solutions to Common Challenges*, 'Too hot: suntraps, hot climates and heat-waves', page 242.

Why some crops need more sun

Tomatoes, chillies and aubergines need lots of sun because they originate from the hot, sunny climate of the South American subtropics and produce substantial fruits that contain sugars. These need the sun's energy to ripen properly.

Keeping It Simple

The key is to observe how much sun your space gets and to identify any particularly sunny or less sunny areas. Then choose and place plants accordingly.

▸ In six hours of sun or more (over half a day) you can grow almost anything you want, including sun-loving crops like tomatoes, chillies and other fruiting vegetables.

▸ In five or six hours of sun (about half a day), peas, beans and most root crops will grow well.

▸ In three to four hours of sun, your choice will be narrowed to leafy crops such as salad and herbs and woodland fruits like blueberry and blackberry – but there are still plenty to choose from.

▸ In less than three hours of sun, growing is more difficult. See *Chapter 11 Solutions to Common Challenges*, 'Too little sun: shady spaces', page 241, for ideas on how and what to grow in such spaces.

▸ Bear in mind that, when starting to grow, it's easy to be over optimistic about how much sun a space gets – observe carefully and try to be as realistic as you can.

▸ Keep learning about the sun in your space and keep moving pots around until you find the best places for them.

Peas grow well in half a day's sun. I grew these purple peas by our front door in London, where they also brightened up the street.

Salad and herbs, on the other hand, require less sun because they only need to produce leaves. Fruits like raspberry and blackberry normally grow in woodlands and their fruits have evolved to ripen in less sun.

How does sun affect flavour?

Crops grown in more sun will often develop more flavour and more sugars. Mediterranean herbs, for example, develop their fullest flavour in lots of sun and books often advise growing them in full sun. But, fortunately for those of us living in places with fewer hours of sunshine, they will still grow successfully with less. Many container growers (myself included) grow rosemary and other Mediterranean herbs in three or four hours' sun – and they still taste great.

Farmers grow woodland fruits like blueberries and blackberries in full sun because they develop more sugars and taste sweeter (to meet the needs of the supermarkets). But these berries will also fruit well and taste good in four or five hours' sun – they will be a little less sweet but, personally, I prefer them.

Step 2: Choose the right container

Containers are one of the most visible parts of your garden, so they have an aesthetic as well as functional role, but the vast array of containers now available can be a bit bewildering. Which to choose? Here are the four main questions you need to ask:

1. What size do you need?
2. What material do you prefer: plastic, metal, wood, terracotta or fabric?
3. Do you want your container with or without a reservoir?
4. New or recycled?

Too Much, Too Soon – A Common Mistake

Early in my growing, I spent a whole weekend building a large wooden (and immovable) container on my balcony. Later, I discovered I'd built it in the shadiest part!

Now I use (free) recycled containers when I'm learning about the sun in a space. Once I've grown in the space for a season or two, I am more confident about investing time and money in it.

Containers come in all shapes and sizes. I made this strawberry planter out of an old plastic bucket.

1. What size?

The general rule is the bigger the pot, the bigger the crop. For example, a kale plant will grow three or four times the size in a 20-litre (5¼-gallon) pot than in a 5-litre (1¼-gallon) pot. And tomato plants will yield a bigger harvest in a larger container.

The *volume* of the pot is usually more critical than the depth, except for root vegetables which can benefit from a deeper pot.

Bigger pots are also easier to grow in. They dry out less quickly, hold more food and provide more space for the plants to develop a healthy root system. Additionally, worms and other valuable soil life thrive better in larger volumes of soil.

However, big pots do have drawbacks. They take up more space, are heavier to move around and are usually more expensive. They also need more potting mix to fill them.

Rhubarb is an excellent container crop – but it's one that ideally needs a big pot to do well.

What size pots do you need?

If your space can take the size and weight, a selection of large pots (or even raised beds) will be hard to beat. But when space is at a premium (or weight is an issue) a mix of pot sizes is often a good compromise. The key is to choose the right size pot for each crop:

Microgreens like pea shoots will grow productively in something as small as a seed tray.

Baby salad leaves such as rocket and mustards will grow well in large trays or window boxes, say 4–10 litres (1–2½ gallons).

Leafy vegetables such as kale or chard will grow to a reasonable size if given plenty of space in bucket-sized pots (10-litres/2½-gallons or more).

Herbs Small herbs can be grown in pots or window boxes with a capacity of 1–2 litres (¼–½ gallon). Larger and more mature herbs do best in 5-litre (1¼-gallon) buckets or bigger. (The pots that supermarket herbs come in are too small, which is why they quickly run out of steam – see *Chapter 9 Your First Growing Projects*, 'Project 2: Supermarket herb plants', page 168).

Root vegetables will usually grow fine in a 10-litre (2½-gallon) bucket or bigger (they like the depth of a bucket), but small spring onions, baby carrots or radishes will grow in a standard window box.

Fruiting crops generally need larger pots to yield well. As a rough rule of thumb, the larger the fruit, the larger the pot you need. So, chillies or a *small* bush cherry tomato can grow well in a 5-litre (1¼-gallon) pot, while larger vining tomatoes do best in 20 litres (5¼ gallons). A big squash probably needs at least 40 litres (10½ gallons) to grow well.

You will find recommended minimum pot sizes for each crop in *Part III: What to Grow*.

Mixed mustard baby leaves in a homemade container (made from pallet slats), about 8 litres (2 gallons) in volume.

2. What material?

The best choice normally comes down to considerations of weight, aesthetics, budget and personal preference. Here is some information to help you decide:

Plastic

Plastic is light and strong, making it ideal for containers. It is widely available and comes in all shapes, sizes and colours. Good-quality, UV-treated plastic will last many years, but try to avoid lower-quality plastics as they quickly deteriorate in the sun and will crack in a season or two. (As a rough rule of thumb, most plastics designed for outdoor use will be UV-treated, while those for indoor use often aren't.)

Wood

Wood looks good, insulates well and it's nice to grow in a natural material. A benefit of making your own wooden containers is that you can cut them to fit your space or create extra volume by making them deeper.

If you don't have woodwork tools or experience, some urban wood-recycling projects offer training, workspace and tools you can hire. Others offer a wood-making service and will even make containers to the dimensions you want.

Be aware that large wooden containers can be very heavy. I once built a deep container out of wood for my windowsill, but when it was full of soil, I couldn't lift it!

Wood also rots after a few years and clearing up rotten containers is not a nice job. Soft wood will usually last two to five years, hardwood for four to ten years. Lining the inside with plastic (such as old compost bags) will prolong its life. Most wood preservatives contain toxic chemicals like fungicides and are best avoided. A safer option is *raw* linseed oil (but NOT *boiled* linseed oil, which contains toxins). There are

Safety and Plastic

Most plastics are generally considered safe to grow in. It's a complicated issue because there are many different types of plastic and each one is different. Also, even when chemicals are leached into the soil, some quickly break down into harmless compounds and others aren't absorbed by the plant. The advice, at the time of writing, is to choose food-safe plastics to grow in. These include:

Polyethylene Terephthalate
(PET or PETE) – Code 1
High-Density Polyethylene
(HDPE) – Code 2
Low-Density Polyethylene
(LDPE) – Code 4
Polypropylene (PP) – Code 5

You can tell the type of plastic by the Code number and abbreviation stamped on the bottom (this isn't mandatory in the UK, but most plastics are marked).

Wooden containers can look good and also be made to fit a specific space. I built these from reclaimed wood to replace some plastic recycling bin containers that looked messy.

Large terracotta pots look good, are nice to grow in and make a fitting choice for Mediterranean herbs and fruit trees.

also a few specialist preservatives on the market that claim to be food-safe. These tend to be expensive, but given the time it takes to make wooden containers, they can represent a good investment.

Terracotta: unglazed

Unglazed terracotta is good to look at, breathes well and is a nice natural material to grow in. If you are lucky, you may be able to source pots made by local craftspeople.

The biggest downside of terracotta is that it can dry out quickly, particularly in small sizes. Pots smaller than 1 litre (¼ gallon) are hard to keep properly watered. Terracotta is also heavy, relatively expensive and can break in frosts or if it falls over.

Unglazed terracotta is particularly well suited to Mediterranean herbs like sage, oregano and rosemary that don't mind occasionally drying out. Larger terracotta pots – 20 litres (5¼ gallons) and bigger – are less prone to drying out and are good for permanent plantings of fruit trees and bushes like apple, blueberry and Chilean guava.

Terracotta: glazed

Glazed terracotta is less porous and so less quick to dry out. It can be very attractive and an excellent choice for a wide variety of vegetables, fruits and herbs. Like unglazed terracotta, the downsides are weight, breakability and cost.

3. With or without reservoirs?

Pots with reservoirs are sometimes called 'self-watering containers', but this isn't a very accurate description: they still need regular watering! How often will depend on the reservoir size and the weather. A spin-off benefit of using them is that, as you fill up the reservoirs, you can learn how much the plants drink in different weather conditions – you might be surprised by how much a mature tomato plant will drink on a hot day. Here are the benefits of using a reservoir:

▶ The plant gets a more constant water supply. This minimises stress and can result in higher yields.
▶ Watering is needed less frequently, but this will depend on the reservoir size – some of mine still need topping up nearly every day.
▶ Watering is easier – just add water until it starts to come out of the overflow hole.
▶ The risk of overwatering is almost eliminated.
▶ Reservoirs reduce – almost eliminate – dirty water runoff.
▶ You can cover the top with a plastic mulch (just cut holes for the plants to come through) to reduce water loss.

Containers with reservoirs are not essential, but I do recommend trying them. They are particularly good for:

▶ Tomatoes, French beans and other fruiting crops that like plenty of water – you'll often get a higher yield.
▶ Hot spaces where containers would dry out too fast otherwise.
▶ If it's hard to keep to a regular watering regime.

Containers with reservoirs are widely available in shops and online. One excellent brand is the 'EarthBox' (this is widely available in the US, but harder to get in the UK). Another, with a reservoir large enough to hold a week's water supply, is the 'Quadgrow'. These models can seem expensive, but often work out as a good investment over the longer term. I've had six EarthBoxes for over ten years and they look as good as new.

You can also make your own. There are many different designs on the internet and some work well. However, having experimented with many of these designs over the years, I can report that they are usually

Containers with Reservoirs

Containers with reservoirs are an excellent innovation and well worth trying. Thirsty plants such as tomatoes and beans grow particularly well in them. This is an Earthbox, a container designed for food growing — and luckily the size fitted my windowsills in London perfectly. (At this stage in my growing, I still hadn't learnt to pinch out tomato side shoots properly.)

Also note the wire to secure the container to the window sill.

These wooden containers had homemade reservoirs (made from old plastic boxes) fitted into the base. They were time-consuming to build, but the results were excellent. Runner beans (*the tall plants on the right*) do particularly well in containers with reservoirs.

Empty olive oil tins can make attractive containers. Be careful of the sharp edges and if the tin will be sitting in hot sun, line the inside with cardboard to prevent it getting too hot. I also added a water reservoir, made out of an old milk bottle, to the bottom of this one.

time-consuming to construct and more work to maintain from year to year. Factory-made pots with purpose-made parts are usually easier to dismantle and clean each season.

4. To buy or recycle?

Recycling is a low-cost way to start a container garden, and it saves resources and reduces landfill. It can also be a rewarding and creative way to grow.

A wide array of recycled objects can make excellent containers. Good choices include flower sellers' buckets; large food tins (for example, catering-size olive oil tins); veg crates; fish boxes; mushroom trays; bags for life; and water-heating tanks. The choice

is endless – see *Chapter 11 Solutions to Common Challenges*, 'The cost of growing', page 227, for more ideas.

With a bit of persistence, it is usually possible to find all the containers you need for free. Look in skips, at veg and fish markets, in recycling centres, outside restaurants and in back alleys. Ask around, keep your eyes open wherever you go, and you might be surprised by what you find.

Avoid using anything potentially toxic, such as old paint tins. Tyres, railway sleepers and any other wood treated with external preservatives are also best avoided.

Remember that all containers need drainage holes unless you are making a container with a water reservoir. If

Airflow

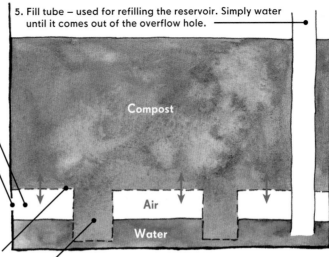

5. Fill tube – used for refilling the reservoir. Simply water until it comes out of the overflow hole.

2. Air gap – enables air to reach the roots.

1. Overflow hole – this is essential to prevent the potting mix becoming waterlogged. It also supplies fresh air into the Air gap (2).

3. False floor – the false floor separates the bulk of the potting mix from the water. Air will permeate the potting mix and the roots through holes drilled in the false floor. (This is a clever feature of these containers – they supply water and air to the potting mix, which are two essentials for growth.)

4. Wicking feet – these conduct water from the reservoir into the potting mix. They usually make up about 5–15 per cent of the total surface area (more than this and the soil can become waterlogged). The wicking feet are usually tubes filled with soil, with holes drilled in the side so water can pass through. But anything that will move water by capillary action can be used as a wick – some models use capillary matting.

Plans for a container with reservoir. There are many different styles and types of reservoirs. Most share the design features shown here.

A vegetable garden on an historic high street – the glazed terracotta pots help it blend with the surroundings.

containers are already full of holes (like mushroom crates), line them with newspaper to prevent the soil falling out.

You'll see pallets used as vertical planters online but in reality these can be heavy, full of splinters and possibly contaminated with chemicals. They can also be hard to water and not very easy to grow in. And, when they rot, there is the physically hard and unpleasant job of clearing up all the mess. Not recommended.

Buying containers

If you need a container garden to fit in with a certain aesthetic, you can buy containers made of anything, from oak and stone to zinc and bamboo, to vibrantly coloured plastic or glazed terracotta. If you are growing in a publicly visible space – on a smart high street, for example, or on a glass and stainless-steel balcony – these can help the garden fit in with its surroundings more easily than a collection of recycled containers.

For the largest selection of containers, look in large gardening stores or online. Supermarkets and discount stores often stock budget-priced containers in the spring, but be wary of buying cheap plastic pots that may only last a few seasons.

Step 3: Use a good-quality compost

The compost you put in your pots is like the foundations of a house: invisible, but essential for strong, healthy plants. Your choice will make a big difference to how well your plants grow. A good-quality compost will support vigorous growth, while plants can struggle to grow at all in anything that is poor quality.

It's important to know that all compost is not equal: the quality in the shops varies significantly. Most brands are okay, a few are very good, but poor and very poor composts are not uncommon. New gardeners often buy poor-quality compost without realising and then get demoralised when their plants don't grow well. It's a shame when this happens as they've usually done nothing else wrong.

Try to get the best compost you can – you'll find tips on how to choose under 'How to find a good-quality compost', page 52.

Keeping It Simple

- ▸ Think about what crops you want to grow and what size containers you need for them (see *Chapter 10 The Best Herbs, Fruit and Veg for Containers*).
- ▸ Remember that bigger is nearly always better (but also heavier!) and that a mix of sizes is often a good compromise for small spaces.
- ▸ Look out for recycled containers – they are a great way to start growing and to learn at minimal cost.
- ▸ Try a few different sizes and styles of container, including some with reservoirs, to find out which work well in your space and with the plants you want to grow.
- ▸ Accumulate containers slowly as you learn what works best in your space and for what you want to grow.

What makes a good compost?

The compost – or potting mix – in your pots is so critical because the plant uses it to drink, breathe and feed. So, a good one will:

1. Retain water well so the plant can **drink**.
2. Be free draining and well aerated, so the roots can **breathe** and the microbes can thrive (most beneficial microbial life needs air).

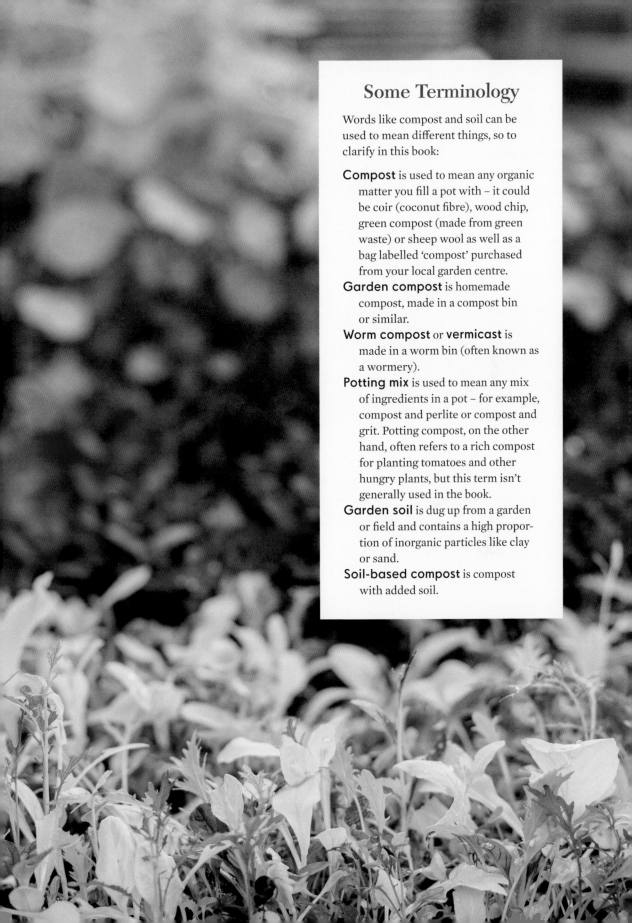

Some Terminology

Words like compost and soil can be used to mean different things, so to clarify in this book:

Compost is used to mean any organic matter you fill a pot with – it could be coir (coconut fibre), wood chip, green compost (made from green waste) or sheep wool as well as a bag labelled 'compost' purchased from your local garden centre.

Garden compost is homemade compost, made in a compost bin or similar.

Worm compost or **vermicast** is made in a worm bin (often known as a wormery).

Potting mix is used to mean any mix of ingredients in a pot – for example, compost and perlite or compost and grit. Potting compost, on the other hand, often refers to a rich compost for planting tomatoes and other hungry plants, but this term isn't generally used in the book.

Garden soil is dug up from a garden or field and contains a high proportion of inorganic particles like clay or sand.

Soil-based compost is compost with added soil.

A good-quality compost should feel nice and crumbly when squeezed between the hands. This is a sign that there are plenty of air gaps for the roots to breathe.

3. Provide a full range of plant nutrients and minerals in the right balance (see *Chapter 4 Eight Steps to Success*, 'Step 7: Feed your crops', page 69), so the plant can **feed**.
4. Be full of beneficial microbial life to help keep plant pathogens at bay and to aid in the breakdown of nutrients for plants.
5. Be free from plant diseases and weed seeds.

A good-quality, shop-bought compost should have all the qualities listed above without you needing to do anything else. There are other ingredients you can add to improve drainage or water retention, as discussed later, but this is usually optional rather than essential.

How can compost retain water and drain well?

When I started growing, I was confused about how a potting mix or compost could retain water *and* drain well. The explanation is that these needs are met in two different ways:

1. Gaps in the mix that hold air and allow water to drain through.
2. Particles that hold water. Two types of particles improve water retention: porous particles, like coir, hold water inside their pores, and tiny particles, such as clay, cling on to water by surface tension.

How to find a good-quality compost

Since compost is heavy and expensive to move, the best brands vary from country to country and even city to city. It's also hard to tell the quality of a mix by looking at it, particularly without much experience. A bit of research or asking around is often needed to help you find a good one. Most often you will be looking for a good *general-purpose* compost or *general-purpose* potting mix, which will be suitable for most food-growing needs. To find these you can:

▸ Ask for advice in a good independent local garden centre (just be aware that not all staff will be well informed about the compost they are selling).
▸ Ask other experienced gardeners in your area or on local online forums.
▸ Look for compost trials and surveys online (in the UK, *Which? Magazine* tests all the main brands each year).
▸ Look at online reviews.

If you don't have time to research, just get what you can and give it a go with an open mind. Trying more than one type is a good idea so you can compare results.

Keeping It Simple

For perfectly good results most of the time, all you need is a good-quality, general-purpose compost or potting mix. Many people I know have grown happily for years without ever doing anything else.

Some dos and don'ts of buying compost and potting mix:

- ▸ Do invest in good-quality products because this gives better results and is usually easier to sustain from season to season. Budget products in discount stores and supermarkets can sometimes be okay, but they're usually more inconsistent and so higher risk – always try one or two bags before purchasing in bulk.
- ▸ Do look for mixes based on **composted bark** or **coir (coconut fibre)**. These tend to be more consistent and easier to reuse. Green compost (made from green waste) is usually okay but more variable.
- ▸ **Don't buy anything containing peat**. Peat is unsustainable *and* harder to reuse year after year. It will soon be made illegal in the UK.
- ▸ Do consider a mix with added **soil (or loam)**. It will retain water and nutrients better, but is also heavier. Good when weight is not an issue.
- ▸ Don't buy stock left over from the previous year (the quality can deteriorate) or left outside in prolonged rain (the nutrients can wash away).
- ▸ Bear in mind that compost is a natural and variable product – even the same brand can vary considerably from batch to batch.

Can I use garden soil?

It's hard to grow in 100 per cent garden soil, as it doesn't usually provide adequate nutrients or drainage. However, good-quality garden soil can be excellent as part of a mix. Include about 25 per cent soil in a mix to add minerals and microbial life and help retain water. Bear in mind, however, that garden soil may be contaminated – see *Chapter 3 How to Design Your Container Garden*, 'Soil pollution', page 32.

Do I need special seed compost to start seeds?

No. Seed compost is finer and lower in nutrients. This can improve germination but also means that seedlings run out of food quicker (this can 'check' their growth – see *Glossary of Gardening Terms*, page 289). It's usually simpler and easier to do everything with a general-purpose compost.

Do any plants have special compost requirements?

Most vegetables and fruit grow well in a general-purpose compost. However, blueberries and cranberries need an acid or 'ericaceous' mix.

How do I make a lightweight mix?

For a lightweight mix for a balcony or rooftop, or to make a container easier to lift, look for one with a high proportion of perlite and/or coir. You can also make your own (see *Chapter 6 How to Make Your Own...*, 'Potting mixes', page 111).

What makes up a potting mix?

To understand more about potting mixes or to make your own, it's useful to know what goes into one and what the different ingredients do.

A potting mix is usually composed of one or two bulk ingredients like coir or bark, with other ingredients added to improve drainage, retain water, add fertility or support soil life.

The bulk ingredients

The common bulk ingredients (see 'Table 4.1 The Pros and Cons of the Bulk Ingredients Used in Commercial Composts', see opposite) all behave a bit differently and have various pros and cons. They are all natural, organic resources and they can vary with every batch. So, you can get coir that is excellent for

(continued on page 58)

TABLE 4.1. The Pros and Cons of the Bulk Ingredients Used in Commercial Composts

Bulk ingredient	What is it	Pros	Cons	Tips for use
Composted bark and wood fibre	Finely screened bits of composted bark and wood fibre	Quite consistent; drains and holds structure well over several years. Usually sustainable.	Not always easy to find (but getting easier). Hard to re-wet if it dries out.	Good all-round choice. Sometimes available with added loam or soil.
Coir	Coconut fibre, a waste by-product from the husks of coconuts. Sometimes sold in dried blocks and reconstituted by adding water.	Drains and retains structure well. Clean to work with. Coir bricks are light, compact and easy to move around. Re-wets well after drying out.	Low in nutrients, so additional feeding required. More sustainable than some composts, but is shipped long distances and so removes organic material from countries it is grown in.	Good lightweight choice and, in brick form, easy to move and store. Mix with worm compost and/or general-purpose fertiliser to add nutrients.
Peat	Mined from peat bogs – a precious habitat. CO_2 and other greenhouse gases are released during the process.	Consistent product, which has made it popular in the past.	Unsustainable. Plus, does not retain structure well over time. Soon to be banned in the UK.	AVOID if at all possible.
Green compost	Made from composted hedge and other clippings, sometimes with added food waste. Often available direct from recycling sites or added to commercial potting mixes.	Sustainable product. Can be good quality. Often low cost or free. Worth trying. If food waste has been added, it can be richer and better for growing vegetables.	Very variable. Sometimes low in nitrogen. Can contain large woody or plastic particles and other contaminants. Sometimes loses structure after a year or two.	Look for PAS 100 compost, a quality standard that checks for impurities, including heavy metals. Will often improve if left to rot down for 6–12 months.

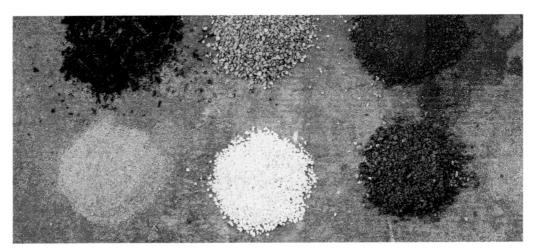

Different growing media, *clockwise from top left*: composted bark, horticultural grit, biochar, rock-dust, perlite and fine vermiculite (for covering seeds – coarser grades are used for potting mixes).

Ways to Learn More

A lot of what happens in compost is invisible – this is one of the harder aspects of container gardening to get your head around. You don't need to know a lot to grow successfully, but if you're interested in learning more, here are some activities to help you build knowledge and experience.

▸ Try more than one compost or potting mix and compare the results. Label each one carefully or you are likely to forget which one is which.

▸ Observe, smell and feel compost when you work with it. Good composts should smell earthy and healthy, and they should crumble between your fingers.

▸ Learn how to rejuvenate and reuse compost each year – see *Chapter 11 Solutions to Common Challenges*, 'Reusing old compost', page 236.

▸ Make some of your own potting mixes – see *Chapter 6 How to Make Your Own...*, 'Potting mixes', page 111.

▸ Try adding one or two of the ingredients in 'Table 4.2 Adding Ingredients to Improve Compost Mixes', opposite, to your potting mix and observe the results.

TABLE 4.2. Adding Ingredients to Improve Compost Mixes

Improving ingredient	What is it	Pros	Cons	Tips for use
Soil, loam or topsoil	The top layer of garden soil which consists mainly of inorganic particles: sand, clay, silt, etc. Sometimes pasteurised.	Holds water well and some minerals and microbial life. Retains its structure well over time.	Heavy! Highly variable. In urban gardens often mixed with builders' rubble or contaminated by past industry.	Excellent addition if weight is not an issue: add 5–30 per cent. Particularly good for long-term plantings, such as fruit trees and herbs.
Biochar	Small pieces of charcoal, usually made from wood, rice or straw. Available raw (without microbes) or treated (with microbes).	Improves drainage; retains water; provides a home for soil life; and a reservoir for nutrients. Long-lasting and sustainable.	Often expensive in small quantities. Good in theory but more variable in practice, though still worth trying. (My own trials have proved inconclusive.)	Buy ready-treated biochar and add 5–15 per cent to a potting mix. If using raw biochar, add to a wormery or compost first to charge with nutrients and microbes.
Rock dust	A waste product from the rock mining industry. Contains a wide range of minerals.	Adds a slow-release supply of minerals and trace elements and can improve structure. Supports microbial life.	Variable. Usually expensive in small quantities (due to transport costs). It will add some minerals but not necessarily in sufficient quantities to meet all the plant's needs.	Add 5–10 per cent as a mineral source to the potting mix. Or add a sprinkling to the surface of established pots – or to a wormery. Probably works best in compost that is very biologically active.
Sand	'Horticultural' sand is graded to include a mix of grain sizes to aid drainage.	May improve drainage and can also add small amounts of minerals.	Heavy. Does not always improve drainage – particles can sometimes block air holes and make drainage worse.	Avoid – unless you are sure sand will improve the drainage of your mix. Add 5–20 per cent.
Water-retaining granules	Usually manufactured from polyacrylamide crystals.	The granules may help water retention.	Some studies suggest the granules make little if any difference. Others suggest that it may be a carcinogen.	AVOID where possible.
Perlite	Volcanic rock, heated to high temperatures until it expands like popcorn.	Lightweight. Primarily improves aeration and drainage; also helps hold water. Lasts for years.	Expensive. High energy to make. Non-renewable. The white lumps can look unattractive.	Useful to make lightweight mixes – add up to 30–40 per cent. Also, to improve aeration and drainage.
Vermiculite	Flakes of volcanic rock heated to high temperatures until they expand.	Primarily improves water retention. Also improves drainage. Holds some nutrients.	Expensive. High energy to make. Non-renewable.	Particularly useful for water retention. Often added to seed-sowing mixes.

growing and coir that isn't. The job of the potting-mix producer is to select and mix good-quality ingredients. The good producers get it right more often than not, but even they can have occasional bad years, and the quality of one brand can vary from year to year.

Improving ingredients

To the bulk, or base, other ingredients are added to improve the drainage, water retention, mineral availability, fertility or microbial activity of the mix. The most common of these are summarised in 'Table 4.2 Adding Ingredients to Improve Compost Mixes', page 57.

A few (often more expensive) potting mixes will have some of these ingredients added or you can add one or two yourself to improve a mix. However, if you have purchased a good-quality potting mix, no further amendment is usually necessary. Indeed, introducing new ingredients can sometimes disrupt the balance. Ask the manufacturer what they recommend.

Still, it can be interesting to experiment with different ingredients and to make your own potting mix – and a lot can be learnt in the process. Good-quality garden soil is often an excellent addition, and biochar and rock dust are interesting to try, particularly if you can find a local source.

Step 4: Check drainage

Good drainage is crucial because the roots of plants need air to breathe. They get this from air gaps in the soil. If drainage is poor, these air gaps fill with water, so the plant can't breathe: it suffocates and dies.

How do you tell if a pot has poor drainage?

The most common signs of poor drainage (and overwatering) are:

Moss or algae growing on top of the potting mix.
Heavy, waterlogged pot
Slightly putrid smells coming from the potting mix.
Slow or no growth or plants dying.

The most common reasons for poor drainage are:

Drainage holes getting blocked.
Pots sitting in puddles and soaking up water.
Low-quality or old potting mix

How to improve drainage

At some stage, you'll probably want to improve the drainage of a potting mix, either to create a free-draining soil for Mediterranean herbs, for example, or to remedy an old potting mix. As a potting mix gets older (over more than one season), the drainage often deteriorates. See how to rejuvenate compost in *Chapter 11 Solutions to Common Challenges*, 'Reusing old compost', page 236.

To improve drainage, more air gaps are needed in the potting mix. This can be achieved by adding something to break up the existing particles and create more air spaces. How much you need to add depends in part on how freely you want your container to drain, but it is usually between 5–30 per cent. Common additives to improve drainage include:

Composted bark or composted wood chip (it is important not to use fresh, uncomposted wood chip as this will take nutrients out of the soil).
Horticultural sand
Perlite
And for very free drainage, use horticultural grit. This is like fine gravel and is often added to mixes for Mediterranean herbs and sometimes mixed into large pots for fruit bushes and trees.

Keeping It Simple

For good drainage, the water must run through the whole growing mix and then out of the holes in the bottom of the container. There are three simple steps to achieve this:

1. Start with a general-purpose compost or potting mix that drains well (any good-quality one will do).
2. Ensure there are good-sized drainage holes in the bottom of the pot. Small holes are prone to block – 1cm (½in) holes are ideal.
3. Ensure the water can run freely out of the holes. If the ground is blocking them, raise the pot using bits of wood or stones or pot 'feet'.

Note: Water can go UP drainage holes too! If your pot is sitting in a permanent puddle on your patio, it will get waterlogged and your plants will drown.

This is why it is NOT recommended that you sit pots in saucers or bowls full of water for long periods (a few hours is usually okay, though).

Sometimes it's necessary to stand a pot on feet to ensure the water can drain freely out through the holes.

Other ingredients such as biochar and rock dust can also improve drainage (depending on how finely they are ground).

Step 5: Space your plants for optimum growth and harvests

What is the optimal spacing for plants in containers to get the best harvests? The answer depends on whether it is a leafy, fruiting or root crop – and whether you want to grow a large or small plant.

Leafy crops

Leafy crops (salads and plants like spinach, chard and kale) can be sown very close together (with seeds almost touching) for a quick crop of microgreens, and a bit further apart (1–3cm/½–1¼in) for a harvest of baby leaves over a few weeks. Or, to grow full-sized leaves that can be harvested over a longer period (often several months), sow at the recommended spacing for that crop usually given on the seed packet – or see *Chapter 10 The Best Herbs, Fruit and Veg for Containers*, 'Table 10.2 Guide to the Best Vegetables for Containers', page 200,

These different spacings all work well but with different results. Microgreens give a high yield of small, tasty leaves very quickly, but need resowing every few weeks. Larger salad leaves take longer to grow, but can be harvested over a significantly longer period. Experiment to find what works best for you. I grow a mix of all three.

Root crops

Like leaves, the more space you give rooting crops, such as carrots, the larger the root will grow. So, for a quick harvest of baby carrots, sow the seeds close together (say, 1–2cm/½–1in apart) and for larger carrots, space them further apart (say 5–7cm/2–3in).

One trick to get more out of a pot of carrots, spring onions or beetroot is to sow them quite close (3cm/1¼in apart), then 'thin' the plants out (pick out some of the roots) as they grow. This will give you first a crop of small roots, then one of medium, then larger.

Fruiting crops

Most fruiting crops need to be given plenty of space to produce a good crop of fruit, often by growing just one plant in a pot. These include tomatoes, aubergines, courgettes, squash, apples and blueberries.

Carrots can be sown close together for a quick harvest of baby roots.

Mixed mustards sown nearly touching for microgreens, slightly further apart for baby leaves and a few inches apart for larger plants.

Keeping It Simple

The more space you give a plant in a pot, the bigger it will grow *and* the longer it will crop for. Most fruiting crops need plenty of space to yield well (though climbing peas and beans are an exception), while leafy crops and roots can be grown close together for a quick harvest of small leaves or roots and further apart for larger leaves and roots over a longer period.

Fruiting crops like tomatoes need plenty of space in a pot to grow and yield well.

Most fruiting vegetables need plenty of space. Climbing beans are an exception – there are 12 plants growing productively in this supermarket veg crate (for comparison, in this size of container I would only plant two tomatoes or one courgette).

The main exception to this rule is climbing beans or peas, which can be grown closer together. For example, eight climbing French bean plants will grow and yield well in a pot measuring 40 × 40cm (16 × 16in).

See *Chapter 10 The Best Herbs, Fruit and Veg for Containers*, 'Table 10.2 Guide to the Best Vegetables for Containers', page 200, for information on the best vegetables for container growing and the recommended number of different vegetables to grow in one pot.

Why some plants need more space than others

The space needed depends firstly on how hungry the plants are and, secondly on how much space their leaves and roots take up.

1. Fruiting crops like tomatoes and squash need lots of nutrients – and therefore soil and space – to produce their fruits. Peas and beans need less space because they are 'nitrogen-fixing plants', meaning they can get their nitrogen needs from the air (see 'Step 7: Feed your crop', page 69, for more on the nutrient needs of plants). Eight climbing beans will grow happily in the same space as one vining tomato!

2. Plants with bushy foliage such as potatoes need more space than tall, thin plants like spring onions. Grow bushy plants too close together and they overshadow each other. Dwarf bush beans are bushier than climbing beans, for example, which means that you can't squeeze as many into a pot.

Step 6: Create a watering routine that works for you and your plants

Watering can be an enjoyable, relaxing part of your day. It can also be the most time-consuming aspect of container gardening. This section focuses on when and how to water. See *Chapter 11 Solutions to Common Challenges*, 'Making watering easier', page 231, for tips on making watering quicker and simpler.

Three reasons why watering is so important

Watering is not just about keeping plants alive; it also affects their health and flavour. If you don't keep on top of watering, you may encounter the following problems:

1. Plants without enough water become stressed even if they survive. When plants are stressed, they get weaker and more prone to pests and disease. Underwatering is one of the most common causes of bad pest problems. A regularly watered garden is a healthier garden.

2. With insufficient water crops can also become less tender and tasty. For example, a tray of sweet, ready-to-eat pea shoots will quickly get stringy, tough and bitter if left unwatered for a few days. Likewise, tomatoes and other fruits from underwatered plants will taste inferior.

3. If the compost dries out, it can stop absorbing water and instead repel it, making it hard to re-wet. A sign that this might be a problem is if you see water rushing out of the holes in the bottom of a container just after watering. The water is travelling down the sides of the container

The secret of watering is establishing a daily routine. Luckily, this can become a relaxing and restorative part of the day – and a great chance to spot produce that is ready to eat for supper!

rather than through it. Adding a drop of washing-up liquid to the watering can can help re-wet the compost as this reduces the surface tension of the water.

The daily watering routine

Watering is a bit like the story of *Goldilocks and the Three Bears*: there is Too Much, Too Little and Just Right.

The secret to getting watering Just Right is starting a daily routine to check your containers. This might sound onerous but for most smaller container gardens (less than 20 pots), it only takes 5–10 minutes.

If you can get into the right mindset, watering can be a lovely way to start (or end) your day. It's a chance to relax, potter round the garden, see how the plants are growing, listen to nature and see if any of your crops are ready to eat for supper.

How to check if your plants need water

There are two easy ways to check if pots need watering – don't wait until the leaves are wilting because by this time the plant is already stressed!

1. Put a finger about 5cm (2in) into the potting mix. It should feel damp like a wrung-out flannel (not soggy or dry). The reason for using your finger is that the surface is not a reliable indicator. Even if the surface is wet, it can often be dry underneath – and vice versa.
2. For smaller pots, a better method is to lift and feel the weight of the pot. You will quickly learn the difference between a well-watered and a dry pot.

Unless you only have one or two pots, it's clearly not feasible to check every pot each day. But do try and check regularly,

New growers often don't realise how much the water needs of plants increase as they grow larger. Mature tomato plants such as this can drink 5 litres (1¼ gallons) of water on a hot day. Containers, with reservoirs, like these, are a good way to learn about the water needs of different crops at different stages.

particularly to start with. It will help you learn how often your plants need watering and soon you'll get a more instinctive feel for this. However, you'll still need to check from time to time. It's easy to get caught out by pots that are much drier than expected.

How to water

Water over the whole surface of the potting mix and keep going until you see water coming out of the drainage holes. This ensures that water runs through the whole growing mix, without allowing dry pockets to form (because dry compost repels water, it can be hard to re-wet). Try to avoid splashing the leaves as this can help spread disease.

Better absorption can be achieved by adding water in two stages – first, a good splash to each container, then a second round. This is particularly useful if a potting mix has dried out a bit as the first splash helps make it more absorbent.

How often to water?

How often to water depends on the following:

- ▸ The size of the pot (small pots dry out *much* faster).
- ▸ The size of the plant in relation to the pot.
- ▸ How warm it is.
- ▸ How windy it is – pots dry out much faster on windy days.

Since there are several variables, checking the dampness of the soil with a finger is the only reliable way to know whether the plant needs water. Usually, an average-sized container needs watering once a day unless it is cold or wet. Very large containers may need less frequent watering (perhaps two or three times a week) and very small containers (such as yoghurt pots) more frequent watering, perhaps two or three times a day – which is why I don't use them.

The key is to check regularly and be vigilant on warm and windy days. You'll soon learn which pots need watering most frequently, and watering will become second nature.

Overwatering

As long as containers have good drainage holes, the potting mix is good quality and the soil is checked regularly, it is quite hard to overwater. Excess water should drain away quickly, but keep an eye out for signs of overwatering, which include green moss or algae on the surface of the potting mix and slow or stunted plant growth.

What time of day is best to water?

Regular watering is the most important thing, so the best time to water is when it is most convenient for you. Where possible, first thing in the morning, before the sun is hot, is ideal. In the middle of the day, more water can be lost to evaporation and evening

Moss or green growth on the top of a pot is often a sign of overwatering or poor drainage. Normally it is accompanied by poor growth, although these garlic chives don't seem to mind!

Underwatering Larger Plants/Overwatering Seedlings

As plants get bigger, they need more water (this might sound obvious, but it took me a while to work that out). So, a baby potato plant might only need water once or twice a week, while a mature, bushy potato will usually need watering once a day. Likewise, a forest of ready-to-eat microgreens will need MUCH more water than the sprouting seeds in the first week or two. Failing to increase watering as plants grow is an easy mistake to make.

While underwatering is common with larger plants, overwatering is more common with seedlings. Baby seedlings often don't need a lot of water and it's easy to lavish too much attention on them. Feeling the weight of the pot or tray is a useful way to judge if seedlings need water.

The network of roots that has developed underneath this tray of fully grown fava bean microgreens shows why they will need more water than they did when the bean shoots were smaller.

Keeping It Simple

Check your plants on a regular basis, ideally daily, and water when needed. The easiest way to remember is to make it part of your daily routine.

Be particularly vigilant in warm and windy weather, and be aware that larger plants need more water. It's important not to overwater, but underwatering is more common, particularly in mid-summer.

Feeding regime: black box – unfed; yellow box – fed with liquid fish emulsion fertiliser; white box – fed with homemade organic fertiliser; blue box – fed with chicken manure and worm compost.

watering creates a nice damp environment for slugs to enjoy at night. But watering at any time is definitely better than not watering.

Is watering needed in the rain?

Pots still need checking in rainy periods because sometimes very little rain actually gets in. This is because buildings create drier areas where the rain doesn't reach, which are known as 'rain shadows'. The leaves of larger plants, such as rhubarb or potatoes, can also act like umbrellas, repelling rain before it reaches the soil.

Step 7: Feed your crops

A new potting mix or bag of compost usually contains enough food for around six weeks. After this, plants need feeding to achieve optimum growth.

The difference feeding makes is shown in the picture above. The four wooden boxes were filled with the same potting mix: one that was a season old (so depleted of many nutrients) and then salad seedlings of the same varieties and size were planted in each one. Three of the boxes were fed, while the fourth was left unfed (and only watered).

It's striking that the plants in the unfed container hardly grew at all, but otherwise looked quite healthy.

There are many different ways to feed plants in containers. Your approach will depend on what is easily available to you (which will vary hugely from city to city), whether you have the time or the inclination to make your own worm compost and other fertilisers, and your ethos for growing.

There is a lot of information in this section. If it seems a bit overwhelming, the most important thing to remember is simply

Keeping It Simple

All you need is a tomato feed, chicken manure pellets (or equivalent) and a 'balanced' fertiliser such as blood, fish and bone to get good results most of the time.

Liquid tomato feed (high potassium) for all fruiting crops (tomatoes, apples, chillies, strawberries, etc). Start feeding fruiting plants when they flower and continue to feed while they fruit. Begin by following the instructions on the bottle: add to the watering can and usually water on once a week, then observe and adjust as you learn and get a feel for how much your plants need. Not all tomato feeds are equal. For optimum results, get the best you can afford (look for added trace elements and minerals).

Chicken manure pellets (or equivalent high-nitrogen feed such as rapeseed meal or fish emulsion) for salads and other leafy crops. Mix into an old compost to replenish the nutrients before planting a new leafy crop.

Blood, fish and bone or a balanced equivalent (there are vegan versions available). A balanced feed has roughly equal amounts of NPK – Nitrogen, Phosphorous and Potassium. Mix the feed into used compost to replenish the main nutrients before planting new crops.

In addition, liquid seaweed and/or worm compost will promote stronger and more resilient plants.

Liquid seaweed Plants grow stronger and healthier with a wide range of minerals and trace elements. Watering (or foliar feeding) weekly or fortnightly with liquid seaweed is simple and effective.

Worm compost Worm compost adds minerals, trace elements *and* valuable soil life. Good-quality worm compost boosts growth and health and improves disease resistance. Mix a few handfuls into a potting mix before planting or use it to mulch hungry crops like tomatoes and squash to give them a boost.

that plants in containers need feeding for optimum growth. Just providing them with some form of feed can make a big difference.

First, let's look at what food plants require in order to thrive. They have three main needs:

1. **Nitrogen, Phosphorus and Potassium (NPK):** As humans, we require three main types of food in our diet: protein, fat and carbohydrate. Similarly, plants need three main elements in their diet: nitrogen (N) for leaf growth, phosphorous (P) for root growth and potassium (K) for fruit growth. These elements are often abbreviated as 'NPK' on fertiliser labels.

   Every plant needs all three elements for healthy growth, but leafy crops will often require a higher proportion of nitrogen (N) and fruiting ones a higher proportion of potassium (K).

2. **Minerals and trace elements:** In the same way that humans need a wide

Nitrogen	Phosphorous	Potassium
N	**P**	**K**
SHOOTS (LEAVES)	ROOTS	FRUITS

High 'N' Feeds	High 'P' Feeds	High 'K' Feeds
Chicken manure pellets	Bonemeal	Tomato feed
Rapeseed meal	Rock phosphate	Comfrey tea
Fish emulsion		
Nettle tea		

'Balanced' feeds contain roughly equal proportions of NPK (for example, blood, fish and bone).

Shoots, roots and fruits is a useful mnemonic for remembering the roles of N, P and K in the plant. This diagram also lists some common fertilisers that are high in each element. The high N feeds are good to promote leafy growth, high P benefits root veg and high K to promote fruiting.

range of minerals and trace elements to stay healthy, so do plants. Some of these elements, such as calcium, play vital roles and are needed in reasonable quantities. Others like silicon and boron are only needed in tiny amounts. See 'Table 4.5 Nutrients That Plants Need and What They Need Them For', page 80, to learn about these different elements and their roles in plant health.

Two of the best ways to add minerals and trace elements to containers are by feeding with liquid seaweed and worm compost.

Alternatively, some of the good-quality general-purpose fertilisers – for example, Biocanna – also contain a wide range of minerals in addition to Nitrogen, Phosphorous and Potassium. Compare different products to see which have the most complete range.

3. **Soil life:** As humans, we rely on billions of microbes in our digestive system to break down the food in our gut.

Understanding NPK labels

Fertilisers in the shops are labelled with their Nitrogen (N), Phosphorous (P) and Potassium (K) ratios. It's useful to understand these, as they can help you choose the right fertiliser.

For example, the NPK of chicken manure pellets is typically NPK 4:2:2, meaning it contains twice as much N (4) as P (2) and K (2). As nitrogen is needed for leaf growth, chicken manure pellets are good for leafy crops like kale. Normally (but not always), the ratio is also expressed as a percentage, so NPK 4:2:2 will usually mean the fertiliser contains 4% Nitrogen, 2% Phosphorous and 2% Potassium. The higher the numbers, the stronger the fertiliser.

Liquid tomato feed, on the other hand, typically has an NPK ratio of something like 4:3:8. In other words, it is highest in Potassium (K) with 8%. As potassium is needed by plants to make fruits, this makes it a good fertiliser for all fruiting crops (and not just tomatoes).

Natural, organic feeds, like well-rotted manure, seaweed, comfrey or compost, are usually less rich, with far lower concentrations of NPK than artificial fertilisers. Worm compost typically has NPK concentrations of 2%:1%:2% while manufactured fertilisers (like Miracle-Gro) can be as high as 24%:8%:16% – about ten times more concentrated than worm compost. In general, I recommend using natural fertilisers as much as you can – and if you do need to use one of the more concentrated, manufactured fertilisers, take extra care not to overfeed.

Chicken manure pellets are widely available, relatively inexpensive and, as they are high in nitrogen, are handy for feeding leafy crops.

Similarly, plants rely on a complex web of soil life: bacteria, fungi, worms and other soil life. The bacteria and fungi break down the organic matter in compost (the bits that the plant itself can't digest), releasing food for the plants. These microorganisms also help suppress some plant diseases in the soil.

The level of beneficial microbial life in purchased compost will vary. However, you can add it by using worm compost, homemade compost or well-rotted manure. Some plant feeds, like liquid seaweed and rock dust, will also feed beneficial soil life, helping it to multiply and flourish.

Spraying the leaves of plants with diluted liquid seaweed feed (gardeners call this foliar feeding) once a week or fortnight is a great way to give them a boost of the trace elements they need.

Homemade organic fertilisers

Organic gardeners love homemade feeds like nettle tea, comfrey tea and well-rotted manure. And for good reason – these are excellent fertilisers, but they are not always a convenient or practical solution for everyone growing in a small space. The ingredients can be difficult or time-consuming to find, and some smell really bad! Find out more in *Chapter 6 How to Make Your Own*, 'Fertiliser "teas" and other homemade fertilisers', page 124.

Feed the soil or feed the plant?

Broadly speaking, there are two approaches, either feed the *soil* or feed the *plant*:

1. Feed the *soil*

The most natural way to feed plants is to add homemade compost, worm compost, well-rotted manure or other organic material. As this slowly breaks down, food is released. The plants help this process by releasing special chemicals from their roots (called exudates), which attract microbial life to help break down the organic matter

and release the food. In this way, plants 'work' for their food, which helps them become 'fitter'. To use an analogy, this way of feeding is a bit like giving a child a healthy diet and lots of exercise, too.

2. Feed the *plant*

Alternatively, plants can be fed with fertiliser or liquid feed that is more directly available to them. Organic matter doesn't have to be broken down, so the plant needs to do less work. To continue our analogy, this is a bit like feeding a child fast food and letting him or her watch TV all day. The plant will usually grow well but it might be less healthy and more prone to illness. (Fertilisers based on natural ingredients like chicken manure or seaweed can fall somewhere between the two, feeding both the soil and the plant.)

Which of these approaches is best in containers? They both have merits. Feeding the soil is arguably more natural and healthier. But, due to the relatively small volume of soil in containers, it can be hard to provide a plant with ALL its nutritional needs in this way. Getting enough organic material into your home may also not be practical. Feeding the plant, on the other hand, can provide plants with all their needs, but arguably in a less healthy way.

Most often, a good compromise is to do both. Feed your plants as much organic matter like worm compost or well-rotted manure as you can easily get hold of and supplement this with other feeds and fertilisers to ensure a plant has all its nutritional needs met.

You can also get perfectly good results with purchased fertilisers alone. This is the easiest and least time-consuming option, and preferable in some circumstances.

Find a way of feeding that works best for you. If you enjoy making worm compost and finding manure in the city, excellent! If not, buy fertilisers, and try to use some that are based on natural ingredients and contain a broad spectrum of minerals as well as NPK.

How to feed plants?

The speed at which the nutrients become available to the plant varies with the feeding method. Liquid and foliar feeding provide an immediate but short-term food supply. Foliar

TABLE 4.3. How and When to Feed Plants in Containers

Feeding method	How to apply	When to use
Mix feed into the potting mix	Simply mix a fertiliser, such as chicken manure pellets, blood, fish and bone, or worm compost, through the soil.	To replenish the nutrients in a pre-used potting mix before replanting.
Topdressing	Add a sprinkling of fertiliser – chicken manure pellets, seaweed meal or rock dust – to the surface of the potting mix.	To give established plants like fruit bushes, tomatoes or kale a boost.
Mulching	Similar to topdressing, but mulching usually refers to adding an organic layer of material, like worm compost or manure, to the top of the potting mix.	Use to boost established plants like fruit bushes or squash.
Liquid feeding	Add a liquid feed, such as tomato feed or liquid seaweed, to the watering can and water on the soil as a root drench. Provides easily accessible food for the plants.	Use regularly to top up nutrients and ensure plants have enough minerals and NPK. How often depends on the feed and type of plant, often once a week or fortnight. It often works well to dilute the feed by more than the instructions and add it more frequently – but don't exceed the recommended weekly dose.
Foliar feeding	Plants can absorb nutrients through their leaves as well as their roots. Dilute liquid feed, such as seaweed, worm tea or comfrey tea, in a spray bottle (an old cleaning bottle, thoroughly washed, is fine), and spray on the leaves on a still day, once a week or fortnight.	Foliar feeding helps a little precious fertiliser go a long way. It's also a good method to add minerals without disturbing the balance of the soil. Nutrients are often absorbed faster through the leaves, providing plants with a quick boost. A very useful way to feed container plants.
'Lasagne' gardening	This is like mulching, except the organic material is added to the *bottom* of the pot. Usually in layers – for example, wood chip or broken twigs, then straw, food waste, worm compost or Bokashi compost, and, finally, potting mix on top.	When planting up a pot this provides a slow release of nutrients as the organic materials break down. It also provides a reservoir of food for soil microorganisms to flourish. Excellent for long-term plantings – and particularly suited to larger pots.

TABLE 4.4. Different Fertilisers and How to Use Them

Feed	NPK	Minerals and trace elements	Benefit to soil life	How to use
Tomato feed	N medium P medium K high	Sometimes (if better quality)	Low	Use on all fruiting crops when the plant starts flowering and throughout fruiting.
Worm compost	N medium P low K medium	High	High. Adds soil life and feeds it.	Use to replenish nutrients in used potting mix. Add as a mulch around hungry crops like tomatoes and squash. Soak in water to make worm tea.
Chicken manure pellets	N high P medium K medium	Low–Medium	Some	Use to replenish nutrients before planting leafy crops and as a topdressing on large, leafy, long-term crops like kale and chard as a boost when needed.
Liquid seaweed	N low P low K medium	High	High	Liquid feed or foliar feed to add minerals and trace elements. Useful for all container-grown plants.
Rock dust	Negligible	High (slow release)	Some	Incorporate into potting mix as a long-term source of minerals. Or add as a topdressing to long-term plantings.
Blood, fish and bone	N high P high K high	Medium	Some	Mix into used potting mix to add major nutrients before replanting with squash, potatoes or tomatoes, for example.
Well-rotted manure	N low P low K low	Low	High	Use as a mulch around hungry crops like squash and tomatoes. Or add to the bottom of large containers before replanting. *Do not use fresh manure on plants.*
Rapeseed meal (flax and cottonseed meal are similar)	N high P medium K medium	Low	Some	Use in the same way as chicken manure pellets. A vegan alternative that has a less unpleasant smell and is easier to mix into the soil than chicken manure pellets. Excellent if you can find it.
Nettle tea	N high P low K medium	Low–Medium	Some	Use as a liquid feed once a week or fortnight. It promotes leaf growth and adds minerals, contributing to healthy plants.
Comfrey tea	N medium P low K high	Medium	Some	Use regularly on tomatoes and other fruiting crops. Adds some minerals, too. Excellent alternative to commercial tomato feed.
Bonemeal	N low P high K negligible	Medium	Some	One of the few fertilisers containing high levels of potassium. May be useful to replenish the potassium in old potting mix before planting root crops (I generally use a balanced NPK fertiliser).
Controlled release fertiliser	Varies (often high)	Sometimes	Low	Will release nutrients over three, six, 12 or even 18 months, depending on the variety used. Particularly useful for trees in pots and other long-term plantings. A benefit of controlled release is that fewer nutrients are washed away by watering.
Epsom salts	All negligible	Contains magnesium and sulphur	Negligible	Best used as an occasional foliar feed – often used on tomatoes, which are hungry for magnesium.

Note: Homemade fertilisers such as nettle tea and worm compost are extremely variable in composition and strength, so the values above are *very* approximate.

feeding is fastest of all – if you spray tomato leaves with Epsom salts (high in magnesium), they will be visibly greener in just 24 hours. Foliar feeding is useful when plants need a quick pick-me-up or to ensure they can access the full spectrum of their nutritional needs. Weekly foliar feeding with liquid seaweed can make a big difference to plant health, and I recommend it.

Organic materials like worm compost, on the other hand, release their nutrients slowly over several weeks and months. They are excellent ways to feed but, as noted before, may not provide everything that a plant in a container needs for optimal growth.

Purchased solid fertilisers can be either 'quick release' or 'slow release' depending on how they are made. Slow-release fertilisers can be designed to feed plants from six up to 18 months. They are good for long-term plantings and nurseries often use them for potted fruit trees to save time on regular feeding.

How much and when to feed?

How much food plants in containers need depends on:

▶ What volume of soil the plant is growing in (larger pots hold more food and need feeding less frequently).
▶ The quality of the potting mix and how much food it contains (some potting mixes have slow-release fertiliser added that can last several months).
▶ The growing conditions (warmth, light, etc) and how fast the plant is growing.
▶ The size of the plant and its stage of growth – most plants need more food when flowering and fruiting, for example.

If this sounds a bit complicated, simply start by following the feeding instructions that come with the fertiliser. Then, be aware that in good growing conditions, or if the plant is growing fast or fruiting, it might need a little more. Also, bear in mind that a little too much or too little fertiliser won't usually make a lot of difference, particularly if you are using natural, organic fertilisers. If you look back at the photograph on page 69 (of the four wooden boxes planted with leaves and fed differently), the starkest difference was between feeding and not feeding – the differences between the different fertilisers was less significant.

Nurturing soil life

One of my favourite gardening quotes comes from the no-dig expert, Charles Dowding, who says in his book, *Organic Gardening: The Natural No-Dig Way*:

> 'The world of gardening is full of chemical ideas. It is vital to ignore most of these and cultivate instead an approach that is based on Life, specifically the life in all soil, the essence of organic gardening. Respect and encourage Life as much as you can...'

Although he is talking about gardening in the ground, his words apply equally well to containers. The more you can nurture the life in the soil of your containers, the better. For this reason, I highly recommend you make your own worm compost. Worm compost is teeming with life and is a brilliant addition to containers. Other natural feeds, such as liquid seaweed and well-rotted manure, will also feed and support soil life, whereas highly concentrated chemical fertilisers may harm it.

Worm compost: the 'black gold' of fertilisers

Worm compost is one of the best plant foods there is – and is the perfect natural plant feed for container growing as it requires little

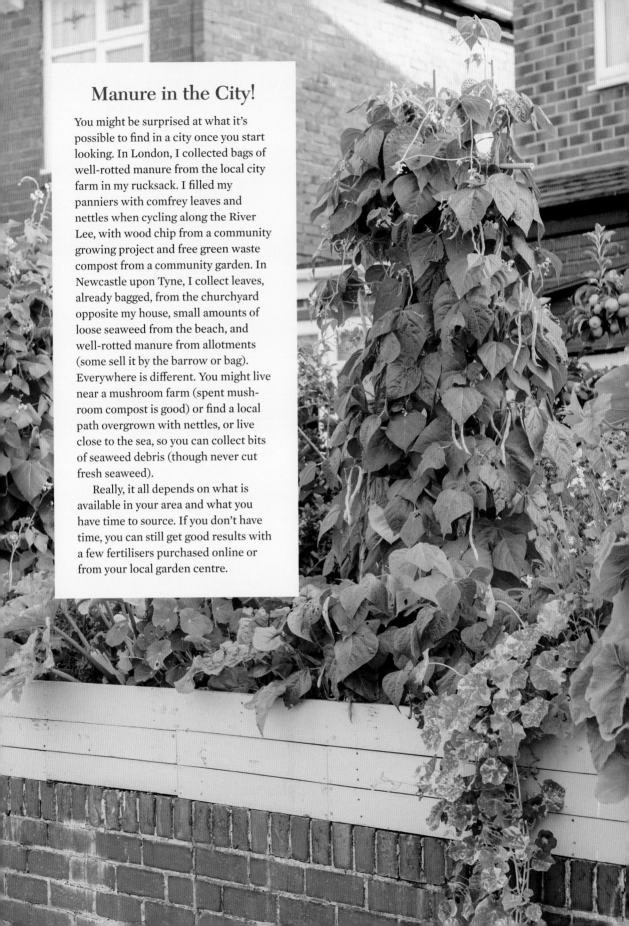

Manure in the City!

You might be surprised at what it's possible to find in a city once you start looking. In London, I collected bags of well-rotted manure from the local city farm in my rucksack. I filled my panniers with comfrey leaves and nettles when cycling along the River Lee, with wood chip from a community growing project and free green waste compost from a community garden. In Newcastle upon Tyne, I collect leaves, already bagged, from the churchyard opposite my house, small amounts of loose seaweed from the beach, and well-rotted manure from allotments (some sell it by the barrow or bag). Everywhere is different. You might live near a mushroom farm (spent mushroom compost is good) or find a local path overgrown with nettles, or live close to the sea, so you can collect bits of seaweed debris (though never cut fresh seaweed).

Really, it all depends on what is available in your area and what you have time to source. If you don't have time, you can still get good results with a few fertilisers purchased online or from your local garden centre.

Freshly sieved compost from my wormery. Getting a wormery transformed my growing, improving the health and vitality of my crops.

space to make. How to make worm compost is covered later in the book (see *Chapter 6 How to Make Your Own...*, 'Worm compost', page 114), but here I want to look briefly at its benefits and how to use it.

The excellence of worm compost is reflected in its price, as Rhonda Sherman, author of *The Worm Farmer's Handbook*, points out – while a tonne of normal compost retails for $30 on average in the US, a tonne of worm compost sells for $200, nearly seven times the price!

In addition to being high in the major nutrients NPK (roughly 2:1:1.5, though this varies a lot), worm compost has many other qualities:

- It's rich in other nutrients, including calcium and magnesium.

- It contains humic and fulvic acids that stimulate plant growth and help make nutrients available to the plant.
- It has a large AND diverse microbial population.
- It retains water well.
- It supports better root and plant growth, and gives higher yields.
- It improves resistance to aphids and caterpillars, and to soil-borne diseases.
- It increases plant vitality and flavour profile.

You can use worm compost in any of the following ways to boost your growing:

- Mix 10–25 per cent into old compost to help rejuvenate and reuse it.
- Add 5–10 per cent to new compost to inoculate it with life. This is beneficial

Worm compost is an excellent mulch for hungry crops like tomatoes – I apply a new layer every few weeks to add both food and soil life.

for seed sowing, transplanting baby seedlings and potting up.

▶ Use it as a mulch on hungry crops (such as tomatoes and courgettes), halfway through the season, or on fruit bushes and trees in autumn and spring.

▶ Use it to make compost tea. Worm compost can be soaked in water for several days to make an excellent fertiliser tea.

The essential elements plants need

A little knowledge of the role that different elements play in plant health can help us understand why it's important that they are included in potting mixes. Plants need both macronutrients like nitrogen and calcium in larger amounts and micronutrients in smaller amounts. Even though the micronutrients are only needed in tiny quantities, plant growth can be significantly affected if one isn't present. The availability of macro- and micronutrients also affects nutrient density – a measure of how nutritious crops are.

The roles the different elements play in plants are summarised in 'Table 4.5 Nutrients That Plants Need and What They Need Them For', page 80 – it's not necessary to remember this information! A good-quality, general-purpose compost should contain all of them. However, if plants aren't growing well, one possible reason is that one of the macro- or micronutrients is present in insufficient quantities. One way to be more certain that plants have everything they need is to buy or make a fertiliser with a full range

TABLE 4.5. Nutrients That Plants Need and What They Need Them For

Macronutrient (Needed in larger amounts)	What the plant needs the nutrient for
Calcium (Ca)	To make cell walls and membranes. Plants do not grow well without calcium being present at reasonable levels.
Magnesium (Mg)	To make chlorophyll for photosynthesis and many other roles. (If you spray tomatoes with Epsom salts, which are high in magnesium, you'll see the leaves green up overnight.)
Nitrogen (N)	Essential to make chlorophyll and protein, but too much can cause 'soft growth' (see 'Table 8.2 Troubleshooting Check Sheet', page 156). It is water-soluble and can wash out of compost (one reason why it's best to avoid buying old stocks of compost).
Phosphorus (P)	A key part of all plant enzymes and determines the speed at which plants grow. Low phosphorus results in slow growth.
Potassium (K)	Needed for the movement of water through the plant. Plants need plenty of potassium, but if potassium levels are too high in the soil, they struggle to take up other nutrients.
Sulphur (S)	Sulphur is needed to make crucial enzymes. When sulphur is abundant, a plant can make a wider range of proteins.
Micronutrient (Only needed in tiny amounts)	What the plant needs the nutrient for
Boron (B)	To make the tubes that plants use to transport water. Too little boron and plants can't drink or feed effectively.
Chlorine (Cl)	For photosynthesis
Copper (Cu)	For the soil ecology and for plant immune systems
Iron (Fe)	Essential to make chlorophyll for photosynthesis and for respiration. Usually, there is no shortage, but iron is harder for plants to access in more alkaline soils.
Manganese (Mn)	For plant photosynthesis and food flavour
Molybdenum (Mo)	Enables plants to utilise nitrogen.
Silicon (Si)	Helps increase stem strength (important in windy growing places) and improves drought tolerance.
Zinc (Zn)	Essential to make proteins and chlorophyll.

of plant nutrients – if you would like to make your own homemade fertiliser, see *Chapter 6 How to Make Your Own...*, 'Complete organic fertiliser', page 126.

Professional growers can get their soil tested to check if nutrients are in short supply. This isn't really practical or cost-effective in small-space growing, but what we can do is keep an eye on the health of our crops, try to buy good-quality compost, make our own worm compost and use quality plant foods that contain a wide range of micronutrients.

Buying fertilisers

Finding suitable fertilisers for food growing in the city is not always that easy. Many urban garden centres are geared more towards ornamental or 'lifestyle' growing with prices to match, but there are other places to look.

Online, eBay has a wide selection and some sellers offer professional-quality products (normally only available in huge bags), split into small, convenient sizes. Discount stores and supermarkets often sell general fertilisers, like chicken manure pellets, in the spring at reasonable prices.

If you get the growing bug in a big way, look for specialist horticultural suppliers who sell good-quality fertilisers with added trace elements, designed for food growing. You may need to buy larger quantities, but it can work out at a fraction of the cost if you have storage space or can share with others.

Signs of under- and overfeeding

Underfeeding is common and easy to do. If plants are growing poorly or have yellowing leaves, the most common deficiency is nitrogen (nitrogen is soluble and easily washes out – and sometimes even new compost is low in it). To address this, try liquid feeding with a high-nitrogen feed like nettle tea or fish emulsion (Biobizz Fish Mix, for example) or topdressing with something rich in nitrogen like chicken manure pellets.

Other mineral deficiencies can present themselves in different ways – for example, purple leaf tints may be a sign of potassium deficiency, while yellowing between the leaf veins can be a sign of magnesium deficiency. This is a huge and complex subject – the most important thing is just to be aware that poor growth, stunted plants or odd leaf colours are often caused by nutrient deficiencies. If you have a particular issue, search engines and growing forums can often help you find an answer. For example, if you search for 'tomato nutrient deficiency' you will see lots of images of tomato leaves with different nutrient deficiencies. The good

news is that, in most instances, a quality general-purpose feed like Biocanna Bio Vega or liquid seaweed and/or a mulch of worm compost will help solve the problem.

It is also possible to overfeed. The more concentrated a fertiliser, the easier it is to add too much. The most common signs of overfeeding are:

▸ Lots of lush growth. Gardeners call it 'soft' growth because the leaves are generally less sturdy and more prone to pest attack.
▸ Bad pest problems, particularly aphids
▸ Lack of growth – sometimes too much fertiliser can cause an imbalance in the soil, suppressing growth. For example, high potassium levels can make it harder for plants to take up the nitrogen they need.

If all this seems a bit overwhelming, my basic message is that if you can feed plants in containers, it will make a big difference. Try it, observe how the plants grow and learn as you grow.

Step 8: Observe and keep learning

If you follow Steps 1–7 in this chapter, you will have many successful and delicious harvests... most of the time. However, things sometimes don't work out as hoped, even for the most experienced growers. You might even have the occasional season when a lot of things seem to go wrong and your plants don't grow well – I know I have. The weather, bad batches of compost or birds and slugs can all conspire against us.

When something does go wrong, don't panic and try not to lose confidence. Remember this happens to all of us. Try to observe what is happening and work out why (see *Chapter 8 Growing in Harmony with Life*,

Feeding Tips
for Healthy Plants

Learning to feed plants, as with much of growing, is trial and error combined with observation and not worrying if things go a bit wrong. Here are some tips to help you:

▶ Like us, plants benefit from a diverse, balanced diet. Try to use a variety of feeds – as many as you easily can.

▶ Plants in containers also seem to do best with a combination of feeds in the soil (like worm compost or chicken manure pellets), a regular root drench with a good-quality liquid feed like liquid seaweed or nettle tea, and regular foliar feeding with liquid seaweed or similar. While it's definitely not essential to do all three, I've found my plants usually look the healthiest when I do.

▶ Try to use feeds based on natural ingredients, such as seaweed, rapeseed meal or chicken manure as much as you can. That said, don't feel you need to dismiss good-quality artificial fertilisers and controlled release fertilisers. They can still be useful, particularly if you can't find natural fertilisers or don't have the time to make them.

▶ Think about what a plant needs and when it needs it. Fruiting plants will benefit from feeds high in potassium and leafy crops from feeds high in nitrogen. Plants that are growing strongly or fruiting heavily will need more feed than those that aren't.

▶ Little and often works well. Professional growers often use liquid feeds (like tomato feed) every time they water, but in a more dilute concentration (the overall amount of feed per week remains the same). I often make up a mix of different liquid feeds (homemade and purchased ones) in a bucket and add a very small amount every time I water.

'Table 8.2 Troubleshooting Check Sheet', page 156). Bear in mind that the seven steps outlined previously can also help you find the underlying cause of many problems in your container garden – for example, too little light, poor compost and not enough feeding or watering are among the most common reasons for poor growth.

A benefit of growing in small spaces is that you can quickly and easily keep an eye on all your plants and hopefully catch any problems early. Try to get into the habit of actively observing all your plants when you water and to spot any pest problems or other issues.

While the essence of growing is simple, there is *always* more to learn. Learning to grow is a slow process that happens over many seasons. In this fast-paced age, this is one of the things that makes it special.

There are several ways to learn more about growing, so choose whichever suit you best:

Growing at home: Learn by trying, getting some things wrong and achieving some successes.

Keep a diary: It is all too easy to forget what you did last year. A diary (or five-year diary) enables you to look back at when you sowed and when you harvested, as well as what went well and not so well.

Take a course: A lot of community growing projects offer day or evening classes in

This was my second year of 'serious' growing on my London balcony. My only 'formal' training at this stage had been gardening evening classes – and I was still making rookie mistakes (such as overcrowding plants). However, I still had some good success. This shows that you don't need a lot of knowledge – or years of training – to grow successfully. Following the 'Keeping It Simple' advice for each of the eight steps outlined in this chapter will get you a long way.

Keeping a close eye on your plants and how healthy they look will help you to spot any problems early. Observation is one of the best ways to learn about growing.

food growing. These are run by tutors experienced at growing in *your* local climate. Unless you are planning a career in horticulture, most people find a practical course more helpful than a theoretical one.

Volunteer at a community garden: A lot can be learnt while gardening with others, chatting and asking questions while you dig, sow and drink tea. Community gardens are also excellent places to pick up local information to help your growing.

Join in online: Join an online gardening forum on Facebook or elsewhere. Or sign up for emails from garden websites that offer seasonal tips. These can help remind you of what to do when and also offer seasonal inspiration.

As I said at the beginning of this book, one of the paradoxes of growing is that the essence is simple but there is always more to learn. The more experience you get and the more you learn, the more confident you will feel and the more success you will have.

Chapter 5

Useful Growing Skills

Once you've started growing, you will probably want to expand and practise your growing skills – whether that's growing from seed, moving plants from one pot to another, taking cuttings or saving seeds. None of these tasks is difficult and many people succeed just by having a try – if you put seeds in compost and water them, they will normally grow! However, as with other parts of growing, a little bit of information (and practise) can improve your chances of success as well as help to raise healthier, stronger plants. My aim is to give you that information here.

This chapter also offers tips on how to harvest and prune your edible crops, and how to tie up and support plants in containers.

You can use a simple homemade 'bottle waterer' (just a plastic milk carton with holes in the lid) to water herb cuttings.

How to grow from seed

Raising healthy plants from seed is an incredibly useful skill to learn as you'll then have access to literally thousands of different varieties that can't be obtained in any other way. It works out at a fraction of the cost of buying plants and watching seeds emerge each spring is one of the wonders of growing.

Growing from seed is straightforward once you get the hang of it. Good-quality seeds and compost are key, and a bright light source is also critical once the seeds have germinated.

To germinate, seeds primarily need three things:

1. **Moisture:** This wakes the seed from dormancy.
2. **Air:** Seeds need air to breathe. They won't germinate if the compost is waterlogged.

3. **Warmth:** Different seeds germinate best at different temperatures. The majority of vegetable seeds will germinate fine in standard room temperatures (16–20°C/61–68°F). Where possible, a steady, constant temperature is better than a fluctuating one. Subtropical plants like chillies, aubergines and tomatoes germinate more quickly and reliably with a little more warmth (ideally between 23–26°C/73–79°F – but normal room temperature is also usually okay). Put these in a warm place, such as above a radiator, or invest in a heated propagator (a tray with an electric heating element).

The quality of the compost affects germination and is a common reason for poor results. Specialist seed compost can give better germination, but it is low in nutrients and the seedlings can run out of food before they are ready to plant out (this is stressful for them). A general-purpose compost is a safer choice for most seeds as it has more nutrients and will sustain seedlings for longer.

How to sow seeds

1. Fill a suitable container, such as a seed tray, pot or modules, with new, good-quality, general-purpose compost about 1–2cm (½–¾in) below the top of the container (new growers often put in too little compost). Lightly firm down to remove any large air gaps. Refill if needed to 1–2cm (½–¾in) below the top.

2. Use a watering can with a fine rose or a 'bottle waterer' (a plastic bottle with holes drilled in the top) to give the soil a good watering – it needs to be damp all the way through.

3. Make a small depression in the compost where you want the seed to go. As a rough rule of thumb, the depth of the depression should be twice the thickness of the seed. Put the seed in the hole and cover with compost.

4. Optional: Put the container in a plastic bag or cover it with a propagator lid (some seed trays are sold with transparent plastic propagator lids). This helps to retain moisture and can speed germination. The bag or lid must be removed as soon as the seeds germinate.

5. Check the container daily until the seeds emerge, ensuring the compost stays damp like a wrung-out flannel (but not too wet). Water with a fine rose if necessary.

6. Once the seeds have emerged, move the container to the brightest place you have – see 'How to raise healthy seedlings', page 92.

Most vegetable seeds germinate in five to 30 days, depending on the variety and temperature, though radish and some mustards can appear in just three to five days, while coriander and parsley can take three or four weeks or more.

Choosing and keeping seeds

Starting with good-quality seeds does make a difference. Look for seeds grown in your country as they will be better adapted to local conditions (and be aware that a lot of seed sold is now imported – up to 80 per cent in the UK). Keep an eye out for small seed companies and cooperatives that save their own seed or those that supply small-scale commercial or organic growers. I also recommend seed swaps if you can find one locally or online. Home-saved seed is another good option (see 'How to save seeds', page 108).

Store seeds in a cool, dry, dark place, perhaps in a Tupperware container or large jam jar in the fridge, or a cool spot in the home. Kept in the right conditions, most seeds will remain viable for three years or more, but there are a few exceptions: the most common are parsnips (get fresh seed every year); onions and leeks (every two years); pea, pepper, aubergine, bean, carrot and spinach seeds (every two or three years).

Indoor versus outdoor sowing

Indoor sowing is useful for starting plants when it is too cold outside and for protecting baby seedlings from slugs and birds. The main challenges of indoor sowing are the light levels (see 'Raising seedlings inside – overcoming the light challenge', page 92) and finding space in your kitchen, living room or bedroom (not to mention the fact that partners and flatmates of particularly enthusiastic growers might not always be keen on having seedlings occupying every available surface!). Chillies, tomatoes, peppers and aubergines are the most

Troubleshooting Seed Germination

Seeds will usually come up okay, but there can be a number of reasons why sometimes they don't. The following list is quite long but don't be intimidated by this: it's normally not difficult to work out which one is the issue.

Old seeds: Germination deteriorates as seeds get older (see 'Choosing and keeping seeds', page 87).

Poor-quality seeds: For example, seed saved from unhealthy plants or that has not been stored well.

Quality of compost: Seeds do not germinate well in poor-quality compost. If you are having difficulty germinating a variety of seeds, compost is often the reason.

Too dry: Seeds need moisture to germinate, so check that the compost feels damp.

Too wet: Seeds breathe and need air to germinate. If the soil is saturated with water, air is excluded and the seeds cannot breathe. Seeds can also rot in wet soil. Overwatering seeds is a very common mistake: always check a seed tray needs it before adding more water. Do this by feeling the compost or feeling the weight of the tray.

Too cold: Crops from the subtropics, such as tomatoes, chillies and French beans, generally need more warmth than temperate crops like peas and broad beans. You can find optimum germination temperatures for each crop online.

Too hot: A few seeds such as lettuce germinate better in cooler temperatures.

Eaten!: Sometimes when seeds don't come up, further investigation reveals they have disappeared. Mice, birds or slugs are the usual culprits.

common seeds started inside, but other tender plants, including squash, runner beans, courgettes and cucumbers can be, too. I sometimes also start seeds of microgreens inside (the mice and birds love the seeds before they germinate), but then move them outside as soon as they come up.

Outdoor-sown seeds will grow stronger in the better light outside and will be more adapted to outdoor conditions from the start. Generally, most things are best sown outside when it is warm enough to do so. Hardy crops like peas, chard, kale, lettuce and beetroot are nearly always started outside (the exception is very early sowings, which can be made inside).

Sowing seeds 'direct' versus in trays and small pots

Seeds can either be sown in their final pot (often referred to as 'direct sowing') or started in trays or smaller pots first. Seeds sown in trays or small pots can be more easily protected from slugs and birds and moved inside if bad weather strikes.

Direct sowing saves on work as plants do not need to be transplanted. It also benefits those plants that don't like to have their roots disturbed, which include parsnips, carrots, coriander and dill. It also makes sense to direct sow fast-growing crops like radish, rocket and pea shoots. For most other crops,

The Difference Between F1, GMO and Open-Pollinated Seeds

You might notice that some packs of vegetable seeds are labelled 'F1'. These seeds are hybrids, created by crossing two different varieties. Hybrids are often more vigorous and higher yielding. However, they are more expensive and seeds that are saved from them will not 'breed true' (that is, they will not be the same as the plant they came from). F1 seeds are not harmful, but they have contributed to a loss of heritage varieties and to a widespread reduction in seed-saving skills – a century ago, nearly all allotment holders and growers saved their own seed.

F1 seeds are created by crossbreeding and are *not* the same as GMO (Genetically Modified Organism) seeds, which are the product of genetic engineering. GMO seeds are developed to confer disease resistance or to improve yields. The balance of evidence so far is that they are safe for both humans and the environment. However, there are other reasons you may choose not to grow them, and there are lots of strong feelings – for and against – GMO. It's a complicated subject and you need to decide for yourself. Personally, although I can see some situations where they have value, I think they're a distraction from finding better ways to farm with nature and I don't grow them myself.

On the other hand, there are heritage and heirloom vegetable varieties, which are also known as 'open-pollinated' seeds. Open-pollinated seeds are the traditional varieties that, if saved correctly, will grow true to their parents. Over time, open-pollinated seeds will also slowly and naturally adapt to the environment and climate in which they are grown. That is why home-saved seeds – or seeds saved in your local area – will often perform better than imported seeds.

Small-space growers can, between us, play a valuable role in helping save our seed diversity. We can support local seed-saving initiatives and buy, swap and save heritage and other open-pollinated seed varieties.

including peas, beans, salads and leafy crops, you can sow direct or start them first in small pots, whichever is most convenient.

Seed sowing: trays, modules, plugs or pots

A variety of different containers can be used for starting seeds.

Seed trays can be bought or improvised from fruit or mushroom trays. They are excellent for starting leafy crops and edible flowers and can be used for microgreens, too. If you are growing to transplant, take care to adequately space the seeds, or to 'thin them out', so that each seedling has plenty of space to grow and the roots don't get too tangled.

Modules give each plant its own space and make it easier to transplant them without disturbing the roots (good for root crops). They are available in different sizes and depths, including deep ones for peas and beans. Rigid plastic modules, if you can find them, are the easiest to use. Care needs to be taken that all the compartments are well watered as the corner ones dry out easily.

Coir Jiffy plugs are neat and tidy and recommended for starting plants like tomatoes and chillies inside. They are first reconstituted by soaking them in water for a few minutes. Once the seedling has grown, the whole plug is moved to a bigger pot.

Small pots can be used to start seeds and you can reuse a wide variety, including yoghurt pots, homemade newspaper pots, toilet rolls and anything else you can find. Add drainage holes if needed. As a rough rule of thumb, start larger plants like squash and courgettes in slightly larger pots, and plants with long roots (peas, beans and root veg) in deeper pots. If you're using paper or card pots, keep a close eye on watering as they can dry out faster.

Coir Jiffy plugs are a clean, neat way to start tomatoes and chillies inside.

Bean seedlings in deep, rigid modules. The seedlings are easiest to move when the roots fill the module, holding the compost together. But there is a fine line here as you don't want to leave them too long or the roots will run out of space in the pot and the available food will be used up.

When to Buy Vegetable Plants?

Growing vegetables from seed has many advantages, but sometimes it makes more sense to buy them as plants – perhaps because you have run out of time to sow seeds, do not have a suitable room to start seeds inside, or don't yet feel confident to grow from seed. Good-quality plug plants (baby plants) can be purchased by mail order from specialist suppliers. Some garden centres also stock them – look for strong, healthy plants and avoid any that look tired or have yellowing leaves.

Slow-maturing crops that need to be sown early, like tomatoes, chillies and aubergines, are good choices to buy as plants, particularly if you don't have a bright window to start them inside.

Salads, leafy greens, root crops, peas and beans are usually better grown from seed. All can be sown outside where light levels are good and, because you need a fair few plants, it can get expensive to buy them as plants. That said, a good-quality set of vegetable plug plants, available from some suppliers in late spring or early summer, will help you create an instant garden with a lot less work.

Most fruits and many herbs are normally obtained as plants or grown from cuttings – see *Part III: What to Grow* for more advice on this.

How to raise healthy seedlings

Once the seeds have emerged, the next step is to grow them into healthy baby plants. This is a key step because plants tend to follow a trajectory that starts very early in life. Healthy seedlings are much more likely to grow into healthy, productive adults, while weak seedlings often continue to struggle and grow into less productive adults. This means that it's worth trying to grow the healthiest seedlings you can. For strong, healthy growth, seedlings primarily need:

Light – and lots of it. Raising seedlings inside poses a particular challenge (see 'Raising Seedlings Inside – Overcoming the Light Challenge').

Water and air for the roots – the compost needs to be kept damp to provide water for the roots, but overwatering will drown the plant (a common mistake with seedlings).

Food – a good-quality, general-purpose compost will contain enough food for the first few weeks. However, if you see signs of lack of food, such as yellowing leaves or slow growth, feed with a mild liquid fertiliser like liquid seaweed.

Warmth – most seedlings need some warmth, but generally less than seeds. Too warm, and they grow tall and spindly. Subtropical seedlings like chillies need more warmth than temperate crops such as peas, which are often best raised outside.

Good ventilation – Seedlings can suffer from 'damping off', a fungus that eats the stems and causes them to fall over. Fungus thrives in a still environment so seedlings benefit from good air flow, which you can improve by opening a window or putting the seedlings outside for a few hours on warmer days.

Love and stroking – stroking plants once a day can help the stems grow stronger and more resilient to wind.

Hardening off

When baby plants are moved outside, they face new challenges: cold, fluctuating temperatures and, perhaps most significantly, wind. This can stress and sometimes kill them.

Hardening off acclimatises plants to these changes. Simply move plants outside for a few hours each day on warmer days to help them adapt and bring them in at night. Putting your plants on trays makes it quicker and easier to move them.

It isn't always essential to harden plants off, but it does help them adjust and reduces stress. The alternative is to choose a period of mild and not-too-windy weather to move your plants into their final pots – or to protect them with cloches or windbreaks for a week or two after moving them. Courgettes, cucumbers and squash in particular dislike windy weather, so do harden these off or protect them if you can.

Raising seedlings inside – overcoming the light challenge

Three issues with light can conspire to make raising healthy plants inside tricky.

First, good light levels are essential to grow strong, healthy plants. Outside, plants receive light from all sides. Inside, even on a bright windowsill, the light only comes from one direction. Surrounding buildings and trees can overshadow and decrease light levels further. The human eye is so good at adapting to different light levels that it's easy not to be aware of how low light levels can be inside. (The difference can be measured with a light meter – there are free apps available for smartphones.)

Tomato plants hardening off – the plastic tray catches drips and makes them quicker and easier to move in and out.

Second, there is a relationship between light and temperature. The warmer the temperature, the more light plants need. As most modern homes are relatively warm, higher light levels are needed for healthy growth.

Third, seeds like chillies and tomatoes are sown in the early spring when days are short and light levels are low.

The result is that the light levels inside many homes are marginal for seedlings, particularly in early spring. Since it's important to raise strong, healthy seedlings (as we've seen), here are some ways to give them the best chance:

▸ Grow them in the lightest room or windowsill you have. Choose a cooler room if that's an option.
▸ Put something behind the seedlings to reflect light, such as white card or reflective foil.

▸ Put seedlings outside for a few hours on warmer (10°C/50°F and above), less windy days, remembering to bring them in at night. This makes a big difference in my experience. While they are outside, using a propagator with a plastic lid will help keep the seedlings warmer and the wind off – leave the ventilation holes on the lid open and bear in mind that it might get too hot under the lid if it's left sitting in strong sun for long periods.

If it still proves difficult to raise healthy seedlings inside, a good-quality LED grow light is a good investment. These are great for raising strong chilli, aubergine and tomato plants early in the season.

Due to the low light conditions, seedlings raised inside often grow thin and spindly. This can be remedied to some degree by burying some of the stem under soil to confer extra support when repotting.

To remove seedlings from a tray, put your fingers in the compost, under the roots, and gently ease them out. Support the seedling by holding a leaf and not the stem.

This is a particularly useful technique for tomatoes and chillies, but can be used with other plants, too.

How to transplant and pot on

Moving plants from one pot to another (known as 'transplanting' or 'potting on' by gardeners) is an essential skill. Plants are similar to humans in that they find 'moving house' stressful. You can help to minimise this stress by choosing the right conditions, moving the plants carefully and giving them a good watering afterwards (the equivalent to a good cup of tea after moving house). As both heat and wind are additional sources of stress, try to avoid transplanting on hot or windy days.

Plants in small pots or modules are easiest to move when their roots fill most of the pot – at this point, the roots and compost will usually slide out in one go. A good sign

that they are ready to move is when you can see roots through the drainage holes.

As you gain experience, you will learn that plants raised in small pots often have a window of a week or two when they are at the perfect stage to move on (this is usually when the roots just fill the pot). If left too long, they can run out of food and lose vigour, which may stall and hamper their future growth. Plants left too long can also become pot-bound (when lots of roots circle the inside of the pot). So, learning to move them at the right stage will help to achieve optimum growth – and will come with practise.

Step-by-step: Potting on

1. Fill the new pot with compost (add a little worm compost if you have it – this helps reduce transplant shock), then water it and make a hole the right size and depth for the plant. If the plant's stem looks a bit thin and fragile, it's often beneficial to bury the stem deeper

Ease plants out by gently squeezing the pot with one hand, if needed, and hold the plant between the fingers of your other hand.

in the new pot to give it extra support – this is common practice with tomato and chilli plants, but works well with most other plants, too.

2. Handle baby plants with care when you move them. When moving seedlings from a seed tray, put your fingers into the compost, under the roots, and carefully lift out the plant with as much compost around the roots as possible. Small plants are best supported with one hand underneath the roots and one gently holding a leaf – and not the stem as this can easily snap, killing the plant.

3. When moving larger plants from another pot, put the fingers of one hand over the top of the pot, with the stem between your fingers. Then turn the pot upside down and, gently squeezing the pot to loosen the compost, ease the plant out. If roots are circling the inside of the pot, tease these out before moving the plant to its new home (it won't matter if a few of the roots break when you do this).

The ideal time to move plants is when the roots fill the pot and hold the compost together, as here, but haven't started circling it. If you see roots in the drainage holes, it's a sign the plant is ready.

4. After moving the plant, give it a good watering (with liquid seaweed if you have it) to help reduce stress and then put it in a shady spot for 24 hours to help it recover.

Plants often experience something gardeners call 'transplant shock' when moved to a new pot. When this happens, they can look unhappy for a few days and often don't grow much for a week or two until they settle. Handling the plants and their roots carefully will help to keep the shock to a minimum.

How to take cuttings

Growing from cuttings is a useful skill to learn. It will help you to expand your container garden for no cost and raise plants that you can swap or give away. It can also feel like a miracle to create new plants from what are essentially twigs. Many herbs are not difficult to grow from cuttings, including mint, rosemary, sage, Vietnamese coriander and basil, while others like lavender, thyme and lemon verbena are also worth a go. You do not need any specialist tools – just a sharp pair of kitchen scissors or secateurs, some pots and compost.

Step-by-step: Taking cuttings

Late spring and early summer, when the plants are growing vigorously, is the best time to take cuttings.

1. Choose a healthy-looking plant that has lots of shoots and fresh growth.
2. Fill a small container (anything that is between 300ml/10fl oz and 2 litres/ ½ gallon) with good-quality, general-

A selection of herbs I started as cuttings three weeks earlier, now nearly ready to move on. *Clockwise from top left*: lemon verbena, savory, Vietnamese coriander, oregano, rosemary, tarragon and sage.

Learning Experiment

A fun and easy way to observe how cuttings work is to pluck a fresh stem of mint or basil, remove the lower leaves and put it in a glass of water. After just a few days, you will see, as if by magic, new roots growing from the nodes where the leaves were removed. Once the roots are a few centimetres long, you can plant the cutting in compost to continue growing into a new plant.

A stem of basil, with lower leaves removed and placed in a glass of water, will grow roots from the leaf nodes in a few days.

Cut the stem just *below* a leaf node.

purpose compost (books often tell you to add about 25 per cent grit or sharp sand, but I've experienced just as good results without), leaving about a 1cm (½in) gap at the top, and water it well.

3. Look for healthy-looking shoots that are about 7.5–10cm (3–4in) long. Choose shoots *without* flower buds and, if possible, cut them first thing in the morning when they are sturdy and fresh. Cut the stem just below a leaf joint, using sharp scissors or a knife, then trim off the lower leaves (at least two pairs) – take care not to tear the stem.

4. Insert four or five cuttings (to improve the chance that some will root) around the pot, pushing them in so that most of the stem is below the compost (the new roots will grow from the stem where you removed the leaves). If the stem is too

Remove the lower leaves, taking care not to tear the stem. Leave on at least one or two pairs of leaves.

flimsy to push into the compost, use a pencil to make a hole, insert the stem and firm the compost around it.

5. Water the cuttings again and label with the date.

6. Cover the pot with a clear plastic bag and secure with an elastic band. You can omit this step, but the plastic bag will retain moisture and help the cuttings establish.

7. Put the cuttings in a bright place indoors, but away from direct sun.

8. Two or three times a week, remove the plastic bag to give the plants air and to check whether the compost is moist, then replace it. Water if needed, but take care not to overwater or the cuttings can rot.

9. When you see signs of new growth, the plastic bag can be removed. (One way to check for growth is to pull gently on a stem – cuttings that have taken will hold; those that haven't will pull out). Most cuttings will have rooted (if they're going to) after eight weeks.

10. Once the new plants look well established, transfer them to their own pots.

Troubleshooting

New cuttings can sometimes wilt and look quite unpromising for the first couple of days. Don't give up yet – quite often they will come round. Success will depend on several things, including the type of plant and how vigorously it is growing. Don't be hard on yourself if the first attempts don't work (success with cuttings is never 100 per cent anyway) – just keep trying and you'll soon succeed.

Since cuttings have no roots at first, they have a limited ability to take up water. *The key to establishing successful cuttings* is

Inserting a few cuttings into each pot increases your chance that one will take.

Covering with a plastic bag helps the cuttings establish.

A cane can be secured by drilling two holes in the side of a pot and then tying it in with string.

helping them to take up enough water so that they don't dry out and die. The steps that help here are removing most of the leaves (to reduce water loss); keeping the cuttings out of strong sun; covering the pot with a plastic bag (to retain moisture); and checking the compost remains damp.

If you are having difficulty starting cuttings, warmth from under the pot can often encourage root growth. A heated propagator is ideal, or you can try putting the pot above a warm (but not too hot!) radiator. I've found that I get a significantly higher proportion of cuttings taking when I put them on my heated propagator.

How to tie up and support plants in containers

Climbers and tall plants need to be sup-ported in containers or they can fall over, and they also need tying in to prevent their stems snapping in strong winds.

The main options for support are canes and sticks, wigwams, cages, trellises and, my favoured option, strings.

Canes and sticks

Canes are widely available and easy to get hold of in most places. But keep an eye out for local coppiced 'bean poles' (usually hazel) or 'pea sticks' (branched sticks for supporting peas). These are far more pleasing aesthetically (and support local jobs and woodland).

A problem with canes and sticks in containers is that they are hard to secure and easily fall over. A solution is to drill two holes about 2.5cm (1in) apart, close to the top of the pot and adjacent to where you want the cane. Push the cane down to the bottom of the pot and then tie it in with string or a cable tie through the drilled holes. For added

Eye Health Warning

A common and serious gardening accident is eyes gouged out by canes. *Always* put an old ball, a cane cap or a bit of gaffer tape over the end of canes to minimise the risk.

strength, make a second set of holes near the bottom of the pot (before filling with compost), and fasten there, too. Occasionally, terracotta pots have holes in the top that can be used in the same way.

Canes are useful for supporting individual small- to medium-sized plants, including aubergines, peppers and chillies, as well as taller plants (if you can secure the cane firmly).

For plants that are grown in a group and which are prone to flop over, like broad beans, canes can be put in the corners of a pot, with string tied around them to box the plants in and give them support. This method also works to keep bushy, straggling plants like potato plants under control.

Wigwams

These are good for climbing peas and beans, blackberries and some other climbers. They are easy to construct – simply poke three or four sticks around the edges of a pot and tie them together firmly at the top. If needed, the sticks can also be tied in at the base for extra stability by drilling adjacent holes in the pot (see 'Canes and sticks', page 100).

Climbing beans will usually wind round and climb canes enthusiastically without much help. Peas, however, find canes too thick for their tendrils to cling onto. They need netting or strings added to the structure, or you can tie them on as they grow.

Strings

Strings are strong and flexible, allowing plants to sway slightly in the wind and reducing the chance of stems snapping. Often used by commercial growers in greenhouses, they work well for vining tomatoes, squash, cucumbers and other tall plants that grow on one stem. Choose a thick string or cord that won't cut into the stem of the plant.

A simple wigwam with three canes tied together at the top. Coppiced sticks can look more attractive than canes if you can find them – these sticks came from a neighbour's garden prunings.

To fix up strings, you need an attachment point above the plant. I screw small eyes into the wall above the windows, or look for an existing attachment point (like an old nail) or rig up a high horizontal line to run vertical lines down from.

To set up, tie a string to the hook above the plant. Then, starting at the top, wind the string round the stem of the plant (not tightly) several times and secure it loosely at the base.

When there's an option, strings are my preferred way to support tomatoes, squash and cucumbers.

Other structures

Other structures to support plants include trellises, cages and netting. There is also creative potential to make support structures using canes and cable ties (see the bean lattice in the photograph), or tying strings to make netting (I know someone who wove

The strings are loosely tied round the base of the plant and wound round it as it grows. They provide excellent support on this windy windowsill.

There is lots of potential for creativity when it comes to building structures for climbers. I spotted this attractive bean lattice while running a workshop on the street.

How to Tie Plants In

When tying plants onto canes or any structure, tie the string firmly to the canes and gently round the plant. This secures the plant while leaving some space for the stem to flex and grow.

For string, jute twine is a good option. For a more flexible tie, cut up old bike inner tubes (most cycle shops give them away) or buy flexi-ties, which are useful for securing fruit trees to stakes, for example.

Harvest leafy crops like lettuce by picking the outer leaves and leaving the inner ones to grow. This way, the plant will produce a higher yield over a longer period than if you picked the whole plant.

string to make a runner-bean canopy) or even a runner-bean or vine arch. For more inspiration, searching online for 'DIY trellis', 'DIY tomato cages' or 'DIY plant supports' will throw up many ideas.

Harvesting, pinching out and other plant maintenance

'Pick, pick, pick' might be a useful gardening motto. It seems counterintuitive, but most edible plants actually produce more to eat if picked regularly. Some simple picking techniques that can improve yields and growth are described in this section.

As the season progresses, plants may also need tying back, dead or diseased leaves removed and excessive growth pruned off.

Picking the outer leaves

Good for higher yields from leafy crops such as lettuce, rocket, sorrel, land cress, mustards, kale, chard, spinach and other similar leafy plants.

Instead of picking a whole lettuce or kale plant, regularly picking the outer leaves, while leaving the rest of the plant to regrow, will give a higher yield over a longer period. Chard and kale can keep supplying leaves in this way for a year or more. Start picking once the plant is well established and before the outer leaves get too tough (finding the right stage is partly trial and error).

Pinching out

Good for encouraging bushy growth of many herbs (including basil, mint, sage, oregano

Pinching out: pick a stem just above a pair of leaves. Two new shoots will grow at the leaf nodes. This will help create a bushy plant instead of a tall, lanky one. Start pinching out before the plant gets too tall.

and rosemary), as well as tall salad plants like orach and indoor chillies. This technique can be used on any plant that has leaves branching from the stem in pairs.

When I started growing, I was picking herbs at the base of the stem and I couldn't understand why they didn't grow nice and bushy. The secret I learnt from Lorraine Melton, at Herbal Haven, was that if a herb such as mint is picked above a leaf node, the plant will grow two new shoots at that point (see the pinching out illustration), which means it will grow back more bushy. For the best results, do this before the plant gets too large – once a plant is tall and lanky, it is harder to bring back. Depending on the size of the plant, you can either pick off just the top pair of leaves (pinching out the tips) or

further down the stem, but be sure to leave at least one pair of leaves on the stalk so it can continue to grow.

This is also a useful technique for tall salads like orach and tree spinach. If left to their own devices, these plants grow tall and thin, but pinched out they grow bushy and produce more new shoots with tender leaves.

Thinning out

Good for root veg (carrots, beetroot and radish), most salads and other leafy crops.

With this technique, more seeds are sown in a pot than will happily grow to full size. While the plants are still small, the excess seedlings are removed (or 'thinned out') to make room for the others to grow to a larger size. The thinnings can be eaten and are often delicious, so the benefits of this technique are twofold: you get extra harvests from the thinnings and sowing extra seeds provides you with some insurance against slugs and poor germination.

Picking fruit regularly

Good for higher yields from fruiting veg.

Regular picking encourages most vegetables to produce more fruits. Some vegetables, particularly runner beans and courgettes, also taste their best when small. It can be tempting to save them up on the plant, but in general it's best to eat them as soon as they are large enough.

Pruning and removing dead leaves

Good for keeping plants healthy, reducing overshading and limiting growth.

Remove leaves that are dead or look unhealthy. Removing leaves with bad powdery mildew, blight or leaf miner (see *Chapter 8 Growing in Harmony with Life,*

By thinning out purple orach seedlings from this crowded tray of microgreens, the remaining seedlings will have more space to continue to grow. The thinnings will make a pretty and tasty addition to a salad. (Note: These are sown so crowded together because they are being grown as microgreens; seedlings grown to transplant to other pots would be spaced much further apart than this.)

Large courgette leaves that cast shade on other plants can be removed. Here, I'm removing a leaf that is overshadowing and slowing the growth of kale in the next-door container.

'Troubleshooting', page 150) can help reduce the spread of the problem.

Larger plants, like potatoes and courgettes, can grow fast and overshadow others with their leaves. Some of these leaves can be pruned off to reduce this problem without harming the plant too much. Try not to remove more than one-third of the leaves at any one time.

When beans, peas and tomatoes climb to the tops of their canes, pinch off the tips of the stems to halt upward growth. This will encourage the plant to put more energy into lateral growth and fruiting.

How to save seeds

Until about a hundred years ago, seed merchants didn't exist and everyone saved their own seeds. Since then, seed-saving skills have been in a slow and steady decline – until recently, that is. Now, seed-saving networks and workshops are popping up all over the place and are certainly worth keeping an eye out for.

Seed saving is a useful and valuable skill, and it's deeply rewarding to sow seeds you've saved yourself (and great to have seeds to give away or swap). Home-saved seeds are also often better quality and can save you money. By saving seeds, you can also select the plants best adapted to your local conditions.

While seed saving is an art that can take years to master fully, the basics are straightforward and you should be able to make a successful start with the information here.

Which seeds can you save?

In small spaces, it is most practical to save seed from self-pollinated plants. Self-pollinated crops carry all the genetic information they need in one plant which means that even if you just grow one or two plants, you can still save healthy seeds. Common self-pollinated crops include tomatoes, French beans and lettuce.

With cross-pollinated crops, on the other hand, the genetic information is spread across a small population. This means that to save healthy beetroot or cabbage seeds, for example, you might need to grow between ten and 50 plants and allow them to flower and mature, which is not so easy in a small space.

Of course, there's nothing to stop you collecting seeds from cross-pollinated plants like kale or rocket, if the odd one goes to seed in your containers – and it can be fun to try this. Just bear in mind that these seeds may not always grow as healthily or vigorously as they should. And, unless you are confident that you have saved good-quality seed (from a large-enough population, if cross-pollinated) do not share it with others, particularly at public events like seed swaps. To maintain healthy varieties, it's important that only strong, good-quality seeds are swapped.

Here are some guidelines for saving good-quality seeds in small spaces:

▶ Choose the strongest, healthiest-looking plants to save seeds from, and avoid any that look feeble or are diseased (the disease can be carried in the seed).
▶ Focus your seed saving on heritage (and other open-pollinated) varieties. Seeds saved from 'F1 plants' will usually not grow true to their parents (see 'The Difference Between F1, GMO and Open-Pollinated Seeds' box, page 89).
▶ Ensure seeds are properly dry before storing – dry them on a plate as they can stick to paper.
▶ Put the dry seeds in paper envelopes – and label and date them.

Easy, first seed-saving projects

The following few crops are self-pollinating, which means you can save good-quality seeds from just one or two plants.

Tomatoes

Saving tomato seeds is easy and you will get plenty of seeds from just one or two tomatoes. It's a great way to have a constant supply of your favourite tomato seed to grow and share.

Tomato seeds are coated in a gel that prevents them from germinating, so this needs to be removed first. Choose two or three ripe, healthy-looking tomatoes (the riper the better), cut them in half and remove the seeds and the tomato pulp with a teaspoon.

Put the seeds and pulp in a glass jar or mug and add a similar quantity of water. Then just leave this mixture in a warm place to ferment for three or four days. It should soon start to go mouldy – this is what you want (the mould helps remove the gel). Rinse the mixture with lots of water, separate the seeds (a kitchen sieve or tea strainer helps), then dry the seeds well on a plate. Your seeds are now ready to pack, label and store.

French and runner beans and peas

To save bean and pea seeds, the pods need to be left on the plant to fully mature (the pods at the bottom of the plant will mature first, so leave a few on the plant). As the pods mature, the seeds will bulge out. When they are dry, brown and parchment-like, they are ready to pick. Bring the pods inside and put them in an airy place to dry out further. When they are dry and brittle, shell them and leave the seeds to dry fully for a few more days before storing.

Chillies

Chillies are mainly self-pollinating, but they can occasionally cross-pollinate. This won't be an issue if you grow just one variety. But if

Save seeds from very ripe chillies.

you grow several varieties and want to save true seeds, net the plants you want to save seeds from with insect mesh.

To save the seeds, simply choose fully ripe fruits, cut them in half, remove the seeds and leave them to dry. If handling hot or large numbers of chillies, it's a good idea to wear protective gloves.

Lettuce

To save healthy lettuce seeds, grow the lettuce in a good-sized container (ideally with a capacity of at least 10 litres/2½ gallons) with plenty of space, so that it can grow into a healthy, full-sized plant.

Leave the lettuce to flower and go to seed. Once about 50 per cent of the seedheads look brown and dry (they will look similar to mini dandelion clocks), cut off the lettuce stalk at the base, pop it in a large paper bag (not plastic as it must be breathable) and put it in a dry place inside. By leaving the stalk on, the remaining seeds will continue to mature inside. After a month or two, give the bag a good shake and collect the seeds from the bottom. The seeds will be mixed with chaff which can be removed with a special seed sieve or by hand on a tray. But a little chaff left in the seeds will not do them any harm.

Chapter 6

How to Make Your Own...

This chapter looks at how to make your own potting mix, wormery and worm compost, and homemade fertilisers. While it's not essential to make any of these, there are lots of benefits if time and space permits. It's a good way to learn more about growing, to save money and to recycle materials that otherwise go to waste. Homemade fertilisers can also be better than any you can buy and, like many things, it's rewarding to make them yourself.

Potting mixes

It's possible to grow food successfully without ever making your own potting mix. Many people do very well with a good-quality, general-purpose compost. However, by making your own you can learn more about soil and make mixes to meet different needs (see the following pages for some examples), or experiment with ingredients such as biochar. In some countries and cities, ready-made potting mixes are not readily available or are priced prohibitively, so making your own becomes essential.

In the same way that there are many different bread recipes, potting mixes can be made from a wide variety of different ingredients. I share some of those I've found most useful here and you'll find a multitude more online. I strongly recommend you look for recipes that use ingredients you can easily get hold of in your local area (availability varies hugely). Shipping heavy ingredients gets expensive and usually isn't necessary. Local information can be invaluable to help you find what you need – check out local gardening forums or community gardening projects.

When you combine ingredients to make any potting mix, bear in mind that you want it to fulfil the following requirements:

▸ Meet all the plant's nutrient needs, in the right balance.
▸ Hold moisture well.
▸ Drain well so that the roots can breathe.
▸ Not contain any large lumps.
▸ Not be contaminated with any toxins or weed seeds.

Mixes can be made up on a plastic tarp or in a large bowl or tray. The recipes that follow are a starting point – try them and see how you get on. And remember that you are working with natural ingredients that can vary a lot from batch to batch. The proportions given are by volume (not weight).

A mix to reuse every year
I have been experimenting with this mix in six containers for the last four years. For comparison, three containers use composted fine bark/wood chip as the base; three use coir (coconut fibre). Both the coir and composted bark are doing similarly well, with the coir just edging it (producing slightly larger, healthier-looking tomatoes), but not significantly so. Coir and composted bark both seem to be excellent bases that retain their structure well, so use whichever is easiest to find. You can also try other bases

– for example, green compost – to see how they do over several years. I can't tell you if they will last as well as coir: you are in the realms of experimental growing here!

> 3 parts good-quality coir or composted fine bark/wood chip as the base
> 1 part good-quality topsoil or loam for structure and minerals. Or, if locally available, experiment by substituting this with rock dust.
> 1 part homemade worm compost (or well-rotted manure) for minerals and soil life
> Handful of dried seaweed and/or a complete organic fertiliser (page 126) – for minerals and trace elements and to help ensure that the plant has everything it needs).

At the beginning of each new season, add 1 part worm compost plus a handful of dried seaweed/organic fertiliser to maintain fertility. If the structure appears to be deteriorating, add extra composted bark or coir, or perhaps a little horticultural grit (see *Chapter 4 Eight Steps to Success*, 'How to improve drainage', page 58).

I have also tried the above mix with an additional one part of biochar. After four years, I think the biochar has helped maintain a slightly better structure, but I haven't noticed a significant difference in plant growth. I will continue experimenting.

A free-draining mix
A free-draining mix is good for most herbs, including Mediterranean ones such as sage, rosemary, tarragon, thyme and lemon verbena, particularly in larger pots (say 3 litres/¾ gallon or more).

> 1 part soil-based (or John Innes), peat-free compost
> 1 part fine composted bark or coir
> 1 part horticultural grit

Or

1 part good-quality, sieved garden soil
1 part homemade compost or coir (if you
    are using coir, add extra nutrients
    such as dried seaweed).
1 part horticultural grit

A lightweight mix

Weight is often an issue on balconies and rooftops as well as when moving large pots around, so try the following ingredients in the mix:

2 parts coir
1 part perlite
Organic fertiliser (most coir suppliers
    will also sell suitable fertiliser and
    recommend the dose required) and, if
    available, ½ part worm compost.

Low-cost mixes

It's possible to make a mix from ingredients that can be found free or for low cost in many cities – for example, leaf mould from parks or churchyards, green waste compost, garden soil or well-rotted manure from city farms or stables. The standard here will depend a lot on the quality of the ingredients you can find – garden soil, for example, is very variable. Experiment and you will find that good results are often possible. Here are some examples of mixes to try:

1 part garden soil
1 part leaf mould (well-rotted leaves
    – they usually take one to two years
    to rot down fully, depending on the
    leaf type).
1 part homemade compost or green
    waste compost (ideally well rotted)

Mixing up a free-draining mix. *Clockwise from top left*: horticultural grit, composted bark and soil-based compost.

Or

1 part garden soil
2 parts homemade compost or green
   waste compost

Or

2 parts garden soil
2 parts homemade compost
1 part well-rotted manure

Worm compost

Good-quality worm compost promotes vigorous plant growth and health, and increases resistance to pests and diseases, as we have seen. Luckily, wormeries are ideal for small spaces. They don't smell, take up little space, and some can even double up as a bench. Having a supply of worm compost can transform container growing and I highly recommend getting a wormery – unless you have a phobia of worms (which is not uncommon) or no space to put one. Wormeries also enable you to recycle all your veg peelings, coffee grounds and any other food waste (including some cooked food).

Learning to run a wormery is like learning to ride a bike: easy once you've got the knack. The most common mistake is to overfeed and I must confess to killing two entire colonies of worms at first. By following these guidelines, I hope you – and your worms – will be saved from this trauma.

Although called wormeries, 'liferies' might be a better description. The process in a wormery replicates what happens on the forest floor and involves billions of microbes (bacteria, protozoa and fungi) as well as the worms and many other small organisms.

The secrets of a successful wormery are design and size, shelter and feeding. The best time to start a wormery is in the spring or early summer so that it is well established by winter.

Wormery design

Three features to look for in the design are good ventilation (worms, like us, need air to breathe), good insulation and darkness. Also consider that square shapes slot more easily into small spaces than round ones.

Most commercial wormeries are made of plastic. These are acceptable, although plastic isn't a good insulator and doesn't breathe well. Before buying, check for plenty of air holes and bear in mind the point about shelter from rain (see 'Shelter', page 115). Wormeries are normally stored outside, but can also be kept in a garage, stairwell or even inside the home. If choosing one for your kitchen, look for a design from which worms can't escape!

Wooden wormeries are superior if you can find one. They breathe better, insulate better and often look better. Some even double up as a bench. You can buy wooden wormeries or make one to whatever size you want – see 'Building a wormery', page 122.

Wormery size

Worms live on or near the surface of a wormery. The surface area is key: the larger it is, the more worms can survive and the more food they will consume. Larger wormeries are also more forgiving and easier to look after.

The size of the wormery you will need is influenced by the number of people in your house and the amount of veg waste produced, which varies hugely according to diet. As a rough rule of thumb, a standard round wormery with a diameter of 76cm (30in) is sufficient for one or two people who have a medium amount of veg waste. A large family that eats a plant-based diet will usually need several regular wormeries or one or two larger ones. For our family of four, we have two large wooden wormeries, which compost all our waste food *and* all the prunings from the extensive container garden.

A typical plastic wormery. This model has ventilation holes in the lid, so it's best kept under some sort of shelter to prevent the contents getting too wet in heavy rain.

A wooden wormery can be attractive and double up as a bench. This one was made by Bubble House Worms.

Once you are committed to wormeries, consider getting the largest wormery that is practical for your space.

Shelter

Wormeries are best kept in a sheltered, shady space, as much out of the wind, rain and hot sun as possible: 15–25°C (59–77°F) is the optimum temperature for worm productivity, but they can survive a far wider range than that, including moderately cold winters (see 'Looking after wormeries in winter and while on holiday', page 119).

It is critical, however, to keep rain out. Excess rain makes the contents wet and anaerobic, and sometimes even drowns the worms. If your wormery has holes in the lid (many plastic ones do), try to shelter it from the rain, perhaps under a table. If this is not possible, try to choose a wormery without holes in the lid or, as a last resort, leave the tap open to reduce the risk of worms drowning.

Sourcing worms and bedding

In the wild, the worms that are used in wormeries live in decaying leaf litter in forests and are common in compost heaps – they are not the same as the earthworms found when digging the soil. Three species of worm commonly used in wormeries in temperate climates are *Eisenia fetida* (also known as brandlings or tiger worms), *Eisenia andrei* and *Dendrobaena veneta*. In tropical climates, look for *Eudrilus eugeniae* (the African Nightcrawler) or *Perionyx excavatus*. You can buy worms online or from a local fishing tackle shop, or get them from a friend with a healthy wormery or compost heap.

The more worms you start with, the faster your wormery will establish. One thousand is ideal. It is possible to start with fewer (starter kits often come with 300), but you'll

An established, healthy wormery has thousands of worms.

need to be patient (and add less food) for at least a year or more while they breed.

The bedding is where the worms predominantly live. It can be worm compost, homemade compost, coir (coconut fibre) or damp, shredded card or paper. Homemade composts are full of microbes – similar to leaf litter in the wild and creating a more natural environment for the worms, these are the best choice if available. Worms bought online will usually come with some bedding, but you may need to add more.

Setting up a wormery

Once you've got the wormery, worms and bedding, you are ready to set up.

1. Site the wormery in a shady place, sheltered from rain if possible.

2. Cover the bottom of the wormery (or the bottom tray if using a stacking type) with a layer of newspaper to prevent worms escaping through the ventilation holes. They often try to escape when they are first put in a new wormery, but will usually stay put once established, provided conditions are suitable for them.

3. Then add a 5–10cm (2–4in) layer of bedding.

4. Put your worms on top of the bedding, followed by a thin layer of finely chopped food like banana skins, tea leaves and greens (avoid acidic food like onions and citrus at this stage).

5. Then add something to exclude the light, like a layer of cardboard or an old towel (anything with 100 per cent natural fibres), and, finally, the lid.

Shredding cardboard – it's essential to add at least 20 per cent 'browns' (such as torn-up cardboard or paper, wood chip or chopped straw) to a wormery to keep it healthy and in balance.

Worms are often traumatised when the wormery is set up, particularly if they have travelled by post to reach you. It may be a week or two before they settle and are ready to feed again. Patience is key.

What to feed worms

Most wormery problems arise from over-feeding or not adding enough 'browns' (torn-up cardboard or paper, wood chip or chopped straw). Initially, little and often is the way to go. A small population of worms in a starter kit will usually only eat a handful or two of food a week at the beginning. If fed too much, the food will putrefy and the worms will try to escape.

As well as feeding in small quantities, it is critical to add a mix of 'greens' (fruit and veg peelings, coffee grounds, food waste) and 'browns'. You need to add a *minimum* of 20–30 per cent browns for a healthy wormery, but you can add 50 per cent or more.

As the worms establish in their new home, they will multiply, doubling in number about every three months in the right conditions. It usually takes 12–24 months for a new wormery to operate at full capacity, by which stage it will contain several thousand worms and be able to process more food – and faster.

As a general rule, try to feed worms as varied a diet as you can. This will help keep the wormery healthy *and* add a wide range of different nutrients to make good worm compost. Don't add too much of any one 'green' ingredient as it risks unbalancing the wormery. For example, don't be tempted to add a whole bucket of free coffee grounds from the local café. Lots of cardboard or wood chip is okay though.

Food chopped into small pieces (but *not puréed*) will be broken down *much* quicker by the microbes and worms. This is recommended, particularly for the first few months. Cardboard and paper can be torn into strips or shredded. Eggshells should be crushed and avocado skins, which are stubborn to break down, finely shredded.

Acidic foods like citrus and onions can be added in small quantities, but it's best to avoid them completely until the wormery is well established.

Observe how quickly the food is eaten and you'll see what your worms like and dislike. Banana skins, for example, often disappear in a day or two. Processed food can take much longer – worms obviously know what is good for them!

When to feed worms

Wormeries are usually fed once, sometimes twice a week (except in winter – see 'Looking after wormeries in winter and while on holiday', page 119). Before feeding, check that there aren't large amounts of uneaten food (don't feed if there is) and that the smell is healthy. If you see worms scouting over the surface, this is usually a sign they are looking for food. But, if in doubt, the safest option is not to feed – or add browns instead of greens.

The amount of food to add will depend on the size of the wormery, how well established it is, the temperature and what else you are adding (nettles and comfrey, for example, will speed up the wormery). The only way of knowing is to observe carefully and adjust as needed. If in doubt, underfeed. *The key is patience while the wormery establishes.*

When adding food, bury it an inch or two under the surface to help it break down more quickly and to reduce the chance of attracting fruit flies.

In stacking wormeries, keep adding food to the bottom tray until it is full, then add the next tray. The worms will slowly move up

TABLE 6.1. Worm Feeding Menu

Yes to: 'Greens' (nitrogen-rich waste): Add 60–80 per cent	Yes to: 'Browns' (carbon-rich waste): Add 20–40 per cent	OK in *small* quantities – but only once wormery is established	No to:
Fruit peelings	Cardboard (torn up, sellotape removed)	Onion skins	Meat and fish
Vegetable peelings – potato, carrot, parsnip, etc	Newspaper/wastepaper, torn or shredded	Citrus	Dog/cat poo
Coffee grounds and tea leaves (but not teabags that contain plastic)	Wood chip, ideally composted (avoid pine wood chip)	Leftover cooked foods	Dairy
Eggshells, crushed		Processed food	Very spicy or salty foods
Cut flowers, chopped up	Mussel shells – roasted and crushed	Grass cuttings	Most fresh manures (but fresh cow manure is okay)
Green waste compost		Bread, rice, cereals, pastries and cake	
Nettles, comfrey and other 'weeds'		Garden prunings, chopped up	Wood ash (too alkaline)
Well-rotted manure		Garden soil	Urine

into the tray above. Be aware that the food in the bottom tray may subside, leaving a gap between trays (worms can't jump!). If this happens, refill the bottom tray with some of the contents from the tray above.

Looking after wormeries in winter and while on holiday

Worms will usually survive outside in most UK winters, unless they are in a very cold or exposed spot. Try to move them into a sheltered spot – a shed or garage if you can (that said, mine always stay outside and seem to do fine). In late autumn, as winter approaches, aim to have your wormery at least two-thirds full. The extra biomass will help keep the worms warm – and, on cold days, they can retreat into the centre.

Worms are less active in the cold and will consume less, so it's important to be extra careful not to overfeed. In freezing and very cold weather, you'll find they need very little, if any, feeding. Check on them every week or two and only add food if needed.

If you want to keep adding your peelings and coffee grounds in winter, one trick is to mix them with Bokashi bran first. Bokashi bran (available online) is inoculated with micro-organisms that will ferment and pre-compost your food waste. Put your food waste in a bucket with a lid, add a handful of bran each time you add more waste, and mix it in. Leave it for one or two weeks, then add it to the wormery. Since it is already partly composted, worms can process it more quickly and the biological activity will add some warmth to the wormery. (In Bokashi composting, the food is usually left to break down and ferment further for several weeks, but I find that the worms prefer it before it becomes too slimy and mushy – and it's nicer to handle, too.) This technique should enable you to process a higher proportion of your food waste in winter – how much will depend on the size of the wormery and the amount of waste you have. Experiment.

When you go away, wormeries are normally fine left for a few weeks. Give them a feed before you leave. I also add an extra helping of torn-up cardboard or wood chip to provide a food source that will break down more slowly.

Troubleshooting

A happy wormery should smell sweet and healthy. The contents should be damp, but not too wet or too dry. An unpleasant smell is often the first sign that something is wrong. Lots of worms trying to escape is another sign (although this is also common in a new wormery until they settle in).

A bad smell is usually caused by over-feeding, which leads to putrefaction of the uneaten food. The solution is to feed less. A too-high proportion of green matter can also cause a bad smell. In this case, simply add more torn-up cardboard, newspaper or wood chip. As a general rule of thumb, if unsure, feed less and add more browns than greens.

If you have inadvertently fed too much (it's easy to make this mistake early on), try to remove any mouldy or smelly pieces of food (not a nice job, admittedly) and then mix in a few handfuls of coir (coconut fibre), composted bark, torn-up cardboard or some general-purpose compost to try to neutralise and stabilise the wormery. Let the wormery settle, then add food in small quantities until the worms start processing it faster again.

The wormery contents should feel damp, like a wrung-out flannel. If they get too wet, the wormery will not work as efficiently and can become unhealthy and anaerobic. Try to keep it sheltered from rain (see 'Shelter', page 115). If it gets too wet, add dry cardboard to help soak up extra water. If too dry, water with a fine spray or add cardboard that has been pre-soaked in water.

Ants can be a sign that the wormery is too dry (ants choose dry places to live).

Rats are fascinating animals and much maligned. However, you don't want one in your wormery. It will eat worms, be unpopular with your neighbours and probably make you jump out of your skin when you open the wormery! Most commercial wormeries should be ratproof, but if yours isn't, wire mesh or chicken wire can be used to seal gaps. Alternatively, try pre-composting food in a Bokashi system (rats do not like 'bokashied' food).

Additional ingredients for superb worm compost

Worm compost is highly variable and the quality of the resulting product depends largely on the ingredients added. The good news is that by feeding a wormery with a diverse range of food scraps and enough browns, you will usually be able to produce a good-quality plant feed.

However, if you want to make top-quality worm compost (it's worth the effort), the following ingredients can help, where they are practical to find and use:

Manure: Well-rotted, organic horse manure is a magical ingredient and will supercharge a wormery. It is teeming with beneficial bacteria that stimulate worm activity and breeding. Well-rotted, organic manures from other animals, like chickens and pigs, are also excellent. Cow manure is less rich and can even be added fresh. When I find a supply (in London I collected it from a city farm near me), I keep it in an old compost bag near the wormery, adding a fresh layer every few weeks.

Wood chip: Wood chip is a brown ingredient, like cardboard, but with the added benefit that it has more structure, helping to keep the wormery (and the worm compost) well aerated. It is best pre-composted, but it can also be added fresh. Avoid pine chippings or treated wood shavings. Tree surgeons and councils often have wood chip they want to get rid of. Composted wood chip can also be bought in bags from good garden centres and sometimes from community growing projects.

Soil: The odd handful of good-quality garden soil will add grit (that the worms can use to help digest food) and beneficial soil microbes to the wormery.

Rock dust: The occasional handful of rock dust will add minerals and structure and stimulate worm activity. This can be purchased online or from good garden centres or local quarries.

Nettles and comfrey: Nettles are high in nitrogen, comfrey in potassium. Both are rich in other minerals and will speed up a wormery. This is a much less smelly way to make good use of comfrey and nettles than making tea (see 'Fertiliser "teas" and other homemade fertilisers', page 124).

Biochar: Biochar is finely ground charcoal that can improve soil structure and support microbial life. Adding raw biochar to a wormery will improve the structure of the worm compost and help to charge the biochar with microbes, ready to use.

By altering the proportion of greens and browns, it is, in theory, also possible to create a more bacterial- or fungal-dominated compost. This might be useful to experiment with as fruit trees prefer a more fungal-dominated soil, while most vegetables prefer a more bacterial-dominated one. To increase the fungi population, add more browns (say 50–60 per cent) as the fungi feed on browns. For more bacteria, add a higher proportion of greens – say, 70–80 per cent green waste.

Harvesting worm compost

Worm compost is ready to harvest when it smells earthy and the constituent parts are no longer recognisable (whole avocado skins and some fruit stones can take longer to disintegrate, so don't wait for them; just add them back in to the top). This can take as little as six weeks in well-established wormeries, but three to six months is more common. In new wormeries, it may take longer, up to a year, so don't worry if yours seems slow.

Harvesting worm compost is a messy job and it's a good idea to wear gardening gloves. PVC work gloves are best as they are strong and easy to wash (avoid using soft leather gardening gloves because they're hard to clean).

To harvest stacking wormeries: By the time the top tray is full, the bottom one is usually ready for harvest. Simply remove the bottom tray, double check it is ready and then empty it.

To harvest box wormeries: Once the box is full, remove the top half or two-thirds and put on one side in an empty container or old compost bag. Harvest the worm compost from the bottom and then add the top half you removed back into the wormery. That's it.

When and how to remove the worms: As most worms live in the top half of a wormery and the worm compost is harvested from the bottom, there aren't normally too many worms in the harvested compost. Adding a few worms to your pots is also no bad thing: they will live there, help aerate the soil, and release nutrients for the plants. However, if you want to remove them, the easiest way is to put the harvested worm compost in a sieve (or any container with holes in the bottom) and place this in the top of the wormery. Keep the wormery lid off so

Worm compost can be sieved to remove any woody bits or pieces of plastic. Return the woody bits to the wormery – they will continue to break down and help create air gaps inside.

that the worms burrow down away from the light, into the wormery below. Skim off the top inch or two of compost in the sieve every hour or two to encourage the worms to keep moving down.

Storing and sieving worm compost

Once harvested, the worm compost can be used straightaway. If you need to store the compost, keep it somewhere it can breathe and out of the rain. I keep mine in a large plastic bucket with a waterproof lid and air holes drilled in the sides.

Sieving worm compost through a garden sieve helps remove large twigs, fruit stones or avocado skins that haven't broken down fully as well as any plastic bits which have inadvertently made their way into the compost (like sellotape from cardboard boxes). It's quite slow work, but satisfying as the sieved compost looks nice and is pleasant to work with. It's a good idea to sieve worm compost if you are mixing it into soil, particularly for seed sowing, but less necessary for mulching.

If worm compost is soggy and wet, it is almost impossible to sieve as it forms a sticky ball and takes ages. Put the compost somewhere to dry a bit first – for example, in a shallow box under shelter. If your worm compost is regularly too wet, it might be an indication that your wormery needs more shelter from the rain.

What about worm 'wee' and worm compost 'tea'?

Some plastic wormeries have a sump and tap to allow for the collection of the liquid runoff (in others, with better airflow, the excess liquid simply evaporates). The proper name for this liquid is leachate (sometimes inaccurately called worm 'wee' or worm 'tea'), which is essentially excess water released from vegetables as they decompose. It's sometimes recommended as a fertiliser (and it does contain some nutrients), but this is controversial as scientific analysis shows that it can also contain toxins and pathogens. Experts recommend it is *not* used on edible plants, particularly if it has a bad smell.

Worm compost tea, on the other hand, is made by soaking a few handfuls of finished compost in a bucket of water for a few days, sometimes aerating it during the process. I can't comment in detail on this as I haven't yet experimented with it properly (simply due to lack of time – it's on the list!); however, it's a safer option than worm 'wee' and some experienced growers highly recommend it.

Building a wormery

When I started growing, I imagined wormeries were complicated things. It was only after using one that I found out how simple they really are. Essentially, all you need is a box with lots of air holes to keep the worms dry, in the dark and protected from birds and other predators.

It's easy to make your own. In my experience, a simple homemade wormery works just as well, and often better, than most commercial models.

From plastic

A wormery made from a large, strong (but not transparent) plastic box is the simplest of all. UV-resistant plastic is best as it won't go brittle after a year or two in the sun (old 50-litre/13-gallon recycling bins are perfect if you can find one – they last for decades). All you need to do is to make lots of air holes in the sides and the bottom (but not the lid or rain will get in), then stand the box on bricks (this improves air circulation). And that is all there is to it. Make sure the air holes are large enough, so they don't clog up easily – say 1cm (½in) holes in the bottom and ½cm (¼in) holes in the sides.

From wood

A wooden wormery can be made to any size to fit a space. It's also one of the easiest ways to get a larger size of wormery (most wormeries you can buy are on the small side). It's basically a wooden box with a lid, a wire mesh base and feet to aid good airflow. For the lid to my wormery, I used a sheet of reclaimed plastic roofing because it is light and waterproof (and it saved me making a wooden lid). But a wooden lid looks more

A plastic box with a lid is all you need to make an effective wormery – drill holes in the bottom and sides and stand the box on bricks to enable good airflow.

My two wormeries. These are large enough to compost all our food scraps as well as all the prunings from the container garden and extra things like nettles, comfrey and manure. They are the main source of fertility in my container garden. Notice how the base is raised and the plastic lid is totally waterproof. Since the lid is transparent, I cover the worms inside with a layer of cardboard to keep them in the dark.

The wire-mesh base (and the feet) both contribute to excellent airflow. It is essential to use a strong mesh that has holes smaller than 2cm (¾in) to make it ratproof. Small bits of compost will occasionally drop through the mesh, so keep a tray or shallow box under the wormery to catch these.

attractive and enables the wormery to double up as a bench, which is handy on a balcony or in other small spaces. I've tried various models of wormeries and, in my experience, these simple, homemade wooden wormeries are by far the best.

Fertiliser 'teas' and other homemade fertilisers

If you can find the ingredients and have the space and time to make them, homemade liquid fertilisers are an excellent additional plant feed.

A fertiliser 'tea' is traditionally made by filling a bucket (ideally with a lid due to the tea's smell) with chopped leaves (nettles, comfrey or any available weeds), covering them with water and leaving them to soak. After two weeks, this will have transformed into a foul-smelling liquid that can be used as a fertiliser. Dilute 10:1 with water and use on your plants once a week or fortnight. If you are able to find it, adding a few handfuls of leaf mould (from the floor of a wood) to the bucket can help reduce the smell.

A variety of teas can be made in this way, the most useful include:

Comfrey tea: Comfrey is high in potassium and minerals, and it makes an excellent liquid feed for tomatoes and other fruiting plants. In cities, it often grows

Warning

Due to their seriously bad smell, some people find traditional weed teas unsuitable for confined spaces or storing close to the home.

Comfrey is often found growing in cities along canals and on railway banks.

along canals, on railway banks and in neglected corners of parks. It's an important bee plant, so only pick in small amounts from areas where it's abundant. If you pick the top half of the plant, the base will quickly regrow or, even better, try to pick it just before the council strims it. Wear gloves because it's a skin irritant.

Nettle tea: Nettles are high in nitrogen and minerals. They make an excellent feed to use regularly on leafy veg and as an occasional boost for most other crops. Avoid picking nettles from May to July as they are an important food for red admiral, tortoiseshell and other butter-flies. If you pinch out the top half of each plant, it will regrow quickly.

Weed tea: A wide variety of plants and weeds can be soaked in water to release some of their nutrients, including dandelion, borage, horsetail, chicory, and even grass and banana skins. In the Americas and Africa, the tree marigold, *Tithonia diversifolia*, is used as a tea as it is rich in nitrogen and other nutrients.

A more concentrated (and slightly less smelly) way to make a liquid is by packing the chopped leaves in a bucket, with a lid, and then putting a brick on top to weigh the leaves down. After two or three weeks, simply pour off the liquid that has collected at the bottom and dilute 100:1 with water.

In his book, *The Regenerative Grower's Guide to Garden Amendments*, Nigel Palmer describes another – less smelly – way to make liquid fertiliser from plants, one that is better suited to those of us growing in small spaces. Mix an equal weight of brown sugar and finely chopped nettle, comfrey or other leaves, and pack them tightly in a large glass jar (I use a 2-litre/½-gallon one), then add a layer (about 1cm/½in) of brown sugar on the top and weigh down the leaves with a stone

or glass filled with water (to keep the leaves under the liquid when it forms). Cover the jar with a cloth and keep it inside (it shouldn't smell strong or unpleasant). Within 24 hours, the mixture will start to ferment and release a dark, sweet-smelling liquid. After a week, strain off the liquid and keep it in a lidded jar until needed. And there you have an excellent liquid fertiliser that is quick, easy and doesn't require a lot of space to make. To use it as a root drench, add one teaspoon to a 9-litre (2¼-gallon) watering can and water as normal, or add half a teaspoon to a 1-litre (35fl-oz) spray bottle and use as a foliar feed.

Nigel's book is full of interesting ways to make other fertilisers at home, including pickling fish waste in sugar and steeping shellfish shells in vinegar. Many of the ingredients he uses are easily sourced in the city, so his book is a great resource for any small-space grower wanting to make more of their own fertilisers – and add a wide range of minerals to their plants.

Another simple (and non-smelly) way to make good use of comfrey or nettles is simply to add them to a wormery or compost heap.

Complete organic fertiliser

In containers, plants are reliant on getting all their needs from a small volume of soil. Without a full range of nutrients, they may grow into low-quality produce or be susceptible to insect and disease attack. Adding homemade compost and fertilisers will help, but can we always be sure these have the full range of minerals and trace elements for healthy growth? Composted kitchen waste, for example, can often be deficient in calcium, phosphorus or silicon.

One answer is to look for a fertiliser that has the full spectrum of minerals and

A variety of homemade fertilisers for foliar feeding and root drenching.

TABLE 6.2. Steve Solomon's Complete Organic Fertiliser Recipe for Containers

Ingredient	Additions
3 litres (¾ gallon) of oilseed meal (rapeseed meal is the easiest to source in the UK, but hemp or cotton can also be used). Can be substituted with chicken manure pellets, but these need to be added to the soil separately as they won't mix well with the other ingredients.	Mainly nitrogen, with some phosphorous and potassium
1 litre (¼ gallon) of seaweed meal (or foliar feed with liquid seaweed throughout the season)	Trace minerals
1 litre (¼ gallon) of bonemeal (or soft rock phosphate)	Phosphorous
1 litre (¼ gallon) of agricultural lime or dolomite (first application only)	Calcium (or calcium and magnesium if dolomite is used).
1 litre (¼ gallon) of gypsum (calcium sulphate)	Calcium and sulphur
75ml (2½fl oz) Sulphate of Potash (aka potassium sulphate)	Potassium and sulphur
Plus, optional but recommended (Needed in tiny quantities and can be toxic in larger doses, so measure carefully)	
1 teaspoon of borax	Boron
2 teaspoons of manganese sulphate	Manganese and sulphur
1½ teaspoons of zinc sulphate	Zinc and sulphur
1 teaspoon of copper sulphate	Copper and sulphur

elements that plants need. This can be purchased from specialist horticultural suppliers or you can make your own.

Steve Solomon, author of *The Intelligent Gardener*, has put together a recipe for a complete organic fertiliser for container growing (see 'Table 6.2 Steve Solomon's Complete Organic Fertiliser Recipe for Containers', page 127). Add some to old compost each time a container is replanted to help ensure a full spectrum of nutrients is present.

I have tried this with excellent results. I should stress, though, that my findings are based on observation and not scientific tests. To make it requires time and investment to source all the ingredients (eBay is helpful). It won't appeal to everyone. However, for those interested in trying to grow nutrient-dense food or learning more about the elements that plants need, it's a useful and interesting exercise. It's more cost-effective to buy the ingredients in larger quantities, which means it also lends itself well to a community project.

Put the ingredients in a bucket, then mix thoroughly, either with your hands or by pouring from one bucket to another (do this outside, wearing a dust mask). Incorporate the fertiliser with your potting mix in the following quantity: 100ml (3½fl oz) per 10 litres (2½ gallons) – this is the equivalent of 1 cup per square foot. As composts vary and plants have different nutrient needs, experiment with how much you add. (I often add about half the recommended dose in conjunction with worm compost.)

Chapter 7

How to Grow More Food in a Small Space

Small spaces vary but there is often the potential to grow quite serious amounts of food in them. I found I could grow far more than I initially thought possible, eating homegrown food every day as I explained in the *Introduction*. The revelation that I could grow a decent amount of (delicious) food to eat was both exciting and motivating. If you are excited by this prospect, too, this chapter is for you.

How much you'll be able to grow depends on the size of your space and its microclimate, among other things. Whatever the size, you'll find a variety of ways to grow more over the next few pages.

To increase yields in small spaces, there are also complex hydroponic tower systems and high-tech vertical walls available, but I'm drawn towards the less costly and more accessible technologies. In my experience these work well, are low cost and easy to look after. This is what I focus on in this chapter.

Growing ladder outside our London flat. This created five new levels of growing in a south-facing space where originally there was only room for bins. The bins are still there, but hidden behind the ladder.

But first a little history. Intensive urban growing is not new. In the 19th century, before the railways, fresh fruit and veg had to be grown in or near the cities. Urban farmers became experts at small-scale, intensive growing. In Paris, for example, growers could get five or six crops out of one bed *in one year*. They achieved this by meticulous planning, by applying lots of manure, by raising plants as seedlings first and by using dozens of glass cloches as mini greenhouses. These growers supplied the whole of Paris with fresh, locally grown veg. You can read more about how they achieved this feat in the fascinating book, *Intensive Culture of Vegetables on the French System* by P. Aquatias.

With the advent of 21st-century transport and distribution systems, most small urban and market farms disappeared, outcompeted by large-scale industrial agriculture. Hopefully, we will move back to more food being grown locally in the future. In the meantime, we can be inspired and learn from urban farmers of the past.

Create a living soil and thriving ecosystem

It's not possible to talk about a high-yield garden without first talking about soil. A healthy, living soil and a thriving ecosystem underpin any productive, healthy growing. In 19th-century Paris, manure was the key.

Depending on how much time you have and the resources available in your neighbourhood, here are some things you can do to create and nurture a living soil:

▸ Learn how to make good-quality worm compost. This will be full of nutrients *and* microbial life. It's a wonderful solution for small spaces, supporting both plant vigour and health.

▸ Use wood chip or leaf mulches to protect the soil and provide food for microbial life. Or experiment with 'lasagne' gardening (see *Chapter 4 Eight Steps to Success*, 'Table 4.3 How and When to Feed Plants in Containers', page 74) and feed the microbial life at the bottom of a pot.

▸ Add a layer of well-rotted, organic manure to the bottom of pots or as a mulch on the top.

▸ Use plant feeds based on natural ingredients, including liquid seaweed, that will promote microbial life.

▸ Try not to let soil dry out completely, keep plants growing for as much of the year as possible, and cover bare soil with a mulch to keep in moisture.

While it can be hard to create a balanced ecosystem in a small, urban space (slug predators, for example, are often lacking), do what you can to nurture life and diversity. As well as supporting a productive garden to feed you, you'll be helping everything else, too. If you are interested in learning more about the biology of the soil, I highly recommend looking into the work of Dr Elaine Ingham.

Vertical and '3D' growing

Thinking of a growing area as a cube can help pinpoint new places to put plants and to make more of a space. Look up and see if higher areas offer new spaces to grow or better light.

There are a variety of simple, effective ways to raise plants and make the most of the vertical dimension.

Growing ladders

Growing ladders are simple genius. They enable four or five shelves of plants in a space where otherwise there would be space for only one. They provide handy storage behind the ladder, which is ideal for compost bags or tools. You can buy ladders (look for 'growing ladders', 'allotment ladders' or 'plant theatres'), make your own or get one made for you. The benefit of DIY models is that you can design them to fit your space and the pots you want to use (I built mine to fit EarthBox containers).

Depending on the model, growing ladders either have legs to stand on or are leant against a wall. Normally they don't need screwing in. I've used mine in three different homes.

Shelves and growing pockets

Shelves can be freestanding or fixed to walls to create new growing ledges or to raise plants up into more light. If you have a power

When I moved some struggling pots of salad from the shady floor of the balcony to this shelf above the door, they flourished. I watered and picked them from a step ladder. If you're making a shelf like this, the weight of containers is significant, and you do have to be confident that it won't fall down!

drill, strong metal shelf brackets are relatively easy to put up. If you are confident at DIY, you can make your own wooden brackets. Low-level shelves can be made with stacks of bricks (though do check they are stable) or trestles, and the space underneath can be used for storage. Paint the shelves in a colour of your choice or seal with external preservatives (unlike containers, they will not be in direct contact with the soil).

Don't overlook the potential that raising plants into more light can have on growing. A lot of backyards and other urban spaces are surrounded by brick walls and the floor is often shady and difficult to grow in. However, by observing the space, you can often identify areas higher up the walls that get more sun.

Growing pockets are an alternative solution. I prefer the flexibility of shelves because you can swap pots around and take them on and off the shelf to replant. However, growing pockets can look good and they are easy to put up, but do be aware of possible damp issues caused by material touching the walls (though well-designed pockets should come with instructions on how to avoid this).

Grow climbers (and trailers)

Climbers help make the most of vertical space and can reach up into sunnier areas. They add height and interest, and many climbing varieties yield better and take up less horizontal space than bush types. For example, tromba (or tromboncino) squash is a good climbing alternative to space-hungry, bushy courgette plants, while climbing beans need less horizontal space than bush beans. Good climbers for small spaces include:

Vining tomatoes
Squash
Cucumbers and mouse melons

Tromba squash growing on strings. It is an excellent climber.

Climbing French and runner beans
Climbing peas
Achocha/fat baby
Malabar spinach – a climbing salad
    (needs warmth)
Nasturtium (climbing varieties only)
Hardy kiwis
Blackberry

Most climbing plants, such as nasturtiums and runner beans, can also be allowed to trail down into lower spaces. When I grew on a balcony, I allowed a squash plant to grow down into my neighbour's (sunnier) garden (with her permission, I should add).

Hanging baskets

Hanging baskets are a neat and cheerful way to fill empty vertical spaces, helping to create

'Cherry Cascade' tomatoes growing in hanging baskets outside my London flat.

a 3D garden. They can be hung outside windows, high on the walls of balconies, by doors – in fact, anywhere there is space to hang one or fix a bracket.

Plant them with small, bright cherry tomato bushes, colourful edible flowers like nasturtiums or violas, or pretty herbs like sage, oregano and thyme.

A challenge with hanging baskets is that, swaying in the wind, they are prone to drying out quickly. Use the largest hanging baskets practical and consider mulching with plastic or adding a bottle waterer (see *Chapter 11 Solutions to Common Challenges*, 'Making watering easier', page 231).

Increase the volume of soil

The size and yield of most crops is related to the volume of the container they are grown in (as we saw in *Chapter 4 Eight Steps to Success*, 'Step 2: Choose the Right Container', 41). The larger the volume, the larger the plant. Using deeper containers is a simple way to increase soil volume without encroaching on horizontal space.

Keep an eye out for deep containers, in the right size, to fit your space or make them yourself out of wood.

It's common sense, but be aware that deep containers, full of soil, can be very heavy. I once made deep containers for my windowsills that I then found almost impossible to lift!

Establish a seedling nursery

A good way to get more out of larger pots (precious assets in a small space) is to allocate a small area (just big enough for a seed tray or two) to raise seedlings to

A small seedling nursery on my London balcony.

transplant when needed. If you have seedlings ready to move when a big pot becomes empty, you will save three to six weeks waiting for seeds to germinate and grow. Urban gardeners in Paris relied heavily on this technique, raising seedlings so that they were ready just in time to plant out when another crop was pulled up.

This can help you to squeeze at least one extra crop in during the year. For example, if potatoes are pulled up in late July, it's on the late side to sow courgettes. But if you have a courgette plant about four to six weeks old that's ready to go, it'll have plenty of time to grow and will be ready to harvest by mid- to late August.

I usually have a tray or two of different salad plants and leafy crops growing as seedlings. Whenever an empty space in a container comes up, I pop one in. If they are not needed as seedlings, we eat the baby plants as tasty microgreens. I also start winter crops like chard and kale in small pots in July, ready to transplant into larger

containers in late August and September as the courgettes and beans finish.

I'm happy to admit that my approach is often a bit ad hoc and relies on finding the time and remembering to do it. You can be more organised. Make a more detailed timetable to raise seedlings throughout the year (see 'Grow Successive Crops in Each Pot', below). It may take a bit of experimentation to get the timings right, but you'll learn lots along the way.

Grow successive crops in each pot

Succession is when one plant follows another. It's probably ambitious to try to grow five or six crops in the same soil as the skilled French intensive growers did, but three or four is within the reach of most of us.

When planning successions, try to avoid plants from the same family following each other. For example, try not to follow potatoes

TABLE 7.1. Succession Planting Examples for Containers

	April	May	June	July	Aug	Sep	Oct	Nov–March
Pot 1	Sow first early potatoes			*Plant* French beans		*Plant* kale		
Pot 2	Sow spring onions		*Plant* tomatoes				*Plant* rocket	
Pot 3	*Plant* peas			*Plant* courgettes		*Plant* Chard		
Pot 4	Sow rocket		*Plant* chillies			Sow mooli (white radish)		

The same mix of lettuces in two pots – one pot with lettuce that is ready to eat and one on its way. This helps ensure a continuous supply.

with tomatoes (both from the Solanaceae family) or rocket with kale (both brassicas), as plants from the same family will use up the same nutrients in the soil and be vulnerable to the same pests. See 'Table 7.1 Succession Planting Examples for Containers', for some ideas for cropping successions that can work well in containers. In this table, 'Plant' refers to ready-grown seedlings being moved into pots (these would need to be sown in small pots four to six weeks before).

For fast-growing crops like microgreens, rocket and salad, you can ensure a continuous supply by sowing new seeds at regular intervals. I try to have a mix of salads ready to eat, halfway there, and just sown.

Catch crops and interplanting

These are two similar techniques that can help you get more out of every little space. 'Catch crops' is a term for fast-growing crops like radish, pea shoots, spring onions or rocket, sown to make the most of temporary empty spaces. For example, three weeks before tomatoes are ready to plant out, grow a crop of pea shoots rather than leaving the pot empty. Or you can sow radishes around the edge of a courgette seedling and harvest them before the courgette leaves overshadow the radishes.

'Interplanting' (or intercropping) is when one plant is grown between another. A well-known example is the 'Three Sisters': sweetcorn, French beans and squash, a combination developed by indigenous groups in North America. The beans climb up the sweetcorn and the squash leaves shade the soil. It isn't really designed for pots (or the UK's cooler climate), and it's not easy to get a good crop. But it's an interesting experiment, it looks pretty and it's fun watching the beans climb the sweetcorn.

Bear in mind that some suggested interplanting combinations may not work well in pots where there is more competition for water, light and food than in the ground. In general, interplanting works best in larger pots, where there is more root space and food for the plants. Here are a few combinations that have worked for me in pots:

- Mixed salads – I often interplant tall salad plants like orach with shorter ones like mustard and rocket.
- Tall, thin crops, particularly spring onions, interspersed between larger plants like kale or chard.
- Herbs or flowers under fruit trees and bushes – for example, I grow mint under a blackberry, and bird's-foot trefoil (a nitrogen-fixing flower) and nasturtiums under an apple tree.
- Trailing nasturtium grown between tall plants like beans or tomatoes because they look pretty hanging down the side of the pot.
- Chard or kale seedlings planted around tomato or chilli plants in late August/September. When the tomatoes or chillies finish, cut them off at the base, leaving the kale or chard to mature.

In summary, interplanting is a useful and interesting method to grow more (and can look great), but this technique may take some experimentation to get it to work well in containers.

High-yielding, high-value and fast-growing crops

Crop choice makes a big difference to the weight and value of food you can grow – by as much as a factor of ten or more. For example, a large (supermarket-crate-sized) container filled with broad beans will typically yield 500g–1kg (1–2¼lb) of beans after podding. However, the same planter with runner beans can yield 10kg (22lb)!

Similarly, a chilli plant might produce over a hundred chillies with a value of £5 to £50 (depending on the variety). However, carrots grown in the same container might typically weigh more but would probably have a shop value of only 30p to £1.

Of course, other factors will determine what you want to grow, but both yield and value are worth bearing in mind. I love a bowl or two of fresh carrots but would much prefer 100 tasty chillies to add flavour to our meals throughout the year.

Runner beans are one of the highest yielding container crops – one large pot can easily produce 10kg (22lb) of beans or more.

High-yielding crops – by weight

Runner beans

Tomatoes

French beans

Courgettes

Microgreens, particularly peas, sunflowers and fava beans

Chard

Peppers (in sunny, sheltered spaces)

Aubergines (in sunny spaces)

Apples, once established

Blackberries and most fruit bushes, once established

High-value crops

Herbs

Microgreens

Salad leaves – rocket, sorrel, etc

Edible flowers

Chillies

Soft fruits

Tomatoes

Unusual/exotic varieties

Some crops like broccoli and cabbage are notoriously slow to grow, but there are sometimes fast-growing alternatives that make more sense in small spaces – see 'Table 7.2 Fast-Growing Alternatives to Slow-Growing Crops'.

TABLE 7.2. Fast-Growing Alternatives to Slow-Growing Crops

Slow-growing crop	Faster alternative
Broad beans	Broad bean shoots
Broccoli	Kailaan (Chinese broccoli) or broccoli microgreens
Cabbage	Chinese cabbage
Onions	Spring onions

Grow in winter

It's possible to grow food all year round in many cities and regions around the world, and this is rewarding if you can. The secret to successful winter growing in temperate climates is to sow seeds in summer or early autumn, so plants are well established before the cold weather sets in. In the cool temperatures and low-light levels of mid-winter, plants will grow slowly if at all, and need to be picked sparingly. But, come early spring, the established plants will grow strongly (and much quicker than seeds sown at the same time). Leaves harvested in the winter and early spring have a particularly good flavour – one of the best and most welcome harvests of the year to my mind.

In addition to the climate in your geographic region, the microclimate of your space in winter (it will be different to the summer) will influence how easy growing is.

TABLE 7.3. Winter Sowing Timetable

Crop	Sow	Harvest	Notes
Chard	Late July–early Aug	Oct–May	Pretty and versatile, ideal for using in salads and cooking.
Coriander and chervil	Late Aug–Sept	Nov–May	The best time to sow coriander (spring sowings are more prone to bolt).
Endive	Early Sept	Nov–May	Pretty varieties, productive, bitter
Jerusalem artichokes	Feb–Apr	Jan–Mar	Tasty winter root veg. Perennial.
Kale	July–early Aug	Nov–May	'Red Russian' and 'Cavolo Nero' look pretty and are also good for salads.
Lamb's lettuce/corn salad/mache	Sept	Feb–Apr	Mild salad leaves, good for bulk
Land cress/American cress	Mid Aug–Sept	Nov–May	Excellent spicy flavour. Perennial.
Lettuce (winter)	August	Nov–Jun	Choose winter varieties.
Mibuna and mizuna	Sept	Nov–Apr	Productive but watch out for slugs.
Mustard 'Red Giant' and 'Green in the Snow'	Late Aug–early Sept	Nov–Apr	Small leaves are nice in salads, larger leaves for cooking. There are many other mustard varieties.
Pak choi	Late Aug–early Sept	Nov–Apr	Slugs also love it.
Parsley	July	Oct–May	Slow to establish.
Pea shoots	Sept–early Nov Late Feb–Mar	Oct–Dec Apr–Jun	Excellent for late and early sowings. Delicious.
Rocket, salad	Late Aug–Sept	Nov–May	Reliable and tasty
Shungiku/chopsuey greens	Aug	Nov–May	Distinctive flavour and pretty leaves
Sorrel, broad-leaved	Aug	Nov–May	Strong flavour and productive
Spinach	Aug	Nov–May	Salad and cooking
Tatsoi	Sept	Nov–Apr	Excellent flavour. Tasty flower buds, too.
Winter purslane	Sept	Jan–Apr	Dislikes wind. Unusual round leaf and pretty flowers.

Kale is one of the hardiest crops for winter – and looks good, too.

Reasons to Grow in Winter

As well as providing a supply of fresh green leaves (when most supermarket salads are imported and lacking in taste), winter growing is worth serious consideration because:

▸ There are fewer slugs, aphids and caterpillars.
▸ Plants need less watering.
▸ Pots look better with plants growing in them.
▸ It's better for the compost (this is less likely to dry out and the plant roots will prevent nutrients washing away and support the microbial ecosystem).

For these reasons, some people even prefer growing in winter to summer.

Some spaces get limited or no sun in winter (particularly if they are north-facing); some are more prone to frosts; others are more exposed to winds (in my front yard, wind is more of a challenge than the cold). On the plus side, many urban spaces are excellent for winter growing, and surrounding walls and concrete often mean they are several degrees warmer than in the countryside.

Experiment with an open mind and you will learn a lot. Try growing a few different winter crops to discover which grow best. Observe or ask around to find out what others in your local area are growing successfully and when they sow them. If unsure, the hardiest winter vegetables to try are kale, sorrel, chard and lamb's lettuce (also known as corn salad or mache).

In colder climates, a cloche or some horticultural fleece can be essential to keep plants alive. In most areas, though, protection will speed up growth, but is optional. The benefits of protection should be weighed up against the unappealing aesthetics and the extra time and work involved in covering pots.

In cool, wet weather, plants need significantly less watering. But remain vigilant, as dry spells in winter are not uncommon. Keep an eye on the forecast and try to avoid watering before freezing weather as freezing water in the pots can damage plant roots.

Winter sowing timetable

The timings I use in Newcastle upon Tyne are shown in 'Table 7.3 Winter Sowing Timetable', page 139. Sowing can be made a week or two later in warmer areas, like London. Local advice is also always helpful as a guide to timings and the best winter crops for your area.

Larger winter vegetables like cabbages, purple-sprouting broccoli, parsnips and

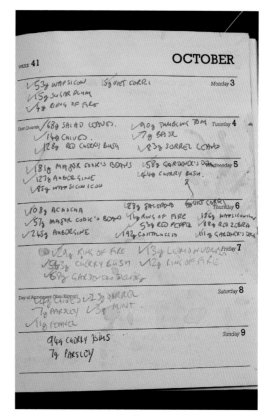

A page from my London growing diary: 'Wapsipinicon' is a tomato variety, 'Ring of Fire', a chilli.

Brussels sprouts are also possible, but I haven't listed them in the table as they take longer to mature and are less suitable for small spaces.

In addition to coriander, parsley and chervil, you can also pick bay, rosemary, thyme and sage sparingly in winter, and mint and oregano in late autumn/early winter before they die back.

Weigh (and value) your harvests

In the same way that measuring time and heart rate can inform and motivate runners, weighing harvests and calculating

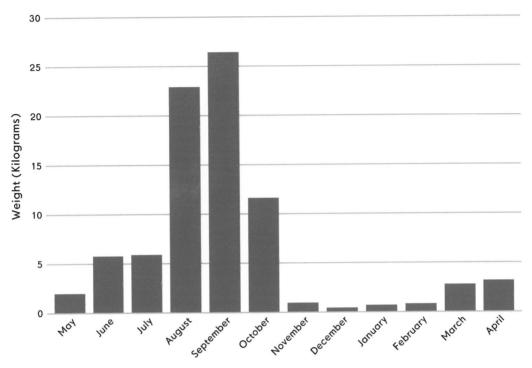

Measuring harvests can give useful insights. After plotting this graph, I decided to try and grow more crops to pick in June and July.

their value is motivating and provides useful information. It tells you which crops yield best and which save the most money. It helps you identify the times of year when you are picking different crops – and plan better for next year. If you make a rule that you can only measure crops that you eat (or give away), it encourages better use of everything (for example, I found a lot more uses for surplus mint once I started weighing it).

Calculating the value is useful because weight alone doesn't mean too much. There is a lot of difference between 4.5kg (10lb) of potatoes and 4.5kg (10lb) of herbs! If you are writing a blog or sharing on social media, the value also tells a better story – and may inspire more people to try growing.

To record your harvests, you can make your own spreadsheets or use an online tool such as the 'Harvest-ometer', developed by Capital Growth.

Chapter 8

Growing in Harmony with Life

Growing can seem easy and straightforward when plants are healthy and happy. However, when they get sick, are eaten by molluscs or just don't grow well, it can feel harder and more mysterious. If problems are serious, it's easy to get demoralised.

When something goes wrong, it's important to remember that *all* growers experience ups and downs and occasional disasters (even if gardening programmes rarely feature them). It's a normal part of growing, and unhealthy plants are *not* a reflection of your ability to grow. If you can keep a positive attitude, and an inquiring mind, gardening problems also offer some of the best opportunities to learn.

When a plant looks unhappy, the first step is to try to identify the cause. Sometimes it's obvious: caterpillars munching on nasturtiums, strong winds snapping stems or plants drooping due to lack of water. But when plants just aren't thriving, a little detective work is often needed. Some cases are harder to solve than others, but hopefully the information here will help.

Seven ways to grow healthy plants in harmony with other life

The secret to a healthy container garden with minimal problems is prevention. There are no magic solutions, but the most important factors are promoting plant health and reducing plant stress. I describe various prevention techniques here and, taken together, they will contribute towards a healthy, lush and vibrant container garden.

1. Promote plant health, reduce plant stress

Like us, plants have a range of natural defences that they deploy against attack from predators and disease. They produce chemicals to make them taste unpleasant to insects, release smells to attract aphid-eating bugs, and some can even send signals through their roots to warn other plants about encroaching predators.

Also, like us, their ability to resist disease and insect attack depends largely on how healthy they are. If stressed or weak, they are less able to respond effectively. The underlying reason for aphids or disease in container gardens is normally not 'a plague of aphids' but stress and poor plant health. Aphids are often a symptom of a problem, rather than the problem itself.

In our culture, it is common to focus attention on the 'pest'. But it's often more helpful to turn this on its head and think about the health of the plant and to try to reduce any stress.

Life can be particularly stressful for urban pot plants. Due to the confines of a container, they are prone to a shortage of

Bright green, glossy leaves are a good sign of strong, healthy plants.

TABLE 8.1. Sources of Stress and How to Minimise Them

Common sources of stress	Minimise by...
Lack of water/irregular watering/too much water	Establishing a daily watering routine and mulching, as well as using large pots and containers with reservoirs where possible.
Lack of minerals, trace elements and soil life	Use a good-quality compost, a range of natural, high-quality feeds, including some containing microbial life like worm compost. Liquid seaweed can help plants recover from stressful events.
Too hot	Use water reservoirs and shade netting, plus select appropriate plants (see *Chapter 11 Solutions to Common Challenges*, 'Too hot: suntraps, hot climates and heatwaves', page 242).
Too cold	Avoid putting plants outside too early in the season – harden off and protect if needed.
Persistent or strong winds	Tie in taller plants. Use windbreaks or cloches. See *Chapter 11 Solutions to Common Challenges*, 'Wind', page 239.
Moving plants/transplanting	Handle plants and roots with care. Water well after moving. Choose an overcast, still day or shelter from strong sun and wind for 24 hours.
Too little sun/light	Select crops according to the sun available. In less sunny places, try to reflect as much sun onto plants as you can.

food and water, and container gardens are often shady or windy. Look at 'Table 8.1 Sources of Stress and How to Minimise Them', for the most common causes of stress for container plants and how to reduce them. Minimising stress will have a major impact when you are trying to grow strong and healthy plants.

2. Observe and remove

However healthy your plants are, they will still sometimes be eaten by slugs, insects and other creatures. A benefit of growing on your doorstep is that it is quick and easy to keep a close eye on this. Spotting and dealing with infestations early is the best and easiest way to manage them. Daily watering offers the ideal time to look out for signs of plants being eaten or in poor health – and to look for the culprits.

Once spotted, the most effective way to deal with slugs, snails and most insects in small spaces is to pick them off. They can

then be fed to the birds (or given to someone with chickens), released in the local park or squished (and added to the wormery). It's often a good idea to leave a few aphids or caterpillars on the plants as these will help attract ladybirds and other beneficial insects to your garden. However, you can't always rely on ladybirds turning up in urban areas, so it is important that you also take on the role of predator and stop the aphid population getting out of hand if necessary.

Always try to identify any insect before removing it (Google or an insect-identification app like 'Seek' makes this much easier). Otherwise, it's easy to unwittingly remove hoverfly or ladybird larvae, two of the best aphid munchers out there!

Not everyone finds it easy to pick off slugs or caterpillars at first, but it's worth trying to get used to it. It might seem cruel but it's far more controlled and discriminate than killing with chemicals. It's also the most effective way to control slugs and most plant-eating insects.

How to Recognise Healthy Plants

Try to become more familiar with what healthy plants look like. Signs of good health include strong, steady growth, a sturdy stem and dark green leaves (the leaf colour will obviously also depend on the variety). They also tend to have shinier and glossier foliage, due to a surplus of fat stored in their leaves, in what is known as a waxy cuticle.

The healthier plants are, the wider range of pests they are resistant to. John Kempf has done some fascinating work in this area and developed the 'plant health pyramid' to illustrate how plants become increasingly resistant to pests as their needs are met.

What Is a 'Pest' and When Are They a Problem?

All life forms have a role to play in a healthy ecosystem. Slugs and snails recycle nutrients in the soil, and are food for thrushes, hedgehogs and ground beetles. Aphids are food for ladybirds and are fed by sparrows to their chicks. Hoverflies are an important pollinator and their larvae eat aphids voraciously. Even the maligned wasp hunts caterpillars and helps with pollination.

Is 'pests' the right word to call this precious life that helps keep everything in balance?

Small populations of slugs or aphids rarely do much damage. It's only in large, uncontrolled numbers that they can. The challenge is that many container gardens are too small to have a full, balanced ecosystem to keep them in check naturally. Most balconies don't have hedgehogs, ducks or ground beetles to eat slugs. Without a predator, slugs multiply uncontrollably and then they *can* make growing difficult.

The upshot is that *you* often need to be the predator and find and remove slugs and other plant eaters from your container garden.

Cultivating a different mindset can help in our relationship with slugs and other animals. In the West, we are taught that 'pests' are bad. But early farmers in some indigenous cultures had a different view. They valued all life and were happy if a proportion of their crops were eaten by other animals. They saw it as a way of giving back to the wider web of life. Making this shift in our own thinking – and realising that our growing can support other animals – makes it more rewarding. And less demoralising if plants are eaten.

3. Grow a diverse mix of crops

A diverse mix of plants makes it harder for insects and animals to see or smell what they want. And if they do find your container garden, they'll often only be interested in one or two plants, leaving the others undamaged. Pigeons, for example, eat mostly kale and other brassicas but won't touch tomatoes, courgettes and most other fruit and vegetables (and, in my experience, they also aren't very good at finding brassicas if they are hidden among other plants).

A diversity of crops also increases the chance that some will do well in our increasingly unpredictable weather. For example, a cold, wet August and September will not suit tomatoes and chillies well, but establishing winter crops like kale and chard will love it.

4. Grow companion plants

'Companion plants' are plants that benefit others around them – by releasing a scent to deter plant-eating insects, for example, or by attracting beneficial insects like pollinators or ladybirds.

The plants listed below make good companions for vegetables in containers and are also all pretty and edible. They are reputed to have the following qualities:

> Lavender deters aphids and the flowers attract pollinators.

A diverse mix of plants makes it harder for pests to find what they want.

Chives and garlic deter aphids and carrot flies, and the flowers are loved by bees.

Pot marigolds attract beneficial insects like ladybirds and hoverflies.

Sage deters brassica pests and attracts pollinating insects when in flower.

Borage flowers are a magnet for bees and other pollinating insects.

Fennel, dill and coriander flowers attract hoverflies and other beneficial insects.

Companion planting alone, however, is not a solution for a trouble-free garden, even if some articles occasionally imply it is. However, it can contribute to a healthy and wildlife-friendly garden and is well worth practising.

5. Use barriers

Barriers like netting and cloches protect plants from hungry wildlife. Fine-mesh insect netting is effective at keeping out aphids, butterflies, leaf miner and other insects, while larger mesh netting keeps out birds, and heavier weight chicken wire does the same for squirrels and animals with sharp teeth.

Netting is effective but it is also unsightly in the container garden. Securing it is time-consuming and a bit of a faff. It's also another thing to buy and store. However, it's useful as a last resort and for bad bird or insect problems, it's sometimes the only practical solution. In our home, without netting, we'd never get any blueberries to eat (the local blackbirds love them).

The Problems with Chemical Control

A wide range of chemicals and pesticides are sold to 'manage' pests and disease. Unfortunately, most also indiscriminately kill other life forms, add poisonous chemicals to the food chain and damage the environment. Even 'organic' slug pellets can harm microbial soil life which, in turn, weakens the plant and its ability to resist attack. It's a vicious circle. I believe that pesticides, even homemade organic ones, are never needed in the container garden.

Chives can deter aphids – and bees love the flowers.

To support netting over leafy crops, make hoops over pots with flexible plastic plumbing pipe, old metal coat hangers or plastic hula hoops. Then drape the netting over and tie it round the base of the pot with string. On fruit bushes, it's often possible to drape the netting directly over the plant and secure it with clothes pegs. Be aware that some birds are very determined and will find a way through surprisingly small gaps.

6. Grow disease-resistant varieties

You can buy specially bred crop varieties that offer varying degrees of resistance against common diseases like blight (see 'Late blight', page 154). Resistant varieties rarely offer total protection, but they do help to delay the onset of the disease or reduce its impact.

7. Edit out difficult crops

If a crop is difficult to grow every year because it gets attacked or diseased, sometimes it's best to listen to nature and just stop growing it, at least for a season or two. I gave up growing New Zealand oca because the tubers were eaten by slugs or vine weevils every year, making it rather disheartening.

Troubleshooting

There are thousands of insects, animals, fungi and other diseases that can live in your container garden and eat your plants. However, only a few of these are encountered regularly by urban gardeners and the ones you are most likely to encounter are described on the next few pages.

Slugs and snails

Slugs and snails are an almost ubiquitous challenge for container growers, reaching most urban places, even high balconies. They do an important job, decomposing rotting plant material (so releasing nutrients back into the soil), and small slug or snail populations do little damage to established plants. However, larger populations make growing difficult (and may cause you distress). For happy growing, aim to keep the population small and try to protect baby seedlings (slugs can make short work of these).

Without many natural predators – like ground beetles, ducks or hedgehogs – in small urban spaces, you'll usually need to hunt for slugs and snails yourself. After trying many different techniques, I've found that the only reliable way to control them is to find and remove them. The three best ways to do this are:

1. **Night-time patrols:** Use a torch once a week or fortnight. This is essential.
2. **Slug hunts:** At the start of the season and whenever you observe new slug damage, look under pots, compost bags and other potential slug-hiding places, removing as many as you can.
3. **Traps:** A simple slug trap is a squeezed orange or grapefruit half, cut side down, on the soil. Slugs will crawl under it and can be collected during the day.

With these simple methods, it's usually possible to keep slugs to a manageable level with just a few minutes' attention each week.

A wide range of products, from copper tape to sheep wool, are sold to deter slugs and snails. While these can offer some protection, few are reliable in wet weather as tests show that slugs just crawl over them. Slug pellets, on the other hand, even organic ones, will harm wildlife and are best avoided.

As a last resort, you can buy a special slug nematode, widely available online, which you mix into a watering can and water on. The nematode is a parasite that enters slugs, stops them feeding and kills them (it is

Not All Slugs Are Equal

Not all slugs eat fresh green leaves and some cause more damage than others. One to watch out for is the Spanish Slug, a large, dark brown beast that is becoming more widespread across Europe. It makes short work of baby plants, and can even be heard munching them!

Other slugs eat predominantly rotting vegetation. They do little damage in the container garden and can usually be left alone to get on with things. A common variety is the Green Cellar Slug, which is often found in wormeries. The John Innes Institute has a good online guide with pictures of the different slugs.

The common Green Cellar Slug mostly eats decaying vegetation and doesn't harm living plants. It's often found in wormeries.

less effective on snails). Despite my fair share of slugs, I've never had to use this, but I understand from those that have used it in their container gardens that it works well.

Protect seedlings

Seedlings and small plants are most vulnerable to slug attack and often need additional protection. Slugs are particularly fond of runner and French beans, pak choi and artichoke seedlings, so take extra care with these.

To protect precious seedlings, put them on a high shelf (although this is never *guaranteed* to keep them safe!), start them inside or protect with a cloche or upturned bottle. Seed trays can be fitted with transparent propagator lids.

Birds

Plants attract birds and watching them is one of the rewards of growing. You might see sparrows collecting aphids for their young, blackbirds eating the odd slug or flamboyant goldfinches feeding on seedheads.

Birds can also bring challenges. Pigeons eat brassicas, sparrows nibble on seedlings and blackbirds eat berries, dig for worms and generally make a mess. But most birds will leave your plants alone for most of the year and sometimes they don't even notice the food under their beaks.

When birds do start to eat your crops, bird netting is the best way to keep them off. Good-quality, modern bird netting seems to trap few, if any, birds. That said, try to avoid putting it on until it's needed.

Netting can be hung over hoops to protect leafy veg or draped over fruit bushes and held in place with clothes pegs. It's a good idea to net fruits like cherries and blueberries just before they are ripe, or they can disappear almost overnight if birds find them first.

Birds can also be deterred with DIY scarers, like shiny CDs, suspended rattling cans or Darth Vader scarecrows. These may

Blackbirds scuff up seedlings, make a mess and help themselves to blueberries, but their antics are also entertaining to watch.

work in the short term, but birds usually get used to them.

Cats

Discovering that a neighbouring cat is using your containers as a toilet is one of the less pleasing possibilities of urban growing. Cats are attracted to bare soil, so fill your containers with plants or find a way to make the bare soil less attractive to them. Try laying something prickly like bramble cuttings or holly leaves on the soil or cover with netting or chicken mesh. Darja Fišer, in Slovenia, discovered that flat stones, laid between the plants, were an effective and attractive solution to keep her cats off containers.

If you have a major problem with roaming cats, you might invest in a water scarecrow. This is a hose with a battery-powered light sensor. When a cat crosses the path of the sensor it gets sprayed with water. This deterrent also works with most other animals that don't enjoy getting wet, including foxes and squirrels.

Other cat deterrents on the market include smelly products like lion poop, but these tend to be more variable in effectiveness.

Aphids

Aphids are small, sap-sucking insects that can weaken plants. There are hundreds of different species in different colours but most commonly they are green ('greenfly') or black ('blackfly'). You can normally spot small colonies with your naked eye. Other signs include distorted leaves or ants running up and down the stem, farming them for the sap.

Aphids target weak, stressed plants. If plants aren't getting enough sun or water, are growing in poor-quality compost or have 'soft growth', they are prime targets. Soft growth occurs when a plant grows fast but weakly because there is too much nitrogen fertiliser in the soil. Soft growth contains lots of sugars and makes a nice, tasty meal for aphids.

Aphids often target weak plants – these were on a runner bean that wasn't getting enough sun.

Symptoms of blight include brown, decaying leaves, brown lesions on the stem and fruits turning brown.

Small numbers of aphids won't do much harm. By letting a few be, you can attract their natural predators like ladybirds and hoverfly larvae, which will only arrive if there is something for them to eat. However, in an urban setting, you can't always rely on ladybirds and hoverflies (insect populations have been drastically depleted in many areas), so it's usually best to take action sooner rather than later.

The best and most targeted control for aphids is to rub them off the plants with your fingers, or, if you prefer, kitchen paper. They can also be sprayed with a diluted soap solution, but I don't recommend this as soap can break down the waxy cuticle on plant leaves (vital for the plant's defence against other pests) and harm other insects. In my experience, it isn't necessary in small-space growing, but if you want to try it, get a proper horticultural soap.

Since aphids tend to target stressed or weak plants, try to work out why your plants might be stressed, so you can address the underlying causes.

Late blight

Late blight is a fungus that attacks potatoes and tomatoes. It makes tomato and potato leaves shrivel and turn brown, and brown lesions develop on the stem. In tomatoes, the fruits will also turn brown. It's more prevalent in some areas than others, so you might be lucky and grow tomatoes for several years without a problem.

Late blight is spread through water on the leaves, so try to avoid splashing the leaves when watering (the lower leaves on tomatoes can be removed to aid this). If blight is a major problem, shielding the plants from rain will reduce the risk significantly – you could, for example, grow them in a mini green-house. In France, they make simple roofs out of plastic to keep rain off their tomatoes.

Blight-resistant varieties like 'Crimson Crush' tomatoes or 'Sarpo' potatoes are also well worth trying.

If blight strikes in tomatoes, remove any badly infected leaves and fruits. Uninfected fruits can still be eaten and brought inside to ripen. In mild attacks, the plants can be left to grow and will usually continue to fruit for several weeks. However, with severe infections, it's best to pull the plant up, saving any fruits you can.

In areas with cold winters (like most of the UK), infected plants can be added to a wormery or compost as the fungus will be killed over winter. However, never save seed potatoes from blight-infected plants as the fungus survives in the potato tuber.

Vine weevil

The vine weevil is a common beetle that eats leaves, but its maggot-like larvae cause most of the problems. These burrow into the soil and eat plant roots. If a plant pulls out of the soil disconcertingly easily and has few roots left, vine weevils are often responsible. They attack most plants, but they seem to favour strawberries. They can be a particular problem in containers as most of their natural predators, like hedgehogs, toads and ground beetles, are usually absent from balconies and patios.

If vine weevils are discovered, the first thing to do is to empty the pot onto a tarp or tray, then hunt out and collect as many of the maggots as you can find (squish them or put them out for the birds). This is time-consuming but effective.

For larger, more widespread, weevil infections, a special nematode is available online. This is watered on, most effectively in warmer weather in late spring or late summer/early autumn. August or early September is a good time, shortly after a new batch of grubs has hatched and before they do much damage.

Leaf miner

Blotches on chard, beetroot, sorrel or spinach leaves are normally caused by a fly larva known as beet leaf miner. The flies, which look similar to house flies, lay their eggs on the leaves, which hatch out and burrow into the leaf. If you hold an infected leaf up to the light, a small larvae can often be seen inside.

Keep an eye out for white vine weevil grubs like this when you empty a pot of soil.

The distinctive blotch made by a leaf miner.

TABLE 8.2. Troubleshooting Check Sheet

Symptom	Possible causes
Plant not growing/weak growth	Many possible causes, including poor-quality compost, too cold, waterlogged potting mix, lack of nutrients, vine weevil, or if growth is 'checked' (see *Glossary of Gardening Terms*, page 289).
Yellow leaves	Sometimes waterlogged soil but most often low nitrogen – a common issue with a poor batch of compost or if a plant has simply outgrown its pot.
Thin, elongated, weak stems	Too little light
Fruits not ripening	Usually too little sun or poor weather, but sometimes because of late sowing.
Fruits not setting	Depends on the crop, but includes lack of pollinators, or too hot or too cold, or other stress (for example, wind).
Lots of soft, lush growth, often attacked by aphids	Usually too much nitrogen
Purple leaves	Normally a nutrient deficiency, often phosphorous
Marbled appearance on leaves	Often a nutrient deficiency, usually magnesium
Tough and bitter leaves/fruit	Normally stress from lack of water but salad crops can also get tough with age, in hot weather or if they bolt.
Leaves eaten	Often slugs or snails but sometimes flea beetles (make bullet-like holes), pigeons (strip leaves back to the veins), or caterpillars.
Plant weakens or dies and has few roots when pulled up	Usually vine weevil
Distorted leaves	Various, including aphids, viruses, bad weather and herbicide residues in manure.
Blotches on leaves, particularly if chard, beet, spinach, sorrel	Leaf miner
Tomatoes or potatoes have withering leaves/brown stem lesions	Late blight is most common, but tomatoes can be affected by a wide range of diseases.

To control, remove infected leaves and dispose of in a bin, not compost (where the flies will hatch and breed). Also, as soon as you spot infected leaves, look on the backs of the leaves for more small clusters of white eggs. Squish these to prevent the larvae hatching.

Commercial growers often prevent leaf miner by covering plants with a fine insect mesh. This is also effective in containers, but the mesh is fiddly to attach, expensive and unattractive.

Hundreds of other leaf mining flies exist, most specific to certain plants. Borage and celery leaf miners are quite common, for example.

Powdery mildew

Powdery mildew is a common fungus that looks like a white dusting on the leaves. Most plants can get mildew, but it is particularly common on courgettes, squash and cucumbers, particularly later in the season.

Try to identify the main cause. Ask questions such as: are the other plants in the same compost growing well? Does the potting mix feel too dry or wet? Is the plant getting enough sun? Has the plant been fed? Finding the cause will help you work out how to resolve it or prevent it happening again.

If low nitrogen, apply a high-nitrogen feed or a balanced feed, ideally in liquid form. If waterlogged, check drainage holes and water less. If plant has outgrown its pot, repot in a larger size.

Move plants to more sun or improve light (for example, by painting a wall white). Move indoor seedlings outside on warm days or invest in a grow light.

Move to a sunnier place, if possible. Consider sowing earlier. Grow crops that need less sun.

Check your climate and growing site is suited to your crop; consider growing more flowers to attract pollinators.

Add less fertiliser next time.

Try to identify which nutrient (the internet will help), then add a feed that contains that nutrient.

Liquid or foliar feed (Epsom salts are high in magnesium).

Daily watering routine, plus watch for warm or windy weather. Don't forget that all plants, particularly microgreens, need more water as they grow larger.

Try to identify the culprit early and take steps to control the population or protect the plant.

Empty the pot and collect up the larvae – see *Chapter 8 Growing in Harmony with Life*, 'Vine weevil', page 155.

If manure, try to get assurance that future manure supplies do not contain herbicides.

Remove and throw away (don't compost) infected leaves – see *Chapter 8 Growing in Harmony with Life*, 'Leaf miner', page 155.

If blight, remove infected leaves and infected fruit in mild cases, and the whole plant if severe – see *Chapter 8 Growing in Harmony with Life*, 'Late blight', page 154.

Plants are more prone to mildew if they get dry or stressed. As a result, the onset of mildew can often be delayed and sometimes prevented by growing plants in larger containers and keeping them well watered. Even with these measures, plants usually succumb eventually.

Powdery mildew isn't fatal. Once infected, plants will usually continue to grow and produce fruit, although productivity can be lowered. Pick off badly infected leaves (these are safe to add to a wormery or compost bin), and keep the plant well watered and fed.

Other animals and diseases

The animals and insects discussed so far are responsible for the vast majority of plant problems. However, there are hundreds of other insects and diseases that you may encounter. Internet searches and online forums now make identifying these far easier than was the case in the past.

Mildew arrives on courgettes in most seasons; the trick is to try and delay it for as long as possible.

As usual, local information is also invaluable. Whether you are troubled by marauding monkeys, squirrels, rabbits, deer, hornworm or Colorado beetle, local gardeners can usually offer ideas to help.

Troubleshooting guide

If you have a problem in your garden, you need to identify the cause to enable you to take the right action. There are often several possible causes for any symptom you observe, but, if you know what these are, you can often work out which one is responsible by a process of elimination. 'Table 8.2 Troubleshooting Check Sheet', pages 156–157, lists the most common symptoms you are likely to encounter and their possible causes. The internet is also useful here; for example, the RHS website lists the most common problems encountered for each crop.

Part III
What to Grow

Radish is one of the fastest and easiest microgreens to grow – and has a very similar flavour to fully grown radish.

Chapter 9

Your First Growing Projects

What to grow first? There are so many possibilities and it's exciting, but the choice can sometimes be confusing. Starting with something quick and easy is a good way to build confidence, get experience and learn about your growing space. It's also motivating to grow something successfully and then to pick and eat it.

In my experience from running workshops, two excellent first projects are growing pea shoots (or other microgreens) and potting up supermarket herbs. Potatoes are also good, particularly if kids are involved. As well as being easy, these projects don't need much stuff, so it shouldn't be difficult to get what you need.

While these are great first projects, don't be deterred from starting with anything else that excites you. Few plants are too difficult as long as you have the right climate and enough sun (do try to check this first) as well as the time to look after them.

If possible, try to grow a few different things during your first year – one or two of the easy projects I've outlined, alongside a few of your favourite veg, herbs and fruits.

Project 1: Microgreens

Microgreens are delicious, easy to grow and usually ready to eat in just 10–20 days. They only need a few hours of sun to thrive and high yields can be produced in very little space. They are also highly nutritious and expensive to buy, but cheap to grow yourself. All this makes them a brilliant choice for growing at home. Even though they are 'easy', they remain one of my favourite things to grow and we eat them most days.

There are many different microgreens, all with different flavours, textures and leaf shapes. I particularly recommend pea shoots to start with because most people love them! Other good ones for beginners include radish (very fast – often ready to eat in just 7–10 days), rocket, fava (small broad beans) and sunflower microgreens.

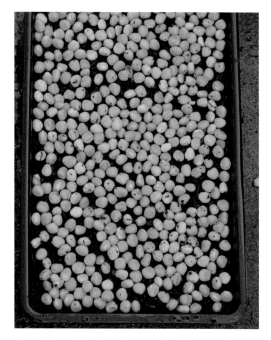

A seed tray showing the spacing for pea shoots.

Collect what you need

As well as a bright place inside or outside, ideally with two hours' sun or more, you will need:

A general-purpose compost or growing medium. Although it is always good to use the best compost you can, most microgreens are less fussy, so a bag of compost from the supermarket will usually do the job.

A tray, crate or container at least 4–6cm (1½–2½in) deep and with drainage holes in the bottom. A seed tray is ideal, or you can use a fruit, mushroom or veg tray scavenged from a market.

Seeds (see 'Where to Buy Seeds for Microgreens' box, page 164).

Watering can or bottle waterer (this is simply a plastic bottle with holes drilled in the lid).

Seed label and indelible pen.

Step-by-step: How to grow microgreens

1. Soak seeds in water overnight. This helps speed up the germination of larger seeds like peas or fava beans but isn't essential.
2. Fill a seed tray to within about 1cm (½in) of the top with compost and press this down lightly with your hands to flatten it and remove any large air gaps. A common beginner's mistake is to put in too little compost– make sure you fill the tray close to the top.
3. Water the compost (it should feel damp like a wrung-out flannel).
4. Scatter the seeds over the top of the compost. Sow thickly for the best yields – and try and space the seed evenly. Large seeds like peas can be nearly touching each other. Small seeds like rocket can be sown about ½cm (¼in) apart.
5. Cover with a thin layer of compost about the depth of the seeds, lightly firm and

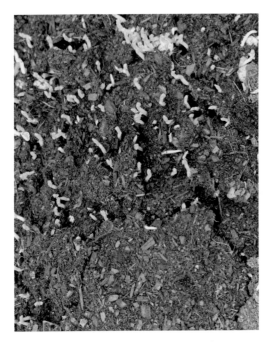

The compost can look like it is erupting when the shoots first appear. Don't worry, this is normal.

After 10–30 days (depending on how warm it is) the pea shoots will be ready to harvest. Simply cut them with sharp scissors.

Harvesting pea shoots.

Where to Buy Seeds for Microgreens

Due to the number of seeds needed to grow a tray of microgreens, it's not economical to buy small commercial seed packs. Luckily, many spice and dried pulse seeds sold for cooking will grow fine, including dried peas, dried chickpeas, coriander seeds (slow to germinate but delicious), black mustard seeds and fenugreek. It's fun to experiment. Alternatively, look for specialist sprout and microgreen seed suppliers who supply large seed packs of excellent microgreens like sunflower, radish, rocket and kale.

water the surface again – do this gently
to avoid disturbing the seeds.

6. Label and date.
7. Put the seed tray in a bright place, ideally
   with *at least* two hours of sun a day.
8. Keep the compost damp, like a wrung-
   out flannel. Check daily and water when
   required. More frequent watering will
   be needed as the seedlings grow.

Most microgreens will be ready to eat 10–21
days after sowing. Sow them thickly to harvest
a LOT of leaves from one tray. With a few
trays, you will find that you can grow a good
quantity of salad – achieving self-sufficiency
in salad is quite possible in a very small space.

How to harvest microgreens

The shoots are edible as soon as they come up.
Most can then be eaten at any size. Keep
picking and tasting them to find the size you
like best. In general, I strongly recommend
eating them sooner rather than later (they may
go tough or bitter as they get older). Pea shoots

are often at their best when they reach 5–10cm
(2–4in). In warm weather, microgreens grow
quickly and the window to harvest them is
much shorter than in cooler months, when
trays can often be picked over several weeks.

1. The cutting method

Harvest by cutting with scissors about 1cm
(½in) above the soil. Sometimes they will
regrow and you'll get a second cut. Cut pea
shoots just above the bottom leaf. This
method is the best for pea shoots, fava beans,
chickpeas, sunflowers and radishes – and
works for most microgreens. Shake off any
dirt and put them straight into a salad
spinner or bowl to wash.

2. The thinning method

With this method, you 'thin out' some of the
leaves by pulling out a few of the baby plants
– see the photograph in *Chapter 5 Useful
Growing Skills*, 'Thinning out', page 106. Try
to do this evenly across the tray. This creates
space for the remaining leaves to grow larger
and stronger – and because of this you can

Sunflower shoots are one of the best microgreens – but they need to be harvested before their
second pair of leaves develop, when they become tough and bitter.

Watering Microgreens

Watering is important because it affects the quality and flavour of the microgreens as well as keeping them alive. If microgreens dry out, they can quickly become tough and bitter. This happens regularly to new growers who often don't realise why.

Until the seeds germinate, they won't need much watering – just enough to keep the soil damp. But as the microgreens emerge and grow larger, they will need to drink more. A fully grown tray of microgreens usually needs watering at least once a day. Keep a particularly close eye in hot or windy weather, when the microgreens will dry out faster.

Coriander microgreens have an intense and superb flavour. These were grown from storecupboard spice seeds.

How to Use Microgreens

Microgreens are versatile and can be used in salads, as a garnish or even as the main ingredient. They can be used to add flavour, colour, texture and interesting leaf shapes. Sunflower shoots are crunchy and nutty. Radish shoots are colourful and spicy. Basil and coriander are intensely flavoured. Pea shoots are pretty and have a wonderful, fresh-pea taste.

A handful of microgreens will transform a supermarket lettuce into a special salad. Or you can make an entire salad by using pea, fava or sunflower shoots as a base. They also make a pretty and tasty garnish for any dish and a good last-minute addition to stir fries and risottos.

often harvest a tray over a longer period. It works well for many microgreens, particularly 'leafy' ones like rocket, mustards, chard, sorrel and coriander. It is less suitable for radishes, sunflowers, pea shoots and fava shoots.

Once you've pulled out your microgreens, chop the roots off with scissors and wash. Or you can experiment with leaving the roots on (coriander roots, for example, have a wonderful flavour).

Project 2: Supermarket herb plants

The easiest way to get and grow herbs – one of the most rewarding crops for containers – is simply to buy and pot up supermarket herbs.

Small pots of living herbs from the supermarket are hard to keep alive for long because the pot is too small and the plants quickly use up all the food and space. As we've seen, when leafy plants are grown close together, they yield quickly but soon run out of steam. Supermarket basil and parsley, for example, have lots of plants crammed close together in one pot, which gives a good harvest of leaves at first, but then the plants look stressed and don't grow well.

However, you can extend their life considerably by moving them to a larger pot. In theory, mint can be kept going indefinitely – I have supermarket mint plants that are at least eight years old.

Collect what you need

Identify a place that gets at least three hours of sun a day. Parsley and mint can be grown outside in most climates, while basil is best grown inside in cooler climates (unless it's a warm summer). You will need:

A good-quality, general-purpose compost – the best you can easily get hold of.

A pot with drainage holes in the bottom. The larger the pot, the larger the herbs will grow and the longer they'll last. Go for at least 1–2 litres (¼–½ gallon) – bucket size is ideal for most herbs if you have space.

Supermarket herb plants. Mint plants are the easiest and a good choice to start with. Parsley and basil also work well, but have a go with whatever herbs are available. (Coriander is trickier, as it doesn't like being moved from one pot to another.)

Watering can or bottle waterer (a plastic bottle with holes drilled in the lid).

Step-by-step: How to grow supermarket herbs

1. Check the pot has drainage holes in the bottom and part fill it with compost, leaving plenty of space in the top to accommodate your new herb plant.
2. Remove the supermarket plant from its container and then:

   For mint, move the whole plant to the new pot (assuming there is just one plant in the supermarket pot – there usually is). First, if the roots are visible and circling round the pot, gently tease them out so they are facing outwards (chop off any extra-long bits with scissors if needed). Then lower the plant into the new pot and fill it with compost, covering the roots with fresh compost. Gently firm the top so that the plant is firmly anchored in the pot.

   For basil and parsley, there are usually lots of baby plants in one supermarket pot. Carefully tease these into small clumps of two or three plants. Then carefully move each of these clumps to a larger pot filled with good-quality compost, leaving plenty of space

Move a whole mint plant to a larger-sized pot with good compost to give it a new lease of life.

Supermarket pots of parsley (and basil) contain lots of plants that need dividing up and planting in small clumps in larger pots.

Once repotted in a larger, bucket-sized container, a supermarket mint will produce an excellent supply of leaves for many months (dying back in winter, then returning in the spring). If divided and repotted each year, it will keep going forever.

between each clump. If there are lots of plants, you might need two or three pots. Remember that the more space you give the plants, the larger each one can grow. Then gently firm the compost around the plants so that they are firmly anchored (see *Chapter 5 Useful Growing Skills*, 'How to transplant and pot on', page 94).

3. Give the plant a good watering – this will help it settle. If possible, move it to a sheltered space, out of strong sun and wind, for the first 24 hours to help it establish in its new pot.

That's it. Once growing, water regularly and feed with liquid seaweed once a week, if available. For the best method for picking herbs and encouraging bushy growth, see *Chapter 5 Useful Growing Skills*, 'Pinching out', page 105.

Troubleshooting

Newly potted herb plants can take a week or two to get established. Parsley, in particular, sometimes dies back after repotting before producing fresh new shoots.

Usually, your herb plants will flourish in their new environment. However, as with all growing, there are lots of variables and occasionally they will not grow so well. Don't be hard on yourself; just see if you can work out what is going wrong. It might be:

▸ The quality of the herb plant and how it was raised. Supermarket herb plants are usually raised under strong lights in warm conditions and can sometimes struggle to adapt when put outside, particularly if the weather is harsh. (If starting them at a cool time of year, try hardening them off, as described in *Chapter 5 Useful Growing Skills*, 'Hardening off', page 92).

▸ The quality of the compost you are using.
▸ The weather, and how much sun and wind there is in your growing space.

Project 3: Potatoes in a bag

It's fun harvesting new potatoes from a pot (and kids love it); they taste delicious and it's not difficult. The trick is to start with good compost, to water regularly (particularly as the plants get larger) and to grow them in a space that gets at least four hours of sun.

Collect what you need

Seed potatoes: The most suitable varieties of potatoes for containers are known as first or second 'earlies'. These are fast-growing varieties (usually ready in 10–12 weeks) and are best eaten young as new potatoes. ('Maincrop' potatoes take longer to grow and are best in larger containers or in the ground.)
Container: Any 10-litre (2½-gallon) or larger container with drainage holes in

Plant one seed potato in a bucket. I'm growing this one in old compost and I've added a handful of blood, fish and bone for fertiliser.

Potatoes don't need much watering for the first few weeks (just be sure to keep the compost damp), but once they are big and bushy, they normally need watering every day.

the bottom. Flower buckets, bags for life or old recycling bins are good options.

Good-quality compost: Potatoes will also grow fine in old compost as long as you add fertiliser – see *Chapter 11 Solutions to Common Challenges*, 'Reusing old compost', page 236.

Fertiliser: Optional if you are using new compost, but essential if using old compost – potatoes are hungry. Options include blood, fish and bone and/or worm compost.

A sunny place: Potatoes ideally need at least four hours' sun.

Step-by-step: How to plant potatoes

1. Put about 10cm (4in) of compost in the bottom of the pot (check it has drainage holes first). If you are using old compost, mix in the fertiliser now.
2. Lay your seed potatoes on top. Put one potato in a 10-litre (2½-gallon) pot and two to three in a large bag.
3. Cover with about 15cm (6in) of compost.
4. Water lightly (omit this step if the compost is already damp).
5. Put in a sunny place.

How to look after your potatoes

Watering

This is critical to get a good harvest. Keep the soil moist and water when needed (remember to put your finger in the soil – it should feel damp like a wrung-out flannel). For the first week or two, they will not need much watering (too much can rot the seed potato). But they will need more as they

Nearly a kilo of potatoes (913g/2lb) was harvested from the bucket with one seed potato (see the photograph on page 170), which is about average from this size of pot (but you may get more or less).

grow – larger plants will need watering every day, particularly if it is warm or windy. Water the soil and try to avoid getting water on the leaves as this can help spread potato blight.

Earthing up

Keep adding compost as the potatoes grow, covering up the lower leaves. This helps prevent green potatoes. Stop about 5cm (2in) from the top, to leave space for watering.

Feeding

You can also liquid feed with a seaweed or general-purpose liquid feed once a fortnight, or add more worm compost. But this is not essential if you start with fertile soil.

When to harvest

Flowering is one sign that your potato might be ready for harvest. But the only way to know for sure is to put your hand in the soil, rummage around a bit and pluck out a potato. If the potato has reached a decent size, it is ready; if not, leave for a week or two longer. If your potato hasn't flowered after 12 weeks, check anyway. New potatoes are usually best eaten when they are about the size of hen's eggs.

Chapter 10

The Best Herbs, Fruit and Veg for Containers

When choosing what to grow in a small space, you want every plant to be special in some way: beautiful, delicious, attractive to wildlife, fragrant, expensive to buy, highly productive or simply something you're excited to grow. And ideally for it to offer several of these qualities.

Based on my experience of growing a wide variety of crops in containers, this chapter covers some of the most reliable, productive, tasty and useful crops to have in the kitchen container garden. Later in this book, you'll find ideas for plants that are good for flavour, nutrition, scent and to attract wildlife and save money. Use these, together with the information in this chapter, to help you make your choices.

A typical July harvest from my container garden. Herbs, soft fruit, tomatoes, courgettes and beans are among the best container crops.

You can grow any crop you like in a container, but bear in mind that some are less well suited to small spaces because they:

▶ Take up lots of space relative to how much you get to eat (like Brussels sprouts and broad beans).
▶ Take a long time to mature (like purple-sprouting broccoli and cabbages).
▶ Are low cost and easy to get in shops (like carrots and onions).

Don't let this put you off experimenting with anything you want, though. Even though the harvest is small, I often grow a few broad beans in containers as they're my favourite vegetable.

It's also worth considering how long a plant can be picked for. Carrots, beetroot and other root veg can only be picked once (so take a lot of space and effort relative to the size of the harvest), while tomatoes and chillies can be picked over several months; chard and kale over a year or more (if the outer leaves are picked); and herbs like thyme, sage and rosemary all year round.

Some crops have the added benefit of several edible parts. Beetroot and turnips have edible leaves as well as roots; nasturtiums have edible leaves, flowers and seeds; and radishes and coriander have edible leaves, flowers, seeds and roots.

Traditional or 'Unusual' Crops?

There is an increasingly wide range of crops available to home growers, including 'unusual' things (for us in the UK) like oca, Sichuan peppers and mouse melons. These enable you to discover delicious new flavours, diversify your diet and eat foods that aren't easy to buy. It can also be fun to share something unusual with friends, like a sorrel omelette, a tomatillo salsa or a snack of Chilean guavas.

The more unusual edibles I like to grow every year include Chilean guavas, Japanese wineberries, sorrel, lovage, New Zealand spinach and society garlic. Even so, I'm not sure that any of these (except perhaps sorrel) would make my 'top ten' if I had less space to grow. With fewer pots, I'd focus on things like tomatoes, chillies, mint, French beans, rocket, raspberries and courgettes – plants that I want to cook with and eat every day.

My advice to you is to experiment with a mix of the unusual and traditional to discover your favourites.

Herbs

Herbs are ideally suited for growing in containers and small spaces, and they have more potential to change the food you eat than anything else that is easily grown in a small space. Just a few pots can provide fresh herbs every day, bring flavour to each meal, smell wonderful, look pretty and support beneficial insects. There are also some excellent culinary herbs that are easy to grow but almost impossible to buy, including lovage, chervil, and savory.

It's quite possible to be almost self-sufficient in herbs in a small space and to eat them every day for a fraction of the cost of buying them. In the kitchen, herbs can be used to make teas, cocktails and pestos, as well as to add flavour to almost any savoury or sweet dishes. They also have medicinal uses and can be used in potpourris and homemade cosmetics.

If you've never had a constant supply of herbs, it can take a bit of time to learn how to make the most of them. There are some ideas in *Chapter 11 Solutions to Common Challenges*, 'Eating the harvests', page 244.

Where to get herbs

With so many wonderful herbs available, a visit to a specialist herb nursery can help you choose what you want: you'll be able to smell the different basils, sages and mints, and get acquainted with the more unusual herbs. Also, look in farmers' markets and fairs, where some herb nurseries set up stalls in the spring and summer. If you can't get to one in person, there are excellent herb nurseries that sell online.

Most herbs can also be grown from cuttings (see *Chapter 5 Useful Growing Skills*, 'How to take cuttings,' page 96) or from divided plants (see 'Repotting and dividing', page 178). If you have a friend or community garden nearby with a herb garden, do ask.

Most gardeners enjoy sharing (my mint, oregano and society garlic plants have been distributed all over Newcastle upon Tyne).

Herbs that are easiest to grow from cuttings include mint, basil, Vietnamese coriander, oregano, rosemary, scented pelargoniums and sage. Lemon verbena, thyme, savory and lavender are also not difficult. Easy herbs to divide (simply dig them up and chop in half) include mint, oregano, chives and society garlic.

How to grow herbs

In general, herbs are low-maintenance and relatively easy to grow. As well as using a

Not much space is needed for a good, daily supply of herbs. On this ladder, 75cm (2½ft) wide, I'm growing fennel, parsley and garlic chives (*top shelf*); marjoram, oregano and society garlic (*middle shelf*); and mint and sorrel (*bottom shelf*).

good potting mix and a large-enough pot, the three things that make the most difference to creating a healthy herb garden are:

1. Feeding with liquid seaweed or similar once a week or fortnight to promote lush, healthy growth.
2. Picking regularly. The best way to pick most herbs is to pinch out the tips, just above a leaf node on each stalk (see *Chapter 5 Useful Growing Skills*, 'Pinching out', page 105) to encourage a bushier plant.
3. Repotting every one to three years, depending on how fast the herbs are growing.

The Mediterranean herbs – like thyme, sage and lavender – do well in terracotta containers. Planting mixed pots like this is an option, but bear in mind that one herb often starts to dominate after a few months. It is usually easier to grow one herb per pot, if space permits.

Sun requirements

Herbs are an excellent choice for less sunny growing spaces. Although some grow and taste best in full sun, most will also do fine in just three or four hours of sun, even the supposedly sun-loving ones like rosemary and basil. They won't develop quite as much flavour, but they still taste great when freshly picked.

Pot size and type

As a rough rule of thumb, move newly purchased herb plants into a pot one size larger. I grow some of my herbs in old 8-litre (2-gallon) plastic flower buckets because they are light, free and a good size for growing decent-sized plants. Terracotta pots are another good option, particularly for the Mediterranean herbs – go for pots of 5 litres (1¼ gallons) or 10 litres (2½ gallons), or larger.

Containers with water reservoirs are useful for herbs that like access to a constant supply of water, including mint, parsley, chives and Vietnamese coriander.

Compost

Most herbs do best in a well-draining soil. A good-quality, general-purpose compost is usually a perfectly satisfactory option and some professional herb nurseries grow most of their herbs in this. Alternatively, you can make a more free-draining potting mix (see *Chapter 6 How to Make Your Own...*, 'A free-draining mix', page 112), which may give better results with some herbs, particularly ones like tarragon and sage.

Watering

Since herbs originate from different habitats, they all have different water needs. Generally, though, they can be divided into herbs that like a constant supply of water (mint, chives and parsley) and those that can survive with more infrequent watering (sage, tarragon, thyme and most Mediterranean herbs). In practice, however, most herbs in

Oregano forms a large clump – when the plant fills a pot, it benefits from dividing in the spring.

containers still need watering regularly in warm weather, particularly as compost can be hard to re-wet if it dries out, as we saw in *Chapter 4 Eight Steps to Success*, 'Step 6: Create a watering routine that works for you and your plants', page 64.

Feeding

It's sometimes assumed that herbs don't need feeding in containers because their natural habitat is often stony soils with low fertility. However, these soils can also be rich in trace elements that contribute to vitality and flavour. Feeding herbs with a feed that is low in major nutrients (NPK) and rich in minerals, like liquid seaweed, once a week or fortnight, will help you grow healthy and lush herbs. If you don't have liquid seaweed, look for something else low in NPK but with trace elements – perhaps worm tea or diluted comfrey or nettle tea.

A few herbs benefit from additional feeding, particularly mint and lovage. Add a light sprinkling of chicken manure pellets or mulch with worm compost every few months.

Repotting and dividing

As herbs grow, they exhaust the available nutrients and their roots fill up the pot. To maintain their vigour, they need repotting every year or two. This is usually best done in the spring or at the end of summer.

If space permits, move herbs to a bigger pot each time. If you are returning them to the same pot, prune off about one-third of the roots (with kitchen scissors or secateurs) or divide the plant into halves or quarters (essential with mint, chives and oregano) before repotting each half or quarter with some fresh compost.

How do you know if a herb needs repotting? The simplest way is to just see if it looks too big for its pot. To gauge more accurately, lay the pot on its side and ease the plant out – if lots of roots are visible circling the pot, it's ready to move.

One herb that always needs repotting and dividing each year is mint. It's a hungry plant that quickly spreads, using up all the available energy and space. If mint plants aren't split up and repotted, they quickly run out of steam, which is a common issue for new mint growers.

Other herbs that benefit from regular division include chives, garlic chives, society garlic, oregano, marjoram and tarragon. Division has the added advantage that you then get extra plants to swap or give away.

Dividing herbs is a simple if sometimes quite physical job, particularly with large plants. Simply remove the plant from the pot and then cut it in half or quarters with a sharp trowel or an old bread knife. Repot each part in a new pot. While it can seem destructive splitting them up, you will often observe that split plants get a new lease of life.

Pruning herbs

Some herbs can become straggly and woody as they age, particularly sage, rosemary and lemon verbena. To keep them compact and neat, cut them back once or twice a year in late spring (after flowering) or early autumn (before any frosts). (Once they get large and woody, the old wooden stems of some herbs like rosemary won't always reshoot, so cutting these right back is risky – but you can sometimes get away with it.)

Usually, it's best not to remove more than a third of a plant at one time to help it maintain its strength.

Herb guide

The easiest herbs to grow are marked with ▲. Those marked with ▲ are also easy. Those marked with ▲ are fussier but still worth a go.

Basil and Thai basil

▲ from seed or plant
Annual, tender
Pot size: 3–4 plants in a 2.5–6 litre
(⅔–1½-gallon) container (or closer together for a quicker, shorter yield)

Basil sings of summer. It's a wonderful herb for salads, pestos and tomato dishes. It's easiest to grow from supermarket plants, though the more unusual varieties can be grown from seed and are well worth trying. The seeds need warmth to germinate, so are usually best started inside or on a heated propagator if you have one.

The essential ingredient for basil is warmth. It hates cold weather and in cooler areas is best grown inside for most of the year, only putting it out on hot summer days. Basil will grow fine in just three or four hours of sun, but more sun will give it more flavour. It doesn't like wet roots at night, so water in the morning if possible.

Varieties: Basil 'Genovese' – a classic Italian variety; 'Mrs Burns' Lemon Basil' has a nice hint of lemon; Greek basil – a small-leaved variety; 'Dark Opal' basil is a pretty, purple variety with an aniseedy bouquet; Thai basil has warmth and an aniseed twist, an essential ingredient for Southeast Asian curries.

Greek basil and 'Dark Opal' basil are two wonderful varieties that can be grown from seed.

Bay

▲ from plant
Perennial, hardy
Pot size: At least 5–10 litres (1¼–2½ gallons), but ideally 20–40 litres (5¼–10½ gallons) for bigger plants

Bay is an evergreen that looks attractive all year round and can add structure to a container garden. It's excellent for flavouring stocks, soups and stews. One medium-sized plant will supply plenty of leaves and last many years – you'll never need to buy bay leaves again.

Bay is best bought as a plant. If you are happy to be patient, buy a small plant and move it to a bigger pot every year or two. Mine has moved from a 2-litre (½-gallon) to a 40-litre (10½-gallon) pot over the last seven years. It's also possible (but tricky) to grow from cuttings.

Bay is an easy and resilient herb to look after once it is established. It seems to enjoy growing in a pot and, unlike many plants, it doesn't mind having its roots restricted, so it will grow quite large in a small pot.

Chervil

▲ from seed
Biennial, hardy
Pot size: At least 1 litre (¼ gallon), but ideally 2.5–5 litres (⅔–1¼ gallons)

Chervil has pretty, feathery leaves and is similar to parsley, but with a mild aniseed flavour. Grow it like parsley. Sow any time from March (for a summer harvest) to the end of August. It is hardy, and late-summer sowings will give fresh herbs in late autumn, winter and spring (pick sparingly in cold weather).

Chives have bright, cheerful and edible flowers from late April to June. Bees also love them.

Chives

▲ from seed or plant
Perennial, hardy
Pot size: At least 2.5 litres (⅔ gallon), but
    ideally 5–10 litres (1¼–2½ gallons)

Chives die back over winter and return with
new shoots like old friends every spring.
Their pretty flowers are edible and an
important source of early nectar for bees.
The flower petals have a strong chive flavour
and look pretty scattered into a salad or on
any dish. The leaves can be snipped into
salads and omelettes and used as a garnish.

Chives prefer sunnier spaces but seem to
do okay in just three or four hours of sun.
Once established, they are low-maintenance
and easy. They grow in a clump that usually
needs dividing every two or three years
when the plant fills the pot or if it looks like
it has run out of energy. Replant the divisions
in fresh compost.

Common lovage and Scots lovage

▲ from seed or plant
Perennial, hardy
Pot size: 20 litres (5¼ gallons) or larger for
    common lovage; 8 litres (2 gallons) or
    larger for Scots lovage

Lovage is a bit of a secret shared by cooks
and keen growers. It has a rich, earthy,
celery-like flavour and is fantastic for adding
base notes to soups, stocks, risottos and
stews. It can also be finely shredded and
added to salads in moderation (it has a strong
flavour). It dies back in winter and regrows
in spring.

Common lovage (*Levisticum officinale*)
can be grown from seed and needs a large
container as it grows 1.2–1.5m (4–5ft) tall. It's
a bit of a thug, so Scots lovage is often a
better choice for container gardens.

Scots lovage (*Ligusticum scoticum*)
grows wild in Scotland and is a smaller plant.
It has attractive leaves and pretty, white,
edible flowers (delicious in salads) and
edible seeds. It's often sold as an ornamental.
The leaves have a similar but different
flavour to common lovage (I prefer it). It can
be grown from fresh seed but it's easiest to
get a plant.

Coriander

▲ from seed
Annual, hardy
Pot size: At least 2.5 litres (⅔ gallon), but
    ideally 2.5–5 litres (⅔–1¼ gallons)

Coriander has a reputation for being difficult
to grow because spring sowings are prone to
bolt. But the upside is that the flowers attract
beneficial insects and have a nice zesty
flavour. What's more, the green seeds (before
they brown and harden) are a well-kept
culinary secret: vibrant and delicious. The
roots can also be eaten – add them at the
beginning of cooking a curry to add depth of
flavour (unlike the leaves which are best
added at the end).

Coriander is often associated with
curries and hot climates in the UK, but it
actually grows best in cool weather and only
needs three or four hours of sun a day. Sow
from March to September in its final pot as it
doesn't like being moved. Late August
sowings are often best because it will grow
through winter (it is quite hardy, even
surviving snow in my experience) into spring
before flowering. The seed is slow to germinate, often taking two or three weeks. To
speed this up, lightly crush the seed husks
(each husk contains two seeds) and soak
them in water for 24 hours before sowing.

For a regular supply of coriander leaves,
sow a fresh pot every few weeks. And for a
large supply (some recipes require

The flowers of garlic chives are edible and have a pleasing crunch.

handfuls!), try growing in large trays, like 50-litre (13-gallon) supermarket veg crates.

Varieties: Supermarket spice packs for cheap seed; 'Leisure' or 'Cilantro', which is a new variety, for leaf production.

Dill

🔺 from seed
Annual, half hardy
Pot size: Ideally 10 litres (2½ gallons) or
    more, and at least 25cm (10in) deep.

Dill is a tall, stately herb with pretty, frond-like leaves that adds height without hogging lots of light. It has umbelliferous (flat-headed) flowers that are magnets for insects, particularly hoverflies. The herb has a distinctive aniseed flavour that goes well in rice salads, with egg dishes and chopped into salads and soups.

Sow dill in its final pot (it doesn't like its roots disturbed) from April to August and thin to about 10–15cm (4–6in) apart. It's a

fussy plant that in my experience either takes off or is reluctant to grow. It does best in a deep pot to accommodate its long tap root and dislikes wind. Like coriander, it can flower and go to seed quickly, so sow regularly for a continuous supply.

Fennel herb

🔺 from seed
Perennial, hardy
Pot size: At least 10 litres (2½ gallons)
    and 25cm (10in) deep

Fennel herb (as opposed to fennel bulb) is similar to dill. It's a tall plant with pretty leaves and flowers that attract beneficial insects. The leaves, flowers and seeds all have an aniseed flavour that go well with fish, salads, pestos and tomato sauces.

Sow fennel in its final pot (it doesn't like its roots being disturbed) from April to July. It does best in a well-draining soil and a sunny, sheltered spot.

Garlic chives

▲ from seed or plant
Perennial, hardy
Pot size: At least 5 litres (1¼ gallons)

Garlic chives look quite different to common chives, with a flatter, garlic-flavoured leaf and edible white flowers that bloom in late summer. Snip the leaves into salads, omelettes, risottos and any dish for a garlic taste or pretty garnish.

Garlic chives return every year and are easy to maintain once a clump is established. Start them from seed from April to July. As with common chives, divide and repot every few years.

Lemongrass

▲ from seed or shop-bought stalks
Perennial (often grown as an annual), tender
Pot size: At least 5 litres (1¼ gallons)

Homegrown lemongrass has a more intense and vibrant flavour than shop-bought. As it grows, it forms a clump of tall grasses that look attractive and wave nicely in the wind. The stalk is widely used in curry pastes and salads, and the leaf makes a nice tea.

Lemongrass can be grown from seed, but it's easiest started from a fresh stalk from the local supermarket or Asian store.

1. In late spring (April–May), choose the freshest-looking stalks you can find.
2. Fill a 2-litre (½-gallon) pot with compost (or a free-draining mix – see *Chapter 6 How to Make Your Own...*, 'A free-draining mix', page 112). Water the compost, then finely trim off the base of each stalk (just enough to expose fresh cells, as this is where the new roots will shoot from) with a sharp knife and push two or three stems an inch or two deep into the pot.
3. Place the pot in a bright place inside, avoiding anywhere too hot or sunny.
4. Check the compost regularly and keep it damp.
5. A new leaf growing from the stalk's centre is the first sign of success, usually appearing two or three weeks after planting.
6. Once growing strongly, move the lemongrass to its final pot, where it will slowly form a clump. It will grow okay outside in most of the UK until the first frosts of autumn. Harvest the stalks by pulling and twisting them off the clump or bring the plant inside for the winter. Surplus stalks freeze well.

This method is not difficult, but success will depend to some degree on the quality and freshness of the lemongrass. Bottom heat will also often significantly improve the success rate – use a heated propagator or put in another consistently warm place.

Lemongrass grown from supermarket stalks on my London balcony.

Lemon verbena

▲ from a plant
Perennial, hardy
Pot size: 5–10 litres (1¼–2½ gallons)
    or larger

Lemon verbena has an exotic lemon fragrance. Just a few leaves are needed for a delicious herbal tea, or it can be made into a syrup for baking or cocktails.

Lemon verbena dies back in winter. Unless the winter is very cold, it will survive in most temperate climates without protection. Some gardeners recommend wrapping it in horticultural fleece to be safe, although mine has survived the last eight winters without any protection.

It is a perennial plant and will grow new leaves in late spring or early summer. It can look very dead in early spring when everything else is growing. But don't give up on it until July.

Lemon verbena will grow woody and straggly and, once fully established (which may take a couple of years), will benefit from being cut back hard in late spring. Simply cut off all the thicker, older stems to about 5cm (2in) above ground with secateurs and this will promote fresh, new, leafy growth.

The easiest way to grow lemon verbena is to buy a plant from a specialist herb nursery or community plant sale. It can also be grown from cuttings.

Mint

▲ from plant, cutting or division
Perennial, hardy
Pot size: 2.5 litres (⅔ gallon) or larger,
    but ideally 10 litres (2½ gallons)

Mint is vigorous, productive, easy to grow and only needs a few hours of sun. It has so many uses, including mint sauce, mint tea, mint chutney, in salads, curries and with peas, broad beans and potatoes, among other things. It's a brilliant plant for small spaces.

The easiest way is to repot a supermarket mint plant (see *Chapter 9 Your First Growing Projects*, 'Project 2: Supermarket herb plants', page 168). It's also very easy to grow as a cutting or from a division (ask a friend with a mint plant).

Mint is a hungry plant and does best with regular watering and feeding (liquid seaweed plus occasional light sprinklings of chicken manure pellets or worm compost). It quickly fills a pot with its roots. It's essential to divide and repot it in spring each year or it will quickly lose its vigour. Remove the plant from the pot, divide it in half or into quarters and repot each piece in a new pot with fresh compost.

Mint dies back in winter and returns with fresh new growth in spring.

Varieties: There are many varieties and they are very different, so choose carefully. Moroccan mint is brilliant in tea and good for cooking. Garden mint (often known as spearmint) is milder, and excellent with new potatoes or peas. Chocolate peppermint makes good tea and goes well with fruit.

Myrtle

▲ from plant (ideally) or cuttings
Perennial
Pot size: 10–30 litres (2½–8 gallons)

Myrtle is one of the prettiest herbs, an evergreen, bushy plant with shiny leaves and beautiful white blossom in summer. It produces edible berries (reminiscent of juniper) and the leaves are used like bay leaves in soups and stews.

Grow myrtle in the same way as bay – buy as a plant and move it into larger pots as it grows. It will grow big if you have space for a large-enough pot.

Oregano/marjoram

▲ from seed, plant or division
Perennial, half hardy
Pot size: 2.5 litres (²⁄₃ gallon) for small
plants; 5 litres (1¼ gallons) or larger
for bigger plants

Oregano and marjoram are similar, related
herbs – some people prefer one to the other,
but I find it hard to see a lot of difference.
They are brilliant in summer salads, on
pizzas and with anything related to tomatoes,
chillies and olives. The flowers are pretty,
bees love them and they make a nice herbal
tea. Both are wonderful, vigorous and easy
herbs to grow – and among our favourites.

They are most often bought as plants, but
are also easy to grow from seed and divisions.
They quickly fill a pot and need dividing every
year or two. They do best in a sunny spot but
will grow okay in just four hours of sun. Cut
back the dead stems to the base in winter
and fresh growth will return in the spring.

Varieties: There are many varieties, so look
around for ones you like. They vary in leaf
colour, size and flavour. We like golden
oregano for its flavour and tender, bright
yellow leaves which look pretty in salads.
Greek oregano has good flavour and dries well.

Parsley

▲ easiest from supermarket plants,
but not difficult from seed
Biennial, hardy
Pot size: 2.5 litres (²⁄₃ gallon) or larger

Parsley is a useful, versatile herb, good for
flavouring salads and many dishes. There are
many different varieties, but the main choice
is between curly or flat-leaf parsley. Some
people prefer one or the other; I like both.

It is easiest to grow parsley by dividing
and repotting a supermarket plant. Or grow

from seed, but be patient as it can take four
to six weeks to germinate. Parsley plants like
to be kept well watered but don't like their
roots sitting in the wet, so be careful not to
overwater. It's normally easy to grow but can
occasionally be fussy, so don't get disheart-
ened if yours doesn't grow well.

Pelargonium, scented

▲ from plant or cutting
Perennial, half hardy
Pot size: 2.5 litres (²⁄₃ gallon) or larger, but
ideally 5 litres (1¼ gallons) or more

Scented pelargoniums have a strong, alluring
fragrance of rose, orange or lemon (depending on the variety) and pretty, geranium-like
flowers. The leaves can be used to make a
sugar syrup (for cakes or cocktails) or
flavoured sugar.

One of the easiest herbs to grow from
cuttings. The plants will survive mild winters
outside (dying back and regrowing in the
spring), but it's safest to take a cutting in
early autumn and grow it inside over winter.

Rosemary

▲ from plant or cutting
Perennial, hardy
Pot size: 5 litres (1¼ gallons) or larger

Rosemary is an attractive evergreen that is
quite hard to kill. It has pretty, violet-coloured
flowers that are edible, delicious and loved
by bees. The leaves are good in tomato
sauces, soups, with chicken or lamb, lemon,
roast potatoes and other roasted veg, and
make a tasty, flavoured olive oil.

Some varieties will grow tall and bushy
and look impressive if grown in a large
(20-litre/5¼-gallon or bigger) pot. To grow
rosemary in smaller pots, choose a more
compact variety.

Grow rosemary from a plant or cutting (easiest in early summer). It's happiest in full sun but will grow fine in just three or four hours, following general, herb-growing instructions (see 'How to grow herbs', page 176).

Society garlic

▲ from a plant or division
Perennial, hardy
Pot size: 5 litres (1¼ gallons) or larger

The flowers and leaves of society garlic are distinctly garlic-flavoured and look pretty in salads or as a garnish. I grow *Tulbaghia* 'Fairy Star' as it produces an endless stream of pink flowers from April right through until late autumn and always looks pretty in the container garden. (*Tulbaghia violacea* is similar but starts flowering later.)

Once established, society garlic forms a clump. These can be split up once every year or two and replanted. It feels harsh cutting the clumps up, but they seem to benefit from it, and it's a bonus to get extra plants to give away or swap – everyone seems to want one!

Tarragon

▲ from plant, cutting or division
Perennial, half hardy
Pot size: 2.5 litres (⅔ galllon) or larger

Tulbaghia 'Fairy Star' produces this pretty shower of pink flowers for seven to eight months of the year – everyone wants one when I take it to swaps!

Tarragon has a distinct aniseed twist that goes well with fish, eggs, mushrooms and chicken. It's also good snipped into salads and as a flavouring for vinegar and mayonnaise. Avoid Russian tarragon as it's far inferior in flavour to French tarragon.

Tarragon is a fussy herb, reluctant to grow vigorously unless it's happy. It does best in a well-draining soil (to make your own, see *Chapter 6 How to Make Your Own...*, 'A free-draining Mix', page 112) in a warm place and dislikes strong winds. It dies back over winter and puts on fresh growth in the spring. Plants tend to run out of steam after three years or so and need replacing. Start new plants with cuttings or by dividing established plants.

Thyme and lemon thyme

▲ from seed, plant or division
Perennial, hardy
Pot size: 2.5 litres (⅔ gallon) or larger

Thyme is one of the most versatile and useful herbs, great for flavouring soups, stews, stuffings, mushrooms, fish and meat. Lemon thyme goes particularly well with stone fruit and fish.

Thyme is a Mediterranean herb that does best in a well-drained soil. It's evergreen and can be harvested in small quantities in winter. Textbooks advise cutting it back hard after flowering to keep it compact, but I usually forget, and it still does okay.

Varieties: Common thyme, 'French' thyme and lemon thyme

Vietnamese coriander

▲ from plant or cutting
Perennial, tender
Pot size: 2.5 litres (⅔ gallon) or larger

A strongly aromatic, spicy herb used in Southeast Asian cooking, particularly in soups and salads. It's a completely different plant to common coriander and tastes very different, too.

Much easier to grow than common coriander, it likes to be kept well watered and does best in a warm spot. Once established, it grows vigorously and one plant can give a plentiful supply of leaves. It's one of the easiest herbs to grow from cuttings (it often looks as if it's wilting and dead for 24–48 hours but then recovers).

Wild garlic

▲ from plant or bulb
Perennial, hardy
Pot size: 5 litres (1¼ gallons) or larger

A pungent, garlic-flavoured herb that thrives in woodland and is a good choice for areas with little sun. The leaves are excellent in salads, pesto and soups and with fish dishes. It has pretty, white flowers in late spring.

A good choice for shady spaces, you can grow wild garlic in the same way as chives, dividing it every few years.

Winter savory

▲ from seed, plant or cutting
Perennial, hardy
Pot size: 2.5 litres (⅔ gallon) or larger

Savory used to be a widely used herb in Europe but is now mainly the preserve of chefs and keen gardeners. It's a lovely herb, slightly similar to thyme, with pretty, violet flowers. It goes particularly well with lentil and bean dishes.

In temperate climates, winter savoury dies back in winter. Cut back old shoots in spring, but otherwise grow it in a similar way to thyme.

Salad leaves

Salad is another brilliant crop for small spaces. With just half a dozen window-box-sized containers, it's possible to eat homegrown salad every day for eight months or more – and to have some leaves all year round. Freshly picked, it has infinitely more flavour than bags of supermarket salad. We've become addicted to it.

There's a huge variety of salads with different flavours, leaf shapes and colours, many of which are almost impossible to buy – and you can grow full-sized leaves, micro-greens and edible flowers. For flavour, there's lemony sorrel, strong-flavoured land cress, salty agretti or spicy mustards. For leaf shape and colour, try pretty, round nasturtium leaves, vivid red orach 'Scarlet Emperor', succulent summer purslane, unusual green and bright magenta tree spinach or frilly salad burnet. Together with a few herbs like mint, chives and basil and a few edible flowers, it's possible to eat a different salad every day.

One way to grow a wider range of leaves is to buy mixed packs of mustards, Asian greens and lettuces, which are widely available. You can also grow a variety of leaves in one container and pop salad plants in any gaps, perhaps a nasturtium trailing over the side of a tomato pot or salad burnet under an apple tree.

If you eat a lot of salad and only have a little space to grow in, a good tactic is to focus on growing the more unusual and strongly flavoured leaves, some herbs and edible flowers, and then bulk these out by buying low-cost leaves like lettuces. A handful of homegrown pea shoots, a few nasturtium flowers and a sprinkling of chives and mint leaves will transform a plain shop-bought lettuce into a gourmet salad.

How to grow salads

Salads are among the easiest crops to grow in containers and are ideal for less sunny places. They can be grown all year round, although most grow best in the cool months of spring and autumn.

Sun needs
Most salad leaves grow productively in just three or four hours of sun, making them a good choice for less sunny balconies and patios.

Pot size and spacing
Salads can be grown close together (seeds nearly touching) for microgreens or further apart for baby leaves and full-sized plants. Closer sowings give a quicker harvest but will need resowing more often.

For full-sized salad plants that can be picked over several weeks, give each plant plenty of space (the recommendations on the side of the seed packet is a good place to start). Experiment with different spacings to find what works for you. I like to grow a mix of leaf sizes.

Similarly, large containers support larger plants and sustain them for longer. For quick, short harvests, growing microgreens in seed trays or small pots works fine. However, for larger plants to pick over a longer period, window boxes or supermarket veg crates holding 20–40 litres (5¼–10½ gallons) of soil are a better choice.

Compost
Salads are not the fussiest plants and will often grow fine in old compost as long as the structure is checked and the nutrients are refreshed (see *Chapter 11 Solutions to Common Challenges*, 'Replenish the nutrients', page 236). Adding chicken manure pellets or rapeseed meal (both high in nitrogen) to old compost works well, as does worm compost.

Homegrown salad is a revelation after supermarket salad bags.

Watering

Most salads like to be kept well watered and will often bolt or start to taste tough and bitter if they don't get enough water. As always, keep a particularly close eye on plants that are large relative to the size of the pot and in hot or windy weather.

Feeding

Although not the hungriest, salads benefit from regular feeding. Regularly watering or foliar feeding with liquid seaweed or nettle tea is beneficial. If you are growing larger salad plants, like lettuces or sorrel, over several months, an occasional mulch of worm compost will give them a boost.

When to sow

Most salads can be sown direct outside from early spring all the way through until early autumn. In the main, they prefer cooler weather and grow better in spring and autumn than in mid-summer. However, there are exceptions, and leaves that grow well in the heat of summer are listed in *Chapter 11 Solutions to Common Challenges*, 'Too hot: suntraps, hot climates and heatwaves', page 242). A few salad leaves (notably rocket and all the Asian greens like mizuna and pak choi) bolt and go to flower quickly in the lengthening days leading up to mid-summer. These are best either sown early in the season (March or early April) or after the midsummer solstice; late August/early September is often the best time to sow them in the whole year. A lot of the salads listed in this section are also winter hardy – and they make some of the best winter crops in small spaces. For a supply of salads through late autumn, winter and spring, see *Chapter 7 How to Grow More Food in a Small Space*, 'Table 7.3 Winter Sowing Timetable', page 139) for suggested sowing dates.

How to grow a constant supply

The secret to a constant salad supply is to sow seeds every few weeks from spring to late autumn. Aim to have pots at different stages: some ready to pick, some maturing, and some freshly sown.

The best salad plants?

Part of the fun of growing is discovering your own favourites. However, if you're looking for ideas to start, here are some we particularly enjoy and grow every year:

Salad leaves: Rocket, nasturtium, orach 'Scarlet Emperor', sorrel, New Zealand spinach, mixed mustards, kale 'Red Russian' and land cress

Microgreens: Pea shoots, sunflower shoots, radish shoots, basil, coriander, beet and fava shoots

Edible flowers: Nasturtium, viola, pot marigolds, chives and society garlic

Salad leaves

There are hundreds of different leaves that can be grown for salad. Here is a selection of the best:

Agretti/salsola

Mild, salty and crunchy, agretti looks and tastes similar to samphire. Larger leaves can be cooked. A fun and unusual one to grow.

Seeds must be very fresh to germinate. Best in warmer areas of the UK and productive once it gets going.

Endive and chicory (winter)

Has a bitter flavour – there are many varieties and colours, some of them pretty.

Sow in late summer for a winter crop.

Kale

Mild. 'Red Russian' and young 'Cavolo Nero' leaves are tender to eat – add whole or finely shred into salads. Both are ornamental and

hardy, and larger leaves can be cooked. Sow any time from early spring to late August.

Lamb's lettuce/corn salad/mache

A mild flavour and makes a good winter salad. Prolific in the right conditions but dislikes windy sites in my experience.

Land cress/American cress

Strong, spicy leaf that is similar to watercress – an excellent choice flavour in winter salads. Perennial and hardy.

Leaf radish 'SaiSai Purple'

Spicy leaf, with radishy flavour. All radish leaves are edible, but 'leaf' varieties are less hairy. The flowers and crunchy, spicy seed pods (eat these young) are also edible.

Lettuce

Mild in flavour. There are many varieties in greens and reds, some speckled. Flavour and texture vary, so try different varieties.

Lettuce is fussy but can be highly productive in containers once it gets going.

Does best in a larger container, at least 15cm (6in) deep. Prefers cool weather and dislikes excessive heat. Fussy – it has a reputation for being easy to grow, but that doesn't always prove to be the case in containers! However, if you can get lettuce established it can be highly productive – a few plants can provide all the leaves you need.

Minutina/Erba stella

Mild with a nice, slightly nutty taste, the unusually forked leaf adds interest to the salad bowl. It's grown and eaten more widely in Italy (*Erba stella* translates as 'star grass'), and also grows wild in parts of the UK. Older, larger leaves can get tough, so it's best picked young.

Mustards: mibuna and mizuna

There are many varieties of mustard, with a range of leaf colours and shapes that look pretty in salads – look for one of the mixed packets of mustard seeds that are available, with names like 'bright and spicy'. They can taste mildly spicy to very spicy, depending on the variety and their age – older leaves tend to be spicier. Mizuna is milder and good for bulk. 'Red Giant' is spicier and, as its name suggests, can grow large. Mibuna has long, thin leaves. 'Green in the Snow' has serrated, green leaves and, like other mustards, grows well in cooler weather.

Best sown in early spring for early-summer leaves, or in late August or early September for a crop in late autumn, winter and spring. All the mustards are fast growing and rewarding to grow – and nice in stir fries as well as salads.

Nasturtium

Mildly spicy, with pretty, round leaves and an excellent flavour. Pick young leaves for salads (older leaves can be tough). There are many nice varieties – 'Blue Pepe' is one I like to grow for its attractive bluish tinge and tasty leaves – or look for trailing and climbing varieties to fill vertical space. You can also eat the young seed pods in salads or pickle them like capers. Overall, a brilliant salad plant.

Young nasturtium leaves have an excellent, mildly spicy flavour – and look so pretty, too.

New Zealand spinach

Mild, slightly crunchy and salty, the young leaves are mild but excellent in salads; cook larger leaves like spinach.

This is a rambling plant, not the prettiest but productive. Doesn't bolt in heat, so ideal for mid-summer growing. Sow in late spring for a supply of leaves into late autumn (undercover it will survive through winter, too).

Orach 'Scarlet Emperor'

Mild but good flavour, a bit like spinach. Pretty and adds height. Pinch out growing tips to encourage bushy growth.

Oyster plant

Mild, with a slight oyster flavour, hence its name. Found growing wild on the coast of Scotland, it has bluish-tinged leaves and pretty blue flowers. Perennial. Can be grown from seed but easier to get a plant.

Pak choi and tatsoi

Mildly spicy and crunchy, there are many varieties of these plants, some fast growing, but they are also favoured by slugs. Sow in early spring or after the summer solstice (they bolt in lengthening days).

Rocket

Mildly spicy – an excellent base leaf and has edible flowers. Salad rocket has large, milder leaves; wild rocket has smaller, spicier leaves.

Can be sown from March to late September, but early-spring and late-summer sowings are most productive (it bolts in lengthening days). We find this one of the most versatile and useful of salad leaves and try to keep up a supply all year round (it's a good winter salad, too).

Salad burnet

Mild with a slight cucumber flavour and pretty, frilly leaves. Add in small quantities to salads. Perennial. Easy to grow once established – and only one or two plants needed for an occasional supply of leaves. I sometimes grow one in the same pot as my apple tree.

Shungiku/chopsuey greens

Slightly bitter with a metallic taste and rich in minerals and antioxidants. They have pretty, yellow flowers, with edible petals and make an attractive and unusual salad. Pinch out tips to encourage a bushy plant.

Sorrel

Lemony and sharp in flavour. Excellent in moderation in salads for a lemony twist. Cooked, sorrel goes well with fish and eggs. Buckler-leaf sorrel has small, heart-shaped leaves; broad-leaved sorrel looks more like spinach.

A perennial, the leaves die back in winter and return in the spring. Can be grown as a perennial or, for optimum leaf production, sown fresh from seed every spring.

Summer purslane

Mild and succulent. An excellent and unusual mild leaf to grow in summer and warm weather. Sow in late spring or early summer – it needs warmth to grow well.

Texel greens/Ethiopian cabbage

Mildly spicy, this is fast growing and unusual with a good flavour. Eat in salads or stir fries. Grow like mustards.

Tree spinach

Mild in flavour, this is a tall, green salad plant with incredibly vivid magenta splashes on its

With a few trays it's possible to grow a lot of microgreens in very little space. *Clockwise from top left*: pea shoots, nasturtium, beetroot, sunflower, orach 'Purple Emperor' and mixed mustards.

leaves. It adds height to the salad garden and a few leaves look pretty in salads. Pinch out the growing tips to get a bushier plant.

Winter purslane

Mild in taste and rich in Vitamin C, this is a pretty winter salad, slightly succulent with round leaves. Pretty, white flowers (also edible) emerge directly from the centre of each leaf.

It can tolerate cold temperatures but does not grow well in exposed, windy areas. The seeds are tiny (cover with a very thin layer of soil), which makes them fiddly to handle, but otherwise they are easy to grow. It self seeds easily – in London, I even once noticed it had seeded itself in the neglected containers on my next-door neighbour's windowsill.

Spice packs from Asian stores and dried pea and pulse packs from health-food stores are excellent sources of cheap seeds for microgreens.

Microgreens

Microgreens are simply the baby, immature leaves of edible plants. Almost any traditional leafy vegetable like rocket or kale, or soft herbs like basil or coriander, can be eaten as a microgreen. In addition, some root vegetables make tasty microgreens, including

TABLE 10.1. Guide to the Best Microgreens

Leaf	Difficulty	Where to find low-cost seeds	Average days to harvest	Notes
Amaranth		Commercial growers	10–20	Spinach-like taste. Purple varieties for vibrant colour. Needs warmth (grow inside or in mid-summer in cooler climates).
Basil		Sprout suppliers and Asian supermarkets (sold as 'Tukmaria')	14–21	Fabulous flavour. Needs warmth and a fairly constant temperature (grow inside or in mid-summer in cooler climates).
Beetroot		Commercial growers	10–21	Colourful with nice, earthy taste. Soak seeds overnight to improve and speed up germination. Grows best in cooler temperatures.
Broccoli		Sprout suppliers	7–14	Easy and nutritious. Sow thickly for good yields.
Buckwheat		Commercial growers	7–14	Mild, tender leaves with a nice texture. Nutritious in moderation (avoid large quantities). Grow from buckwheat *seeds* (with hulls on), not groats.
Chard		Commercial growers	14–28	Nice, earthy taste. Look for mixes of bright colours. Soak seeds to improve germination. Grows best in cooler temperatures.
Chia		Health-food stores and supermarkets	7–14	Nutritious
Chickpeas		Supermarkets	14–28	Nutritious and easy to grow with pretty leaves. Most dried chickpeas grow fine.
Coriander		Asian stores and commercial growers	18–28	Eat the leaf *and* root for a fabulous zingy taste. Cracking the seeds and pre-soaking overnight can help speed up germination. Grows best in cooler temperatures.
Dill and fennel		Supermarkets, Asian stores and health-food stores	14–30	Add to your salads. Slow to germinate.
Endive		Commercial growers	12–21	Produces low, flat seedlings – so space seeds further apart. Bitter taste. Grows best in cooler temperatures.

Key: ▲ = Easiest ▲ = Easy ▲ = Not too difficult

TABLE 10.1 (*continued*)

Leaf	Difficulty	Where to find low-cost seeds	Average days to harvest	Notes
Fava beans	▲	Middle Eastern stores, Asian stores, health-food stores and online	14–21	Mild, bean-like taste, nice crunch. Good salad base or for stir fries. High yielding. Grows best in cooler temperatures.
Fenugreek/ methi	▲	Asian stores and sprout suppliers	7–14	Fast and easy to grow. Distinctive, unusual flavour. Use fresh or dry the leaves for enhanced flavour.
Haloon	▲	Asian stores	5–14	Tastes like cress. Very fast and easy to grow. Red seeds are easy to see – good for kids to sow.
Kale	◿	Commercial growers	10–21	Any kale. 'Red Russian' has pretty, serrated leaves. Grows best in cooler temperatures.
Land cress/ American cress	▲	Commercial growers	10–21	Strong, spicy flavour that's similar to watercress. Adds a kick to your salads. Grows best in cooler temperatures.
Mustards – mizuna, mibuna, etc	▲	Commercial growers (for mixed mustards) and Asian stores (for black mustard)	10–21	Spicy and pretty leaf shapes. Grow a mix for a variety of leaf shapes and colours. Asian store mustard grows well, but a 'mixed mustard' seed pack has more interest. Grows best in cooler temperatures.
Nasturtium	▲	Commercial growers	10–21	Pretty, round leaves and a good spicy flavour. Super garnish or salad addition.
Parsley	◿	Commercial growers	14–28	Slow to germinate. Grows best in cooler temperatures.
Pea shoots	▲	Supermarkets and health-food stores	12–28	The queen of shoots and fantastic for small spaces: delicious, beautiful and productive. Use any variety, but 'Marrowfat' is good. Grows best in cooler temperatures.
Purple cabbage	◿	Commercial growers	10–21	Purple stems make a pretty addition to salads. Grows best in cooler temperatures.
Radish	▲	Sprout suppliers	7–14	Easy and super fast. Excellent radish flavour and crunchy texture for salads and garnishes. The variety 'China Rose' has pretty, red stems.

Key: ▲ = Easiest ◿ = Easy ◿ = Not too difficult

TABLE 10.1 (*continued*)

Leaf	Difficulty	Where to find low-cost seeds	Average days to harvest	Notes
Rocket	▲	Sprout suppliers and commercial growers	7–21	Good spicy flavour and great for salads. Thin stem – so water gently to avoid it collapsing. Grows best in cooler temperatures.
Shiso perilla	◢	Commercial growers	14–21	Unique flavour with hints of mint, basil, coriander and cinnamon. Grows like basil. Purple varieties are the prettiest, but the green variety has the best flavour. Prefers warmth (in cooler places grow inside).
Sorrel	◢	Commercial growers	10–21	Strong, lemony taste that adds zing to salads. Use in moderation. Grows best in cooler temperatures.
Sunflower	▲	Sprout suppliers (you need sunflower seeds with hulls *on*)	8–20	Delicious microgreen with a mild, slightly nutty flavour and pleasing crunch. Harvest *before* the second set of leaves appears (the second set is bitter). Protect seed trays from birds and mice if needed.

Key: ▲ = Easiest   ◢ = Easy   ◿ = Not too difficult

turnip, beetroot and radish (it's the leaf, not the baby root that is eaten). Other tasty microgreens include sunflower and buckwheat. Microgreens are easy and fast to grow, packed with flavour and highly nutritious. They are very productive in small spaces and only need two or three hours of sun. They make an excellent addition to any container garden and I always try to have a tray or two growing.

'Table 10.1 Guide to the Best Microgreens', summarises some of the best microgreens, and where to get the seeds in the large amounts needed economically. The steps to grow microgreens are summarised in *Chapter 9 Your First Growing Projects*, 'Project 1: Microgreens', page 162.

How to be self-sufficient in microgreens

The key to getting a constant supply of microgreens is to sow trays regularly, ideally every week or two. You want to aim for trays at different stages – for example, two that have been recently sown, two that are maturing, and two ready to pick from. If you sow thickly, you can grow so much in one tray that you'll probably find you can be self-sufficient in salad (even if you eat it every day) with six to 12 trays. Growing mixed trays (sow in blocks) is a good way to grow a wider variety of leaves. Radish, for example, is delicious but strongly flavoured, so you may only want to sow a half or a quarter of a tray.

Edible flowers

Edible flowers add colour and flavour to salads and can be used as a beautiful garnish to lift any dish. As home growers, we're among the few people with easy access to these precious jewels as they are hard to get hold of in the shops.

Edible flowers add beauty, attract and support insects, and you can eat them: a win, win, win. Every small container garden should have a few. The flowers of most herbs are edible, as are many vegetable flowers and even some plants that we normally think of as ornamentals, like tulips.

You'll find long lists of edible flowers online. Some flowers are packed with flavour like nasturtium; others look pretty but don't taste of much, like cornflowers. My favourites for containers include:

Nasturtiums – for tasty flowers and buds that have a spicy kick.

Violas – for pretty flowers with a delicate flavour in late autumn and often right through winter (I've picked them in the snow).

Pot marigold – separate the petals and sprinkle into a salad for colour and a mild citrus flavour.

Society garlic, *Tulbaghia* 'Fairy Star' – pretty, pink flowers with a strong garlic flavour. Superb. Flowers from April to later autumn. Perennial.

Other good edible flowers for containers include sunflowers (use the petals), French marigold (*Tagetes patula*), dahlias, daylilies (*Hemerocallis* species only – other lilies are poisonous) and roses (the stronger the fragrance, the better the flavour).

Vegetables that have tasty flowers to eat include:

Courgettes – subtle, beautiful flavour. Stuff the flowers or stir them into risottos or pasta, or use for tempura. (Squash and cucumber flowers are also edible.)

Shungiku/chopsuey greens – use the petals in salads or stir fries.

Rocket and mustard flowers – scatter into salads.

Broad bean, pea and runner bean flowers – scatter into salads or through pasta dishes.

Freshly picked nasturtium, pot marigold, cornflower, borage, society garlic and runner bean flowers.

Courgette flowers, a culinary treat, growing alongside a nasturtium.

Rosemary flowers garnishing an orange salad.

Herbs have some of the most strongly flavoured and delicious flowers, usually with a taste similar to the leaf, sometimes more perfumed or intense. Here are some great ones to try:

Rosemary – a lovely garnish and goes nicely with oranges, among other things.
Lavender – for baking and also delicious with blackberries (try blackberry and lavender sorbet).
Fennel – crunchy, aniseed flavour; use to garnish savoury and sweet dishes.
Chives – break up the cluster and sprinkle into salads or use as a garnish.
Garlic chives – break up the flower heads for crunchy shards of garlic.
Scots lovage – scatter into salads; this is unusual and very delicious.
Coriander – delicate white flowers that have a wonderfully pungent coriander flavour.

Vegetables

Vegetables need a bit more space than herbs and salads, but make excellent container crops if you can fit them in. Tomatoes, chillies, courgettes, kale, French beans, spinach and chard are among my favourite harvests of the year.

'Table 10.2 Guide to the Best Vegetables for Containers', pages 200–203, summarises some of the best container vegetables, what size container they need, how many plants to put in a pot, and the approximate times each one takes to mature. More details on how to grow them is given on the following pages.

Fruiting vegetables offer the advantage that they often crop over a long period. Tomatoes and chillies, for example, can fruit from mid-July all the way through to October or November.

Tomatoes, chillies, peppers and aubergines are all part of the Solanum family, hail from South America and need sun and warmth to do well. They take a relatively long time to fruit (18–24 weeks), so usually need starting inside in spring. They can be grown in old compost, but new compost gives more reliable results.

Let's look in more detail at some of the best fruiting veg for containers and how to grow them.

Tomatoes

Homegrown tomatoes are one of the most delicious and productive container crops. There are hundreds of varieties that vary in size (from 20cm/8in to 3.6m/12ft tall), size of fruits (from tiny currants to the size of small melons), colour, shape, flavour and how early they ripen.

Vine (or 'indeterminate') tomatoes are grown on one main stem and the side shoots pinched out (see 'Pinching out', page 204) – good for making the most of vertical spaces.

Bush (or 'determinate') tomatoes are left to grow bushy, so the side shoots are not pinched out. Some varieties are small and compact, making them perfect for hanging baskets. Others are big and rambling, needing a larger container and are greedy for horizontal space but often highly productive.

Try to choose a variety suited to your climate, space and the size of pot:

▸ Cherry tomatoes ripen far more reliably and are a good choice for containers, particularly in cooler areas. Good, early-ripening vine cherry varieties include 'Gardener's Delight', 'Black Cherry', 'Stupice', 'Latah' and 'Sungold' (F1 hybrid).

▸ For hanging baskets or small pots (5–10 litres/1¼–2½ gallons), choose a small, compact cherry bush variety like 'Tumbling Tom' (F1), 'Cherry Cascade' (F1), 'Hundreds and Thousands' (F1) or 'Balconi Red'.

Cherry vine tomatoes ripen well and make good use of vertical space – I grew these on my windowsills in London.

TABLE 10.2. Guide to the Best Vegetables for Containers

Vegetable	Difficulty	Sun	Weeks to maturity*
Achocha/fat baby	▲	●	12
Aubergine	▲	●	20
Beans, broad	▲	◑	16
Beans, French, climbing	▲	◑	10
Beans, runner, climbing	▲	◑	10
Beetroot	▲	◕	12
Cabbage, Chinese	▲	◔	9
Carrots, finger	▲	◑	14
Chard 'Bright Lights'	▲	◔	10
Chilli	▲	●	14–20
Choy sum	▲	◔	9
Courgettes	▲	●	10
Cucumber	▲	●	12
Florence fennel	▲	◑	14
Garlic	▲	◑	36
Kailaan (Chinese broccoli)	▲	◔	9

* Weeks to maturity: This is an average – useful for planning, but may be slower in adverse conditions.

† Minimum pot size and plants per pot: This gives you a very approximate minimum size of pot that will give you a worthwhile yield – and a suggested number of plants to grow in that size of pot. Other factors like variety will also influence the optimal spacing – use my suggestions in this table, along with spacings on seed packets, as a starting point and experiment. Remember that fruiting crops, like tomatoes, need plenty of space to yield well, with the exception of climbing peas and beans.

Minimum pot size and number of plants per pot (spacing)†	Notes
5 litres (1¼ gallons) 1 plant	Vigorous climber, useful for covering walls and fences. Produces spiky fruits with a flavour that is a cross between cucumbers, lemon and peppers.
10 litres (2½ gallons) 1 plant	Needs an early start, sheltered spot and lots of sun to produce well.
20 litres (5¼ gallons) 6–8 plants	Low yield in containers. Sow in October for a June harvest. Growing tips are edible.
20 litres (5¼ gallons) 6–8 plants	Use climbing varieties to maximise space. Attractive flowers. For bush beans, grow 4 plants per container.
20 litres (5¼ gallons) 6–8 plants	Very productive and ornamental. Need plenty of water and grow better in a 40–50-litre (10½–13-gallon) container if space permits. Pick beans small for best flavour.
10 litres (2½ gallons) 6–12 plants	Thin out small roots to allow for 3–4 larger roots. Edible leaves.
10 litres (2½ gallons) 3–6 plants	Fast growing. Harvest outer leaves.
10 litres (2½ gallons) 6–12 plants	Baby or finger carrots are best in pots.
20 litres (5¼ gallons) 4 plants	Ornamental, tasty and can be picked over a long period. Can be grown closer together for smaller leaves.
5–10 litres (1¼–2½ gallons) 1 plant	Needs an early start and lots of sun. Very productive in the right conditions. Grow early-ripening varieties in cooler locations.
10 litres (2½ gallons) 4 plants	Oriental vegetable, nice in stir fries.
20 litres (5¼ gallons) 1 plant	Better in containers of 30–40 litres (8–10½ gallons), if possible. Needs lots of sun, water and food. Bushy and takes up space. Tromboncino is a good climbing alternative.
10–20 litres (2½–5¼ gallons) 1 plant	Likes warmth and shelter. Climbs well. Choose outdoor varieties.
10 litres (2½ gallons) 3 plants	Edible leaves and bulb. Ornamental.
10 litres (2½ gallons) 4 plants	Slow grower. Needs cold at start – best planted in October/November.
10 litres (2½ gallons) 2–4 plants	Fast-growing alternative to broccoli.

Key

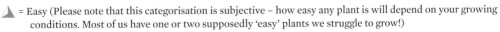 = Easy (Please note that this categorisation is subjective – how easy any plant is will depend on your growing conditions. Most of us have one or two supposedly 'easy' plants we struggle to grow!)

= Not too difficult

= Needs full sun (6 hours-plus) for a good crop

= Needs part sun (5–6 hours) for a good crop

= A good crop can be achieved in 4 hours' sun (may grow even better in full sun)

TABLE 10.2 (*continued*)

Vegetable	Difficulty	Sun	Weeks to maturity*
Kale	▲	◖	16
Leeks, baby	▲	◗	12
Mooli (white radish)	▲	◗	12
Mouse melon	▲	●	12
Oca	▲	◗	30
Onions, spring	▲	◖	8–12
Peas, mangetout/sugar snap, climbing	▲	◗	14
Peas, podded, climbing	▲	◗	14–16
Peppers	▲	●	20–24
Potatoes, first and second earlies	▲	◗	10–14
Radish	▲	◗	4–6
Spinach	▲	◖	10
Squash, winter	▲	●	14
Tomatillo	▲	●	18
Tomato	▲	●	18
Turnip	▲	◗	10

* Weeks to maturity: This is an average – useful for planning, but may be slower in adverse conditions.

† Minimum pot size and plants per pot: This gives you a very approximate minimum size of pot that will give you a worthwhile yield – and a suggested number of plants to grow in that size of pot. Other factors like variety will also influence the optimal spacing – use my suggestions in this table, along with spacings on seed packets, as a starting point and experiment. Remember that fruiting crops, like tomatoes, need plenty of space to yield well, with the exception of climbing peas and beans.

Minimum pot size and number of plants per pot (spacing)†	Notes
10 litres (2½ gallons) 1 plant	Good winter crop. Ornamental and nutritious. Grow in 20–40-litre (5¼–10½-gallon) containers for stronger, larger plants.
10 litres (2½ gallons) 6 plants	Good alternative to adult leeks that take 25 weeks.
10 litres (2½ gallons) 4 plants	Useful winter crop. Edible leaves and root.
5 litres (1¼ gallons) 1 plant	Climber with grape-sized melons that have a cucumber flavour. Needs warmth.
10 litres (2½ gallons) 1 tuber	South American tuber, similar to potatoes, but with a lemony twist. Edible leaves (contain oxalic acid, so eat in moderation). Plant in May and harvest after the plant is killed by frost in late November/December.
10 litres (2½ gallons) 10 plants	Quick to grow. Tall and thin – can be interplanted between other salads and vegetables.
20 litres (5¼ gallons) 6–8 plants	Higher-yielding alternative to podded peas. Attractive flowers.
20 litres (5¼ gallons) 6–8 plants	Small yield from containers after podding, but pretty and great for kids.
10 litres (2½ gallons) 1 plant	Look for an early-ripening variety. Need warmth, but productive in the right conditions.
10 litres (2½ gallons) 1 tuber	First or second earlies are good in containers. Maincrop potatoes can be grown in larger containers and take 18–20 weeks.
10 litres (2½ gallons) 10–12 plants	Fast and prolific. Good 'catch crop'. Edible leaves that are nice stir-fried in olive oil.
10 litres (2½ gallons) 4–6 plants	Nice winter crop. Harvest outer leaves.
30–40 litres (8–10½ gallons) 1 plant	Hungry plants, they need a big pot and plenty of feeding (e.g. with liquid tomato feed and worm compost). Most are good climbers – trail up a sunny wall.
20 litres (5¼ gallons) 1 plant	Produces green fruits, similar to tomatoes, but with a tart flavour. Two plants are needed for good pollination and a good yield.
10 litres/2½ gallons (for cherry) 20 litres/5¼ gallons (for plum or beefsteak) 1 plant	Brilliant container crop, both productive and tasty. Different varieties vary in size considerably, so choose the container size accordingly.
10 litres (2½ gallons) 8 plants	Eat golf-ball size for best flavour. Edible leaves that you can steam or stir-fry.

Key

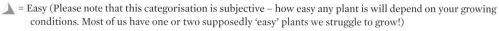

= Easy (Please note that this categorisation is subjective – how easy any plant is will depend on your growing conditions. Most of us have one or two supposedly 'easy' plants we struggle to grow!)

= Not too difficult

= Needs full sun (6 hours-plus) for a good crop

= Needs part sun (5–6 hours) for a good crop

= A good crop can be achieved in 4 hours' sun (may grow even better in full sun)

How to grow tomatoes

Start from seed in a warm place inside from mid-March to mid-April or buy plants in late May or early June. Be warned: tomatoes grow fast and quickly take over indoor space if sown too early – many of us learn this the hard way!

Move seedlings into progressively bigger pots as they grow. When repotting, bury the lower part of the stem under the compost to give the plant extra support (this is particularly useful if seedlings are 'leggy' from growing inside). Move tomatoes outside into their final pots once the threat of frost has passed, usually late May/early June.

Containers: The smallest tomato varieties will grow in pots of 5–10 litres/1¼–2½ gallons), but 20 litres (5¼ gallons) or larger is a better option for most other varieties.

Watering: Tomatoes are thirsty – large plants can drink a full watering can on a hot day. They grow well in containers with water reservoirs. When watering, try to avoid splashing the leaves as this can spread blight (see *Chapter 8 Growing in Harmony with Life*, 'Late blight', page 154).

Feeding: When tomato plants start flowering, feed with a high potassium feed (liquid tomato feed or comfrey tea) once or twice a week. For healthier plants, foliar feed with liquid seaweed fertiliser once a week and mulch with worm compost mid-season.

Tying up and staking: Vine tomatoes need support or they fall over. Use a cane, make a tomato cage (a frame round the pot) or use string supports (see *Chapter 5 Useful Growing Skills*, 'How to tie up and support plants in containers', page 100).

Pinching out: Vining tomatoes are grown on just one (sometimes two) main stems. When side shoots appear between the main stem and each leaf, they need to be 'pinched out' with fingers or cut with scissors, otherwise the tomato will grow into an unruly bush. To grow a tomato with two main stems (this sometimes gives a higher yield), simply leave one of the side shoots near the base to develop and support it with a separate cane or string.

Tomato side shoot. These are pinched out on vining tomatoes.

Chillies

Homegrown chillies, if you choose the right varieties, knock the socks off supermarket ones in terms of flavour. If you enjoy spicy food, and have a sunny growing space, it's almost essential to grow a few.

Depending on the variety and growing conditions, each plant can produce a hundred or more chillies and it's often possible to be self-sufficient in chillies with just a few plants. Any surplus can be chopped and frozen for a fresh chilli taste, dried for a warmer, fruitier flavour (thin-skinned chillies dry best), pickled or made into a chilli sauce.

If you're not experienced at cooking with hot chillies, they can take a bit of getting used to. For example, half an 'Alberto's Locoto' chilli has more heat – and a lot more flavour – than two average supermarket chillies. Sometimes, just a few slivers are enough to add depth of flavour to a dish.

Chillies need more sun to thrive than tomatoes and yield best in a sheltered spot. In cooler areas of the UK, they often need to be grown in a mini greenhouse or similar to yield well. European varieties, like 'Padron' from Spain or 'Espelette' from France are a more reliable choice for cooler areas than the heat-loving 'Habanero' varieties, like 'Scotch Bonnet'.

There are hundreds of different chilli varieties that produce fruits of different sizes, colour, shape, flavour and heat. Different varieties also vary in size of plant and how easy they are to grow. Varieties that grow well in containers and have excellent flavour include:

Hot: 'Alberto's Locoto' chilli (large, round fruits with unusual black seeds – our favourite at home), 'Aji Lemon' (yellow chillies, slight lemony taste, superb), 'Ring of Fire' (early to ripen, productive). Or, for *very hot* chillies, 'Bhut Jolokia'.

Chillies can be very productive and many varieties have much more flavour than generic supermarket ones.

Medium: 'Jalapeño' (the famous, versatile green chilli), 'Hungarian Hot Wax', 'Espelette' and 'Cherry Bomb' (a round, red F1 chilli)

Mild: 'Padron' – delicious stir-fried with garlic as a tapas dish.

How to grow chillies

Sow inside in February or March for fruits in August. They germinate best in a warm place (20°C/68°F or more) or with a heated propagator. They usually come up in 10–14 days, although some varieties are slower.

When chillies are sown inside early in the year, light levels are marginal for healthy growth – see *Chapter 11 Solutions to Common Challenges*, 'Sowing, planting and raising seedlings inside', page 249. Move the seedlings to larger pots as they grow and, like tomatoes, bury some of the stem when replanting to give extra support. Move the plants outside into their final pot once the threat of frost has passed.

Container: A size of 5–10 litres (1¼–2½ gallons) is usually sufficient, although

Courgettes grow well in containers, but they do have large, bushy plants – great if you have space for them.

larger varieties like 'Espelette' can grow over 1m (3ft) tall and will benefit from a larger container if space permits.

Watering: Professional chilli growers advise letting the compost dry out between waterings. In practice, this is tricky unless you are on hand to keep a careful eye on the plants every day. It's easier to use a well-draining compost and water as normal.

Feeding: Chillies are not as hungry as tomatoes but still benefit from weekly liquid feeding once they start flowering. I often alternate between tomato feed one week and liquid seaweed the next.

Tying up, staking and pruning: Taller plants can need support with a cane or string. If indoor plants grow tall and lanky, pinch out the growing tips to encourage more bushy growth.

Sweet peppers

Grow peppers in the same way as chillies, using a 10-litre (2½-gallon) pot or bigger. They can be vigorous and productive in a warm, sheltered space. Varieties with small fruits are a good choice for containers.

Aubergines

Aubergines, like chillies, need a warm, sheltered spot where they will grow well in containers, but they're marginal for outdoor growing in cooler regions (they need a polytunnel for a good crop here in Newcastle upon Tyne). Look for varieties with small fruits and grow in the same way as chillies.

Courgettes, squash, cucumbers and achocha

Courgettes and squash crop well in containers but they need a sunny space and big pots. Cucumbers will grow in smaller pots but like more shelter, while achocha grows fast and easily and has fun, alien-looking fruit.

Young plants in this group dislike wind and can wilt alarmingly if moved suddenly into windy conditions. Harden them off carefully and move outside in less windy weather or protect with a windbreak or

Unlike courgettes, squash are excellent climbers. This one is off to visit my next-door neighbour!

cloche. They usually cope with wind better once established outside.

How to grow courgettes

Homegrown courgettes are firmer, juicier and better flavoured than shop-bought ones, and the flowers are a gourmet treat. They form bushy plants with large leaves that can overshadow other containers, so bear this in mind in very small spaces.

To grow, sow seeds inside in small pots in late April or May, or outside in June, and move to the final pot outside after the last frost. Pots of 30–50 litres (8–13 gallons) are optimum for good harvests, but 20 litres (5¼ gallons) are possible. They usually grow fine in old compost as long as the nutrients are replenished. They are hungry plants: feed weekly with liquid tomato feed and mulch with worm compost or well-rotted manure in mid-season, if available. Regular watering is needed and helps keep powdery mildew at bay (see *Chapter 8 Growing in Harmony with Life*, 'Powdery mildew', page 156).

Courgettes have both male and female flowers. Only the females produce courgettes from the base of the flower. Plants often produce only male flowers at first, then females later in the season. If females still don't appear later in the season, it's usually a sign the plant is stressed. Pick the fruits small for the best flavour and to encourage the plant to produce more.

Large leaves can be removed with kitchen scissors to help reduce any shade they cast on other plants, but try not to remove more than one-third of the leaves at a time.

In theory, courgettes climb (there are videos on YouTube) but, in practice, it's not always as easy as it looks. Tromba or tromboncino squash is a good climbing alternative.

How to grow squash

Squash varieties with small- to medium-sized fruit, such as the bright orange 'Uchikci Kuri' make a good choice to grow in containers. Tromba or tromboncino is a fun, climbing alternative to courgettes – the young squash have a similar flavour or you leave them to grow to 1m (3ft) long. Larger squash call for bigger containers – 50 litres (13 gallons) minimum for something like a pumpkin.

Squash are grown like courgettes, the main difference being that most varieties climb vigorously. Support them with a string (wind the string round the stem of the plant as it grows) or with trellis – or let them trail over the ground. The fruits sometimes need extra support if they get heavy. In Italy, they support them in slings made from old stockings or tights.

How to grow cucumbers

Homegrown cucumbers have a more intense, perfumed flavour than shop-bought varieties and sometimes spiny skins. Choose an outdoor variety – 'Marketmore' is a reliable choice.

Cucumbers don't need as big a container as squash (10–20 litres/2½–5¼ gallons is large enough) but otherwise are grown and supported (they also climb) in a similar way. Cucumbers don't grow well in windy places but, in a sheltered space, they can be very productive. They also grow well on a sunny windowsill inside.

How to grow achocha/fat baby

Achocha has spiny, alien-like fruit, and prehistoric-looking seeds. It's unusual, fun and easy to grow. The fruits taste like a cross between cucumbers and peppers, with a hint of lemon. Cook them like peppers (remove the seeds first) or slice and add to salads or salsas. It's a fast-growing, vigorous climber and will quickly cover unsightly walls or fences.

Plant out after the last frosts and grow in a sunny place in a 5-litre (1¼-gallon) container or bigger.

Climbing French beans and runner beans

French and runner beans are among the most productive crops: one 40-litre (10½-gallon) container can produce 5kg (11lb) or even 10kg (22lb) of beans. A teepee of flowering beans also adds height and a splash of colour – and looks great in any container garden.

Climbing beans are often grown up a teepee and don't usually need tying in once

Achocha is a vigorous climber with unusual, spiny-looking fruits.

Bush beans can be better on windy sites and they cast less shade than climbing beans.

French beans are tall, ornamental and productive, but watch out for the shade they cast over other plants.

they get going (see *Chapter 5 Useful Growing Skills*, 'How to tie up and support plants in containers', page 100). The teepee will cast shade, so think carefully about where to put it. Pinch out the tips of the beans once they reach the top. There is also creative potential to climb beans over netting, to make a bean canopy or even to grow them trailing from a hanging basket.

Good runner varieties include 'Scarlet Emperor' (very productive but must be picked small or it gets tough); 'Enorma' (relatively 'stringless'); 'White Lady'; or 'Lady Di' (white flowers).

There are many excellent French beans, including: 'Blauhilde' (purple bean and tender even when large); 'Cherokee Trail of Tears' (carried by Cherokees on their infamous march after forced displacement); or 'Major Cook's' (excellent flavour).

While climbing beans make good use of vertical space, on windy sites, bush beans, which are only 30–60cm (1–2ft) tall, can be a better choice.

How to grow French and Runner beans
Sow inside in late April/May, or outside in June, in pots at least 10cm (4in) deep (they have long roots); move outside after the last frost. Seedlings raised inside hate the wind and cold: harden off carefully and avoid planting out on a windy day. Slugs also love the seedlings, so watch out and protect with plastic bottle cloches if needed.

Beans yield best with a constant supply of water and don't like to dry out, so grow them in a big pot (20 litres/5¼ gallons minimum; 40–50 litres/10½–13 gallons is a better size) or a container with a reservoir.

Beans will usually grow fine in old compost as long as the nutrients are replenished (but avoid a high-nitrogen fertiliser like chicken manure pellets as this will result in too much leaf growth). Beans benefit from occasional feeding with liquid tomato feed and a mulch of worm compost mid-season, but they are not as hungry as tomatoes or squash (one reason for this is that they can fix nitrogen from the air).

Runner beans are best picked small and tender, and some varieties are almost inedible when large. Any beans that inadvertently grow too large can be left to harvest for next year's seeds (see *Chapter 5 Useful Growing Skills*, 'How to save seeds', page 108) or hulled and eaten like kidney beans.

French beans vary, but some varieties, like 'Blauhilde', stay tender even when large. Experiment.

Broad beans

Broad beans grow okay in containers, but the cropping season and yield is small. For comparison, from a similar-sized container, a runner bean harvest will often weigh ten to fifteen times as much.

Sow a winter-hardy broad bean variety, like 'Aquadulce Claudia', outside in October for an early-summer harvest, freeing up a container for a summer crop like courgettes. Other varieties can be sown outside from February to April.

Peas

Podded peas make a lovely garden snack and kids love them. However, you will get more to eat by growing mangetout or sugar snap peas. All pea varieties have lovely flowers and some even have pretty, purple pods.

One benefit of growing peas is that early sowings are ready to harvest in June or early July, making space for another crop over the summer. Climbing peas usually give better harvests, but bush peas are a good option on windy sites. Climbing peas can grow from 60cm (2ft) to over 2m (6½ft) tall, depending on the variety – check this when choosing.

Mangetout-type peas give a more worthwhile yield in containers than podded peas.

Start the seeds inside in deep modules or pots in March or outside in April. Pea tendrils are unable to cling onto canes (they're too thick). For support, they are best grown up netting, chicken mesh or 'pea sticks' (often hazel prunings, but any young tree branches with thin twiggy ends will work).

Peas are not particularly hungry but will benefit from the occasional feed with dilute tomato feed when fruiting and occasional liquid seaweed like other plants.

Leafy vegetables

Leafy veg can be grown all year round in most temperate climates and most varieties grow productively in containers in just four hours of sun. The most suitable for containers include chard, kale, spinach and Asian leaves. They usually grow fine in old compost as long as fertiliser is added (I usually mix in chicken manure pellets and worm compost).

Asian leaves

A wide variety of Asian leaves grow well in all temperate climates, even surviving mild frosts, including Chinese cabbage, kailaan (Chinese broccoli), tatsoi, pak choi and choy sum, and many more. They are all delicious in their own right – brilliant for stir fries or they can make a good, fast-growing alternative to some traditional crops like broccoli (use kailaan) or cabbage (use Chinese cabbage).

All can be sown in early spring (late March) for leaves in early summer, but the optimum time is usually August or early September for late-autumn and winter pickings. May and June sowings tend to bolt and quickly go to seed.

Kailaan/Chinese broccoli: This has a thick, tender stem with lots of flavour, similar to broccoli. In optimal conditions, it is ready to eat in just eight weeks. Harvest by picking off the florets, leaving the rest of the plant to continue to grow. If grown in a large-enough container, it can be harvested over several months in winter and spring.

Choy sum: A stir-fry leaf that has a good taste.

Mustards: The large leaves of mustards like 'Red Giant' and 'Green in the Snow' can be left to grow a bit bigger and steamed or added to stir fries (the large, spicy leaves become milder when cooked).

Pak choi: Stems with a lovely crunch that are excellent for stir fries. There are many different varieties – look for fast-growing ones – and watch out for slugs.

Chinese cabbage: Fast growing and excellent for stir fries.

Chard

Chard tastes similar to spinach, with a thicker, crunchier (and tasty) stem. It's a versatile green and is used a lot in Mediterranean and Middle Eastern dishes. It's becoming better known in the UK but is still not widely available, so growing your own is the best way to have a regular supply. Some varieties like 'Rainbow Chard' or 'Bright Lights' have bright yellow and red stalks that look cheerful in the container garden.

Sow the seeds outside any time from late April until July (earlier sowings are prone to bolt prematurely if there's a cold snap). I often sow it thickly in its final pot and thin out the pretty baby seedlings to eat in salads.

Chard can be grown in almost any sized container, but for large plants, go for something with a capacity of at least 20 litres (5¼ gallons) and, ideally, 15cm (6in) deep. It likes a mineral-rich soil, so watering or foliar feeding with liquid seaweed and/or mulching with worm compost will help. A light surface sprinkling of chicken manure pellets in early autumn and spring helps boost leaf production.

Once the plant is well established, pick the outer leaves, ideally before they get too large and tough. Pick sparingly in winter and it will grow back lush and strong in spring.

Kale

Kale is nutritious, full of flavour and very hardy. There are many varieties, some of which are ornamental and look great in containers: 'Cavolo Nero' has blue-green leaves that look like beautiful plumes, 'Red Russian' has pretty, serrated leaves, and 'Redbor' is stately, bright red and frilly. If you're used to tough kale leaves, you may be surprised at how soft and tender some homegrown kale varieties can be: 'Red Russian' and young 'Cavolo Nero' leaves, in particular, are delicious shredded in a salad.

Nice heritage varieties include asparagus kale and Sutherland kale, and there are

As well as being a tasty and nutritious vegetable, chard is a colourful crop. In London, I sometimes grew it in the window box above our front door.

several perennial kales, including Daubenton's kale and African kale that can be grown in a large pot, if you can get hold of them.

Sow, grow and pick kale in the same way as chard. Late July sowings are excellent for a supply of winter leaves. For large, sturdy kale plants, give each one plenty of space, at least 9 inches (23 cm) apart.

Spinach

True spinach (as opposed to beet spinach that is often sold in supermarkets) is a delicious and versatile vegetable that grows well in containers in the spring and later in the year (it goes to seed quickly in summer).

Sow in spring (March or April) for summer leaves or late summer (late July or August) for leaves in late autumn and winter. It's best to use fresh seed, no more than two years old.

Please note that other leafy crops can be used like spinach in the kitchen, including New Zealand spinach (keeps its leaf shape when cooked), orach, chard and tree spinach.

Root vegetables

The smaller, fast-growing roots like radish and spring onions are good choices for small spaces. Potatoes and Jerusalem artichokes also do well. Carrots are tasty and fun if you have kids, but not particularly productive. On the other hand, the slower-growing, space-hungry roots like parsnips and celeriac are perhaps better in allotments, but can be grown in containers if you fancy – exhibition growers grow huge parsnips in dustbins! Some roots have the double benefit of having tasty edible leaves, including radish, mooli (also known as daikon), beetroot, turnip and oca.

In theory, most root veg should be easy to grow. However, in containers, it's quite common to get an excellent crop of leaves but small roots, particularly with beetroot and sometimes radish (potatoes, spring

Beetroot grown in a bucket – one of my more successful attempts.

onions, oca and artichokes are usually more reliable). I've never quite got to the bottom of this, but I think it is more related to the nutrient balance in the compost rather than the container size or weather conditions.

Beetroot

Fickle in containers (some people find it easy; others, including me, struggle), but it's great to have when it grows well. The leaves can also be eaten like spinach (they wilt quickly, so eat freshly picked). The variety 'Chioggia' has pretty, pink-and-white rings, while 'Burpees Golden' is yellow. Sow any time from March to September in a deep container, ideally bucket-sized or larger. Thin the plants as they grow (it's delicious to eat at golf-ball size) to give the remaining beetroot space to grow.

These beetroots have developed an extensive, deep root system – showing why they benefit from a deep container.

Carrots

Sow quite thickly (say, 3cm/1¼in apart) and harvest by thinning out as they grow (baby carrots make a tasty snack). Watch out for slugs – sometimes they eat the baby seedlings before you even realise they have come up!

Jerusalem artichokes

These are tall plants (1.8m/6ft or more), related to sunflowers, that grow surprisingly well in containers given their large size. They have tasty edible tubers with a flavour reminiscent of globe artichokes. It's impossible to mention them without reference to jokes about flatulence, but this wears off the more you eat them! Since they grow tall and fast, they can also be used as a windbreak.

Like potatoes, they are grown from tubers, planted in the early spring (tubers from a farmers' market or veg box will usually grow fine). Put one tuber in a 10-litre (2½-gallon) bucket or five or six in a 50-litre

Jerusalem artichokes at the front of one of our rented homes in Newcastle upon Tyne. Surprisingly, they also grow well in containers as small as buckets.

Oca growing in a container.

(13-gallon) veg crate. Prune the plants back if they get too tall. Harvest the tubers once the foliage dies back – any time from late December to the end of February or early March. Save a few of the smaller tubers to plant again next season.

Mooli/daikon

Similar to radish, except with larger, white roots. The leaves are also edible. Sow in early September for a harvest in late autumn/early winter.

Oca

An interesting and fun alternative to potatoes with the benefit of pretty, edible leaves in addition to brightly coloured, slightly lemony flavoured tubers. They are high in oxalic acid (like rhubarb), and it's advised to avoid eating them in very large quantities. They are relatively easy to grow, although unfortunately can be prone to slugs eating the tubers in containers.

Plant the tubers (one in a large bucket) in May or early June. They can be slow to start but grow best after the midsummer solstice. Leave in the container as long as possible before harvesting and for a few weeks after they have been killed by frost (after the foliage has died back, the tubers will continue swelling under the compost).

Potatoes

Potatoes are one of the most productive and reliable root crops for containers. Be aware that they do grow big and bushy, so place them carefully so they don't cast too much shade over neighbouring pots. The superb taste of home-grown new potatoes (sold as first or second earlies in garden centres), combined with how quickly they grow, makes them the best choice to grow in containers. Good varieties include Arran Pilot, Casablanca and International Kidney.

It's also possible to grow main crop potatoes in containers, they just need larger containers (ideally at least 50 litres /

13 gallons), and they take several weeks longer to grow. A good main crop variety to try is Pink Fir Apple – productive, tasty and one not commonly found in the shops.

Details of how to grow potatoes can be found in *Chapter 9 Your First Growing Projects*, 'Project 3: Potatoes in a bag', page 170.

Radish

Fast growing, with some varieties ready to eat in just 30 days. The leaves are a treat when lightly stir-fried with lemon and garlic, but eat freshly picked as they wilt quickly.

Radish is also a useful catch crop (see *Chapter 7 How to Grow More Food in a Small Space*, 'Catch crops and interplanting', page 137). Sow the seeds directly into their final pot any time from March to September. In theory, it's a very easy crop to grow, but I've found it doesn't always bulb up as much as I would like.

Spring onions

Grow relatively fast (ready in 60–90 days) and don't take up much space. Spring onions can be picked at any size and it's handy to be able to pick a fresh handful as and when needed.

Sow any time from March until September. Keep sowing regularly as gaps appear to keep up a constant supply or interplant in a larger container with salads.

Interesting and unusual vegetables

Many other vegetables can be grown in containers and trying different things can be all part of the fun. Here are a few worth considering:

Florence fennel/bulbing fennel has pretty, frond-like leaves that look great in a potager-style garden. Sow in July and harvest the bulbs in autumn before the first hard frosts.

Globe artichokes – these are impressive perennials that grow 90cm–1.2m (3–4ft) tall and have huge, purple, thistle-like flowers. They need a large container (50 litres/13 gallons or more). Start from seed in March or April or buy a plant.

Mouse melons are tiny fruits, the size of cherry tomatoes, that taste more like cucumbers than melons. They are pretty little things and fun to grow. Grow them like cucumbers in pots of 5 litres (1¼ gallons) or bigger. Like cucumbers, they need warmth to do well.

Tomatillos are related to tomatoes and are grown in a similar way except two plants are needed for a good crop (they need to cross-pollinate). The fruits are green or purple, look similar to tomatoes, but are less sweet. In Mexico and South America, they are key ingredients in salsas and green sauces.

Other possibilities include **mashua** (looks like nasturtium and has edible tubers and leaves); a climber with tasty tubers called **potato bean/American groundnut**; **Chinese artichokes** (look similar to Jerusalem artichokes but have a nuttier flavour); **Hooker's onion** (a perennial onion that is fabulous for bees); and **yacón** (a perennial root vegetable with a water chestnut-like texture).

More tricky vegetables

While anything can be grown in a container, some vegetables are trickier. Brussels sprouts, purple-sprouting broccoli and cauliflower are large plants that take a long time to grow. Sweetcorn looks impressive and stately in containers, but it's hard to get good pollination with just a few plants (it is wind-pollinated and does best with a large number planted in a block formation).

Fruit

You are spoilt for choice when it comes to fruit in containers: strawberries, apples, blackberries, cherries, raspberries and blueberries are among those that do well, along with more unusual things like Japanese wineberries and Chilean guavas. Fruit trees and bushes also add height and structure to a container garden, and many have pretty blossoms in spring (which is good for bees) and attractive red foliage in autumn. Soft fruits like raspberries and blackberries are pricey in the shops and do not store or travel well – another reason to grow them at home.

With a bit of planning and a large enough space, it's possible to have fruit from March to November. As an example, 'Table 10.3 Month-by-Month Fruit Harvests from My Container Garden', shows the fruits grown in my front yard and when we harvest them.

Most fruits are not difficult to grow, but they usually need looking after for a year or two (and sometimes longer) before fruiting productively. Bear this in mind before you buy. My apple tree, now over ten years old, has only been really productive for the last four or five years.

Choose the right fruit and variety

As well as what you like to eat, points to consider when choosing fruit to grow include how much sun your space gets and how big a pot you can squeeze in – see 'Table 10.4

Chilean guavas produce small, compact fruits the size of blueberries, late in the year from October to December. Their taste is reminiscent of strawberries.

Guide to the Best Fruits for Containers', page 222. Once you've chosen a fruit you would like to grow, it's then vital to select a variety suitable for a container, and one that suits your local climate and that ripens at the right time (a blueberry that ripens in August isn't so good if that's a month you are normally away, for example). Also, bear in mind that not all fruits are self-pollinating, which means you might need two plants (or a neighbour with one). Furthermore, some trees like apples and cherries are grafted onto

TABLE 10.3. Month-by-Month Fruit Harvests from My Container Garden

March–June	June–July	July–August	August–September	September–October	October–December
Rhubarb	Raspberries, strawberries and cherries	Blackberries	Blueberries and Japanese wineberries	Apples	Chilean guavas

Apple tree in our front yard in Newcastle upon Tyne – the blossom is always a cheerful sight in spring.

different rootstocks. The choice of rootstock determines how vigorously and how large the tree will grow, so a 'dwarf' rooting stock will be less vigorous and produce a smaller tree. A specialist nursery can advise on the best rootstock for your situation.

As you can see, fruit trees are a specialist area, and I can't recommend enough the value of using a specialist fruit nursery to help you choose. You'll pay more than the supermarkets or discount stores, but you'll get far better-quality plants, more suited to your needs and often accompanied by invaluable growing and pruning advice. Fruit trees can live and fruit for many years, and investing in one that will give a lot of pleasure (and fruit!) is worth every penny.

The widest choice of fruit trees, and the best value, is available in autumn and winter when 'bare-rooted' fruit trees are sold. These come, as the name suggests, bare rooted and need planting up straight away. Fruit trees in pots are also available all year round.

Another excellent option is to look out for community orchard projects in your area.

These sometimes offer the chance to graft your own tree as well as pruning workshops.

Planting up

Once you've got a fruit tree or bush home, a good rule of thumb is to repot it into a container that is one size larger (move from 5 litres/1¼ gallons into 10 litres/2½ gallons, for example). This gives it the space and fresh food it needs for its next stage of growth.

A 'soil-based' potting mix is a good choice as it holds nutrients for longer and is heavier, stabilising the pot and reducing the risk that it will blow over. In large pots, it can work well to add an inch or two mix of twigs, straw and food waste to the bottom to break down and slowly release nutrients for the plant, otherwise known as 'lasagne' gardening – see *Chapter 4 Eight Steps to Success*, 'Table 4.3 How and When to Feed Plants in Containers', page 74).

Note that blueberries and cranberries need an acid compost mix – often labelled 'ericaceous' compost.

Choosing a good variety of fruit for containers is key. This purple raspberry, 'Glen Coe', is an excellent choice because it is high yielding and fruits on this year's growth.

Feeding fruit trees

As with other container crops, fruits benefit from feeding. The easiest ways to meet their essential nutrient needs is to:

- ▶ Feed with liquid tomato feed once a week while fruiting. Comfrey or seaweed-based tomato feeds are a good choice.
- ▶ Or mix slow-release fertiliser granules like Osmocote into the potting mix. Most professional growers choose this option as it saves time, works well and reduces the amount of nutrients washed away with watering.

To boost the health of your fruits, you can also feed with:

Liquid seaweed, watered on or foliar fed once a week or fortnight, for minerals and trace elements. (I often alternate tomato feed one week, seaweed the next.)

A layer of worm compost added to the top of the container in spring, mid-summer and autumn for minerals and beneficial soil life.

A wood chip mulch to support fungal life, which benefits fruit trees.

Repotting

Fruit trees benefit from regular repotting, once a year or every other year, depending on how fast they're growing. Check if your fruits need repotting in winter when most are dormant: lie the pot on its side and carefully slide the bush or tree out. If there are lots of roots visible, circling the pot, this is a sign it's ready for repotting.

When repotting, there are two options. If space permits, the ideal option is to move the tree or bush to a pot one size larger, to give the roots more space to grow. However, if space is limited and you need to return it to the same size pot, try to remove about a third of the soil and prune back some of the roots, particularly any circling the edge of the pot. Take care not to remove more than one-third of the

This blackberry, 'Loch Tay', gives us several kilos of fresh berries in July each year.

This apple tree spent its first four years in a 20-litre (5¼-gallon) pot (while we moved house three times!), then three years in a 40-litre (10½-gallon) pot and the past three years in an 80-litre (21-gallon) pot. It now produces around 100 apples a year.

The Best Herbs, Fruit and Veg for Containers | 221

TABLE 10.4. Guide to the Best Fruits for Containers

Fruit and a few suggested varieties	Final pot size	Minimum sun needs (hours)	Self-pollinating
Alpine strawberry	1 litre (¼ gallon) or several plants in a window box	3–4	Yes
Apple	30–100 litres (8–26 gallons)	5–6	Normally no, but some varieties yes
Blackberry 'Loch Tay' (thornless)	40–80 litres (10½–21 gallons)	4	Yes
Blueberry 'Bluecrop' (highbush variety)	20–60 litres (5¼–16 gallons), depending on variety	4	Partially – best to grow two different varieties.
Cherry 'Stella' (self-pollinating, sweet)	25–60 litres (6½–16 gallons), ideal for a dwarf variety	4 (for acid/sour cherries); 6 (for sweet cherries)	Varies – some self-pollinating varieties
Chilean guava	20–50 litres (5¼–13 gallons)	4	Yes
Cranberry	10–20 litres (2½–5¼ gallons)	4	Yes
Fig 'Brown Turkey' (for UK climate)	50–80 litres (13–21 gallons)	6-plus	Yes
Hardy kiwi 'Issai' (self-pollinating variety)	40–60 litres (10½–16 gallons)	6-plus	Varies
Honeyberry	20–30 litres (5¼–8 gallons)	4	No. Two plants needed.
Japanese wineberry	20–50 litres (5¼–13 gallons)	4	Yes
Raspberry 'Glen Coe' (purple variety)	20–60 litres (5¼–16 gallons)	4	Yes
Rhubarb	40–80 litres (10½–21 gallons)	3	N/A
Strawberry 'Mara des Bois' (perpetual variety)	5–20 litres (1¼–5¼ gallons)	5–6-plus	Yes

Good choice for small and less sunny spaces. Produces small berries over several months. Small yield, but good flavour. Ideal for snacking or as a pretty garnish. Kids love them. Can be grown from seed.

Pretty blossom in spring. Can be very productive in a large pot but may take a few years to establish. There are many varieties which vary in hardiness and flavour, when they ripen and how long they store for. Choose a variety and dwarfing rootstock suitable for a container – Minarette trees are a good choice.

Needs a big pot but grows well in containers and can be very productive. Requires support (for example, a simple wigwam). Thornless and early-fruiting varieties available – blackberries in July are a treat.

Can be productive but it is fussy. Needs ericaceous compost and, ideally, rainwater (not tap water) if possible.

Doesn't like overfeeding – feed every three or four weeks with liquid seaweed or dilute tomato feed.

Pretty flowers and some varieties have vivid autumn foliage.

Fruits best with two or more varieties. Varieties vary in flavour, fruiting time and size – highbush varieties need larger containers.

Fruits well in four hours of sun but for sweeter fruits, grow in full sun.

Pretty blossom. Many varieties, both sweet and sour. Sour varieties tend to have more flavour and are excellent for cooking and jam. Sweet varieties are the choice for snacking. Choose a cherry on a dwarfing rootstock (such as 'Gisela 6').

Fruits about the size of blueberries but with a peppery/strawberry flavour. Delicious as a snack and kids love them. Can grow into a large bush in a big-enough container. Berries ripen in October/November time.

Needs acid soil. Similar looking, but smaller plants to blueberries – yet grown in a similar way. Can be grown in a hanging basket.

Climber. Needs plenty of warmth, ideally a south-facing sunny wall, and will crop well in the right conditions. May need protecting with fleece or moving inside in winter.

Climber. Small, grape-sized kiwis can be grown in cooler climates like the UK, but it needs a sunny and sheltered wall (it dislikes wind). Usually takes several years to fruit well. Self-fertile varieties are available. Very pretty blossom.

Pretty plant that is related to honeysuckle. Berries taste similar to a tart blueberry.

Bright red berry, somewhat similar in look and taste to a raspberry. Spiny, red stems that look pretty in winter. An excellent fruit for containers.

The best variety for containers as it is delicious and productive.

Autumn varieties, or any variety that fruits on this year's growth, are also a good choice. Cut the canes back to the base after fruiting.

Summer-fruiting raspberries are less suitable as they fruit on the second year's growth (and need larger pots).

Great choice for places with less sun. Needs a big pot and regular feeding but grows well in containers. Some varieties can be picked as early as March, right through to July or August. Stop picking towards mid-August to allow the plant to regain strength for winter, when it dies back to return in early spring.

Grow in containers, strawberry planters or good-quality grow bags. They run out of steam and need replacing every three years or so. The plants produce 'runners' – small baby plants on stems. Remove these (they can be planted in a new pot and will grow into new plants). Different varieties fruit at different times – 'perpetual' varieties fruit over a longer period.

roots in one go. Then return the tree to its pot with some fresh compost. Now is usually a good time to prune the top branches, too, to balance the plant now that it has less roots.

The best results are often achieved by steadily increasing the pot size (so, 10 litres/2½ gallons, 20 litres/5¼ gallons, 40 litres/10½ gallons, and so on), rather than using the largest pot straight away. This provides more food and space for the roots as the plant grows. The final pot size depends on how much space you have and how big you want the tree to grow. Apple trees, for example, often do best in a 60-litre (16-gallon) pot or larger, but can be kept going in smaller pots, too.

Pruning

Most fruit trees benefit from regular pruning, usually in winter when the tree is dormant. How to prune depends on both the type of tree and the shape you want. The details are beyond the scope of this book because every tree is different. A specialist pruning book, YouTube videos or a local workshop will help, particularly if you want to do anything fancy like a fan or espalier tree. Fruit bushes like blueberries and Chilean guavas need less pruning and can be shaped more or less how you like (just avoid removing more than a third in a season). With autumn and purple raspberries, and blackberries, cut the stems that have fruited back at the base at the end of the season.

Harvesting

It's recommended that you remove most of the blossom in the first year you plant a fruit tree – do this when the blossom starts to die back. This enables the tree to channel its strength into establishing itself. The same goes for rhubarb – let it establish in the first year and try to resist the temptation of picking it.

Fruit guide

'Table 10.4 Guide to the Best Fruits for Containers', (pages 222–223), summarises the sun needs (the minimum for fruits to grow but note that they will usually be sweeter in more sun) and the final pot size for the best container fruits.

Japanese wineberries are pretty with an excellent flavour, somewhat similar to raspberries.

Pretty autumnal leaves are another benefit of growing fruit – this is a blueberry.

Chapter 11

Solutions to Common Challenges

Growing in containers in small spaces poses unique challenges that aren't usually addressed in traditional gardening books. These include shortage of space, not enough sun and too much wind, as well as factors like the cost of buying materials (which quickly adds up), shifting heavy bags of compost without a car, keeping spaces neat and tidy, or avoiding getting compost on your new carpet.

It's often possible to find a way round these challenges and grow successfully. This chapter looks at how. Bear in mind that whatever challenges you face, it's likely that other people who live and grow in your area have already found solutions. Balconies on blocks of flats, for example, often have similar growing conditions or are subject to the same animal raids, whether that be from squirrels in London or monkeys in Mumbai. It can be invaluable to connect with others and learn from each other about what works and what doesn't.

Hedvig Murray created this garden in her local park.

A few of the common challenges are covered elsewhere in the book. For instance, water dripping onto neighbour's washing is discussed in *Chapter 3 How to Design Your Container Garden*, 'Will water drip on the neighbour's washing?', page 25, and raising seedlings inside urban homes in *Chapter 5 Useful Growing Skills*, 'Raising seedlings inside – overcoming the light challenge', page 92.

Not enough space to grow

Many urban homes have a balcony, rooftop, patio or front yard that can become a productive edible garden. But other homes may have a space that is difficult to grow in (perhaps because of a severe lack of sun), rules against growing plants or no outdoor growing space at all. Even those of us lucky to have some space often want more!

How can we find more space in crowded cities? Sometimes it's possible to get an allotment, but there are other options, too. It's worth exploring these with an open and positive mind as most people who really want to grow do find somewhere eventually.

A common solution is to grow in a neighbour's garden or front yard (look online for local and national garden share schemes or simply ask around). With their permission, I grew in the front of both my downstairs and next-door neighbour's homes when I lived in London. Another option is to explore possibilities in local community spaces. For example, permaculture trainer, Hedvig Murray, in Brighton, East Sussex, was given permission to create a small edible garden in her local park and another in the churchyard next door. Another grower, Azul Thome, built a large container garden on the roof of her local supermarket. Francesca Hardy created one in the communal space outside her block of flats. Check also whether there is any space

Supermarket crates make excellent containers for growing vegetables. Line with newspaper or card to stop soil falling out.

to grow at work – many offices have rooftops or bits of car parks that are underused. Or take inspiration from the guerrilla gardening movement and grow in untended planters or patches of ground nearby.

The cost of growing

If everything is bought from the shops, the costs of a container garden can quickly add up. This is a common barrier to starting or creating a large and productive container garden.

However, with a bit of knowledge and time, it's also possible to grow at low cost. I know people who have created entire container gardens for almost nothing and many others who find a lot of what they need for free or very little.

It's usually possible to find containers, make your own worm compost, save seeds, take cuttings and swap plants and seeds with other growers. As you gain experience and knowledge, you'll learn more about what

works and where to find things for free and then costs can drop further. As well as saving money, many people find this way of growing to be more rewarding, fun and creative.

Finding what you need

Every city, region and country have different treasures to offer. Some have city farms with manure, plumbers' skips filled with old sinks, bathtubs and hot-water tanks or markets with discarded veg crates – and more.

Keep an eye out everywhere you go and you'll be amazed at what you can find. Local growing networks are also invaluable sources of information on what and where to find things. The search is often a fun way to explore the local area and meet new people.

Containers

People are always discovering new and creative ways to make containers. Use 'Table 11.1 Guide to Recycled Containers and

Rules of Engagement

Skips can be treasure troves, but do ask permission before taking anything (by law, the contents still belong to the owner).

If you're unsure about anything else you want to take or any plant you want to pick, double check that it's ethical and that you have permission.

TABLE 11.1. Guide to Recycled Containers and Where to Find Them

Containers	Comments	Where to find
Plastic flower/ food buckets	Excellent for a wide range of crops: tomatoes, chillies, herbs, etc.	Flower sellers, supermarkets and restaurants
Metal tins	Large olive oil or food tins can be attractive. Line insides with cardboard to insulate from sun.	Restaurants and back alleys
Bags for life	Good for potatoes and larger veg crops. Only last a season or two – not for life!	Everywhere
Water tanks	Useful large containers – for potatoes, squash and other bigger crops.	Skips, central heating contractors and plumbers
Recycling bins (50 litres/13 gallons)	Strong and long-lasting containers; UV treated.	Recycling centres and skips
Pallets	Heavy and full of splinters. Often treated with toxic preservative or contaminated with chemical spillage, but useful as staging to raise containers or deconstructed to use the slats. Often used as vertical planters but watering can be an issue and dealing with rotten pallets is a nasty, dirty job.	Back alleys, skips and builders' merchant yards
Baths/basins/ even toilets	Fun and can look good.	Skips and plumbers' yards
Wood	Useful to make containers to size but avoid treated wood. Also useful as cladding to hide unattractive plastic containers and to make ladders and shelves.	Back alleys, skips and local wood-recycling centres
Mushroom boxes	Good for microgreens or alternative seed trays.	Vegetable markets and greengrocers
Wooden crates/ trays/boxes	Attractive, nice for salads and pea shoots.	Vegetable markets and wine merchants
Plastic crates	Not the most attractive (but you can hide them behind wood). Good for a wide range of veg.	Supermarkets and fishmongers' back alleys

Where to Find Them', see above, as a starting point for ideas, but don't be limited by it. Avoid any container that might have contained toxic chemicals (paint buckets, for example) and steer clear of old tyres (toxic).

Remember to add drainage holes to containers if needed. Containers that have too many holes can be lined with newspaper or card to prevent soil falling out.

Compost and fertiliser

Chapter 6 How to Make Your Own... includes various methods for making your own compost and fertiliser with ingredients such as nettles, worm compost and comfrey that can be sourced for free in many places. Other fertilisers can also be made out of weeds, shellfish shells, bones, fish waste, eggshells and other food scraps.

Tools and accessories

Where there is a need, there is usually a free solution. 'Table 11.2 Recycled Tool Options and Where to Find Them', page 230, provides suggestions for places where I have been able to find useful tools and accessories.

TABLE 11.2. Recycled Tool Options and Where to Find Them

Tool/accessory	Free/low-cost alternative	Where to find
Plant ties	Cut up old bike inner tubes for flexible plant ties.	Bike repair shops
Sieves	Plastic mushroom boxes with holes in them make good garden sieves.	Veg markets and independent green grocers
Pea sticks and bean poles	Coppiced sticks and poles	Tree surgeons and neighbour's trees that are being coppiced, etc.
Cloches	Cut in half water cooler bottles or large plastic bottles. Make hoops with plastic plumber's piping, covered with plastic sheeting or bubble wrap.	Offices, skips and home waste
Plant labels	Many options – for example, cut strips from plastic milk bottles or use coffee-stirrer sticks.	
Seedling waterer	Punch holes in the lid of a plastic milk or juice bottle.	Everywhere
Platforms to raise containers	Pallets, bricks and brown plastic bread trays turned upside down.	Back alleys, skips and markets

Mushroom boxes can be used as seed trays or to grow microgreens (line with newspaper first), as a sieve, for drying chillies and herbs, or stacked for storing tools and string, for example.

Low-cost options

Most garden centres in urban areas are set up to cater for the needs of homeowners with large gardens. Prices are often high, and the needs of food growers aren't always well catered for. Look out for and research other options in your local area, including:

Community plant sales and seed swaps: these are enjoyable places to get seeds and plants (and local growing advice)

at a fraction of the cost, but they are not always well advertised.

Allotment shops often sell compost, fertiliser, seeds and sometimes plants at cost price. Some are open to members of the public.

Some community growing projects sell compost, fertiliser, seeds and plants at cost price or for a small markup to help fund their work.

Discount stores and supermarkets often stock containers, fertiliser, compost and plants (sometimes fruit trees, too) in the gardening season. They can be useful, but be wary of cheap plastic and bargains that may not be as good as they appear (for example, fruit trees are often of poor quality and unsuitable for containers).

Online sites like Freecycle, eBay and Gumtree are excellent places for picking up free or low-cost containers, barrels, water butts, garden tools and things like bird netting and fertiliser.

Through my work with Vertical Veg, I've been lucky enough to talk to and learn from container growers improvising to create amazing container gardens on almost zero budget with reclaimed materials, both in the UK and around the world. Murhula Zigabe, in the Democratic Republic of Congo, for example, reclaims bottles from rubbish tips to use as containers, makes liquid fertiliser from weeds, banana skins and cow dung that he collects, and potting mix from soil and homemade compost. He uses his container gardens to teach children to grow food in his hometown of Bukavu, kindling an interest and enthusiasm for food growing.

Making watering easier

Watering is the one element of container gardening that requires the most regular commitment and time. With the right mindset, it can be a relaxing and rewarding part of the day. But it can also be a challenge if you're very busy with other commitments, travel a lot or simply have lots of containers.

Even if time isn't an issue, it's still worth implementing a lot of the suggestions here. As well as making watering easier, they reduce the risk of plant stress. Easier watering also makes the task less onerous if you need to ask friends and neighbours to water while you are away.

There isn't really one magic solution. Even an automatic watering system needs setting up and keeping a close eye on. But there are lots of simple things you can do to make watering easier and to reduce the frequency. One of the best ways is to have a water source – a tap, hose or water butt – close to the plants, as I have already discussed in *Chapter 3 How to Design Your Container Garden*, 'Where is the nearest water source?', page 24, but here are some other suggestions.

Use the largest pots practical

The larger the volume of pot, the more water it can hold and the less quickly it dries out.

Murhula Zigabe's bottle garden in Bukavu, in the Democratic Republic of Congo.

Although large pots are not practical in all small spaces, try to avoid lots of very small pots (like yoghurt pots) unless you are happy to water two or three times a day on hot days.

Choose containers with water reservoirs

Reservoirs reduce the frequency of watering that is needed. Depending on the size of the reservoir, however, they often still need topping up once a day in warm weather. If you need to leave plants for longer periods, look for containers with very large reservoirs, like the 'Quadgrow'. This has a 30-litre (8-gallon) reservoir and an optional kit to link it to a water butt, which is perfect if you want to grow tomatoes but are not able to water daily. I've left mine for over a week in peak season without any problems.

Quadgrow planters have large reservoirs that hold enough water for several days.

A homemade bottle waterer, which is buried in the compost to drip water near the roots. The bottom is cut off for easy watering. Adjust the size of the holes for quicker or slower water release.

Use bottle waterers or ollas

For containers without built-in reservoirs, a bottle waterer or olla can be added if needed. A bottle waterer is simply a plastic bottle with two small holes drilled in the screwtop lid (you can also buy adjustable dripper lids that screw on), placed upside down in the soil so that it slowly drips water. Cut the base off the bottle so that it can be refilled easily. They are particularly useful in hanging baskets which are prone to drying out quickly.

Ollas are porous, unglazed clay pots that are buried in the soil and then filled with water. The water seeps into the soil as it is needed by the plant. They were developed thousands of years ago and are still used in Sri Lanka, India and other hot countries. You can buy beautiful handmade ollas or make your own by joining two terracotta pots together (look for DIY instructions online).

Mulch

Adding a layer of pebbles, grit, composted wood chip, chopped leaves, straw, cardboard or even plastic reduces evaporation and helps keep moisture in. Gardeners call this technique 'mulching'. Organic mulches such as chopped-up leaves, composted bark or wood chip will also support microbial life and release a small but steady stream of nutrients for the plants. I highly recommend adding some sort of mulch to your containers, particularly to large and hungry plants (for example, tomatoes, courgettes and fruit trees).

For plastic mulches, I use old compost bags, cutting holes in them for the plants. They retain water particularly well and make a good choice for thirsty plants like tomatoes and courgettes. Black plastic absorbs warmth well (good for cooler areas); white plastic

An olla – the unglazed part is buried under the soil.

Mulching an apple tree with wood chip.

reflects heat and more light onto the plant (useful where light levels are marginal).

Make a water-retentive potting mix

Additives that improve water retention in a potting mix include vermiculite, perlite, biochar and worm compost, usually added in the region of 5–30 per cent, depending on the water retention needed. Vermiculite (derived from volcanic rock) holds water particularly well, but is energy intensive to make.

It's probably best to avoid the water-retaining crystals sold in gardening shops (tests show mixed results and some brands may even be toxic) and the crystals found in disposable nappies, an idea that I've seen doing the rounds on the internet.

Automated watering systems

The techniques outlined so far reduce plant stress and help to extend the time between waterings. However, if you go away regularly or are struggling to keep up with the number of pots you need to water, an automated system is another option. They can save a lot of time, but none are foolproof – batteries run out and pipes get blocked or leak.

Drippers and timers

Drip systems consist of water drippers (in different shapes and sizes), piping and a battery-powered timer that attaches to a tap or water butt. Piping is laid round the container garden, then drippers are run off the main pipe into each pot. Most timers can be set to water once or twice a day. Some

A dripper system on most of these pots saves me 15 minutes a day – more time for seed sowing and other jobs. To ensure that plants aren't over- or underwatered, I still water by hand several times a week, time permitting.

drippers are adjustable, enabling more water to flow to some pots as needed. They are not too difficult to set up, but they can be a bit fiddly and time-consuming, particularly the first time. Dipping the end of the pipe into a cup of hot water makes it more pliable and easier to attach the drippers.

Be careful that dry pockets don't form in the compost, particularly if the water drips down in just part of the pot. Check all pots regularly and water by hand at least once a week.

Gravity-fed reservoir systems

A neat alternative is to link together several containers with reservoirs, join them to a water butt and then use gravity and a ball valve system (which works in a similar way to a toilet cistern) to keep the reservoirs topped up. To work, all the containers need to be on a flat surface at the same level.

Making your own is a good DIY project and, if you're confident in simple plumbing tasks, it shouldn't be too difficult. I managed with limited plumbing skills, albeit with a little stress. The reward is a gravity-powered, self-watering garden. Details of how to make one were published by the Canadian Rooftop Garden Project in their free and excellent publication, *Guide to Setting Up Your Own Edible Rooftop Garden*, and more details of mine are on my Vertical Veg website (see *Further Reading*, page 287).

Another solution, using similar principles, is the rain gutter grow system, which uses a gutter as a reservoir. It needs a large, flat surface like a rooftop. Look for videos online.

The inner workings of the gravity-powered, self-watering system that I built. The blue reservoir and ballcock are linked to the water butt to keep them topped up.

A couple of manufacturers also sell systems based on similar principles. Quadgrow pots with reservoirs, for example, can be linked together and attached to a water butt. Or you can buy a system to link up to 12 EarthBox containers to a mains water supply.

Reusing old compost

Replacing the compost in every pot each year (as gardening advice sometimes recommends) is impractical, costly and takes up time and precious resources. Luckily, *good-quality* compost can be reused for several years, perhaps even indefinitely.

It's not difficult to reuse compost, you just need to do three things: 1) replenish the nutrients; 2) check the structure is still good; and 3) bear in mind that some crops are easier to grow in reused compost than others. There is some guesswork and luck involved, but the results are often good.

Replenish the nutrients

Most of the readily available nutrients in compost are used up during the growing season and need to be replenished to grow a new crop. Commercial farmers do soil tests to measure nutrient levels and accurately calculate what to add, but this is unrealistic in container growing. Knowing what to add is therefore more of an educated guess.

You might add some fresh, new compost, homemade worm compost, well-rotted manure or fertilisers such as seaweed meal or chicken manure pellets. When choosing what to add, try to think about what the crop will need (see *Chapter 4 Eight Steps to Success*, 'Step 7: Feed your crops', page 69). For example, for leafy greens, add something like chicken manure pellets that are high in nitrogen to support leaf growth. For fruit and root crops, add a balanced fertiliser (equal NPK) like blood, fish and bone to support fruit and root formation. Also try to consider how hungry the plant is likely to be. For example, add more food for a squash plant than for a nasturtium or rocket crop.

If you have access to a variety of feeds, using small amounts of several different ones often works well. For example, to grow salads in used compost, I might add 15 per cent worm compost, a handful of chicken manure pellets and a small handful of seaweed meal. But to begin with, just experiment with what you can easily get, note down what you have done and observe how your plants grow. Even just adding a few handfuls of fresh compost to the top of the container will add some nutrients to help new plants establish and then you can apply liquid feeds as they grow.

Worm compost is particularly useful for rejuvenating compost because it contains soil life and a wide range of minerals as well as NPK. And, because it's composed of organic matter, it's more forgiving and harder (but not impossible) to add too much. You need to be more careful with stronger fertilisers like blood, fish and bone. Read the recommended dosage level on the side of the pack – start with those, then experiment.

The most important thing is to add *some* fertility back in, so your plants can get off to a good start. Remember that you can always apply a liquid feed, mulch with worm compost or add a topdressing of fertiliser to feed the plant more as it grows.

Check the structure

The air gaps that exist between particles of compost are needed for the roots to breathe and are vital for plant health. However, as compost ages, the particles slowly wear down and the number and size of the air spaces reduces, making it harder for the roots to breathe. When this happens, you

The squeeze test – compost that is losing its structure becomes a soggy ball after squeezing.

The squeeze test – compost with good structure remains crumbly after squeezing.

need to add some fresh material to the compost to help open up the air spaces again, otherwise plants will grow poorly.

An easy way to test the structure is to do what I call a 'squeeze test'. Take a handful of moist compost and squeeze it in your hand. If it becomes a soggy ball after squeezing, this is usually a sign that the structure has become poor. However, if it remains loose and crumbly after squeezing, the structure is good. Try this with new compost and you should see what I mean.

How much and how quickly the structure deteriorates depends on the material. Coir, composted bark and wood chip, for example, seem to retain good structure for several years, at least. Peat, on the other hand, tends to degrade in just a season or two (which is yet another reason to avoid it). Every material is different. Some soil-based composts perform poorly in the 'squeeze test' but still breathe well because the

inorganic soil particles create small air gaps that are too small to see. As with most growing, it's a case of observing, experimenting and learning.

To restore the structure, the easiest thing is to add a few handfuls of new general-purpose compost or whatever potting mix you are using. Or you can try adding composted bark (I use this a lot), fresh coir, treated biochar, horticultural grit, vermiculite or perlite. Homemade compost and worm compost generally do *not* add much structure unless you include a fair bit of wood chip or similar when you make it.

Select what to grow

Some plants seem to be easier to grow in used compost than others. Those that I've had consistent success with include potatoes, Jerusalem artichokes, most salads and leaves, courgettes and squash, peas and beans, mint

By replenishing the nutrients, I've been growing these tomatoes in the same compost for four successive years – and they still yield well.

Coir comes in neat bricks that are easy to carry and store. They are then reconstituted in water. Coir is an excellent growing medium.

and microgreens. Different crops have different nutrient needs, so if you've used compost for kale, for example, grow something from a different family next time, like potatoes.

Tomatoes, chillies and aubergines, on the other hand, are fussier about their nutrient needs and are easiest to grow in new compost each year. It is still possible to grow these in old compost, although yields may be lower. As an experiment, I've grown tomatoes in both coir and Sylvagrow (mainly composted wood chip) for four years in a row and they've done well every year so far.

Carrying heavy compost and getting it without a car

If you don't have a car, struggle to lift bags weighing 30kg (66lb) or live in a high-rise flat without a lift, getting heavy bags of compost to where you need them can be a challenge. If you've had to carry several bags of compost up lots of flights of stairs, you'll know exactly what I mean.

There are some obvious solutions to explore first, such as local garden centres that offer delivery (some will even carry bags to where you need them), online suppliers (although delivery is often expensive), or getting help from friends.

Another option is to buy coir (coconut fibre) bricks (see *Chapter 4 Eight Steps to Success*, 'How to find a good-quality compost', page 52). A typical coir brick weighs just over 500g (18oz) and expands to make 9 litres (2¼ gallons) of growing mix when soaked in water. They're infinitely easier to move around and store than large bags of compost. Coir is also pleasant to handle, clean to work with, and an excellent growing medium. However, it doesn't contain a lot of nutrients, so these will usually need to be added. Companies that sell coir usually recommend what and how many nutrients to add. Coir is shipped long distances, often from Sri Lanka, so only use it if you really need to.

The easiest place to get coir bricks is normally online – orders of 20 bricks or more often work out substantially cheaper.

Perlite is another lightweight material that can be added to potting mixes (up to 50 per cent, but normally 10–20 per cent). It's bulky but ultra light – a 20-litre (5¼-gallon) bag can weigh as little as 2kg (4½lb).

Wind

Some air movement is good for plants, but persistent or strong winds are not. Wind is a common issue because balconies and rooftops are often exposed, and patios and windowsills sometimes sit in wind tunnels created by rows of buildings.

Why is wind a problem? In persistent winds, plants have to close their leaf pores (called stomata) to reduce water loss. This limits their ability to breathe, slows their growth and reduces yields. Strong winds also cause physical damage, snapping stems and ripping leaves. It's heartbreaking to watch lovingly raised tomato plants being ripped to shreds in a storm.

There are several ways to reduce the effect of wind. These include windbreaks, cloches and mini greenhouses to shelter plants. Ensuring plants are securely tied in and well watered also helps. As a last resort, it's also possible to choose plants that cope better with wind – or even to bring them inside in a storm.

Observe the wind

First, observe the wind, working out what direction it normally comes from and how it

My northwest-facing London balcony was exposed to cold northeasterly winds early in the year. Baby courgettes and runner beans hated it. Rigging up a temporary windbreak like this helped the young plants get established.

varies during the year. This will help you work out the best way to reduce it. If the wind normally comes from one direction, a windbreak on one side may solve the problem. Since buildings can funnel and bounce winds, every space is different and it may take a year or two to learn how it varies.

Try to learn about the seasonal pattern of prevailing winds in your area. For example, across much of the UK, cold, dry and persistent northeasterly winds through much of the winter and spring are followed by warmer, wetter and more blustery southwesterly winds from early summer to autumn. Plants particularly dislike the dry, persistent north-easterlies and usually need more protection from them.

Windbreaks and shelters

A windbreak can change a marginal growing space, such as an exposed rooftop, into an excellent one. To be effective, windbreaks need to be 40–50 per cent permeable. Solid barriers create turbulence on the 'sheltered' side, making them less effective.

There are a variety of ways to construct a windbreak. Horticultural suppliers sell windbreak material (used by farmers on exposed fields) or you can improvise with permeable materials like scaffold netting or hessian bags. Woven rush, bamboo or willow panels are attractive options. Secure windbreaks to walls, posts or railings using string or cable ties. Lack of attachment points is a common challenge, and a solution that works in some situations is to fix posts to hold the windbreak onto the sides of large containers or other heavy objects (posts can be screwed onto wooden containers).

Alternatively, plants can be used to make an attractive living windbreak. Good windbreak plants for containers include Jerusalem artichokes, the dog rose (*Rosa rugosa*), which has edible flowers and fruits,

sea buckthorn (*Hippophae rhamnoides*), with its edible berries, bamboo, willow (*Salix*) and holly (*Ilex*), if you have the space.

Cloches, fleece and mini greenhouses

A cover or 'cloche' (like a plastic water cooler bottle) provides an effective wind shelter for smaller plants, which is particularly useful while they become established. Hoops for temporary cloches can be made out of plumber's tubing and covered with clear plastic sheeting or fleece. Alternatively, horticultural fleece, anchored loosely over a container and laid over the top of plants, will give some protection from the wind. Another option is to buy or make a mini greenhouse for starting plants early in the season – just make sure that it can't be blown away!

Tying in plants

Tie climbing and tall plants to sticks or frames to support them and to reduce the damaging effect of wind. Keep an eye on the forecast and double check everything is tied in well if strong winds are on the way.

Select more wind-resilient plants

Plants that do better in windy areas include kale, low-growing varieties like bush beans (instead of climbing beans) and some herbs, including parsley, rosemary, lavender, thyme and fennel. Plants that do less well in windy sites include warmth-loving plants like chillies and tomatoes and plants with big leaves such as courgettes, cucumbers and rhubarb.

Plant care

Plants that are kept well watered, well fed and healthy are stronger and better able to resist the wind. Feed them regularly with something like liquid seaweed and try to nurture soil life. Silicon is an element that can help plants produce stronger, thicker stems but is sometimes missing, so you may also want to experiment with a liquid silicon feed, which is available from horticultural suppliers.

Too little sun: shady spaces

Urban growing spaces are frequently overshadowed by tall buildings, walls or trees and often get less sun than is ideal for growing. As long as a space gets four hours of sun or more in mid-summer, it's usually possible to sustain a healthy, vibrant container garden, providing you choose the right plants (see *Chapter 4 Eight Steps to Success*, 'Step 1: Match the crops to how much sun your space has', page 36). But with less than four hours' sun – and certainly with less than two or three hours – it gets trickier. Even so, it's still often possible to create a rewarding edible garden with a little experimentation. When I first moved to Newcastle upon Tyne, I had a backyard that had no direct sun, but I still managed to grow a few herbs, salad leaves and microgreens.

To grow successfully in a less sunny space, plant selection is key. You can also try to identify which areas get the most sun and try to increase the light available. Plants that grow in low light levels are weaker and more prone to pests, and so need extra care.

Woodland fruits like raspberries are among the crops worth trying in less sunny places.

Fruit: Blackberries and blueberries, rhubarb, raspberries, gooseberries and redcurrants

Vegetables: Jerusalem artichokes, rocket, sorrel and kale

Herbs: Mint, wild garlic, parsley, coriander and wasabi

Microgreens: Most microgreens can be grown successfully; harvest young before they grow too tall and thin.

For spaces with even less than two hours' sun, try microgreens and herbs like wild garlic, mint and wasabi.

Plants for shady places

In less sunny spaces, look for plants that are better adapted to the shade, such as woodland plants that have evolved to prosper in dappled shade. Plants worth a try in two to three hours of sun include:

Look for the sunniest places

By observing a space carefully, it's often possible to find a few areas that get more sun. Often these are higher up and can be reached by using shelves, hanging baskets and ladders or by growing climbers.

Increase reflected light

In marginal light conditions, any extra light can make a difference. Use white paint or a white material to reflect light from walls or the floor (plants can use light reflected onto the underside of their leaves as well). Mirrors are another option, but use them with care: they can result in accidental bird deaths and scorched plants, and even start fires.

Too hot: suntraps, hot climates and heatwaves

Heat is a common challenge in tropical countries, but even in cooler climates, a sheltered and sunny concrete balcony or patio can be a heat trap. Large volumes of concrete in urban areas absorb and radiate heat. And, as our climate changes, more of us are experiencing extremes of heat, wherever we live.

While most edible crops benefit from plenty of sun, they don't grow well if it gets *too* hot. High temperatures adversely affect plants in several ways. They struggle to replace lost water, vital proteins are damaged, and photosynthesis is affected. This results in stress and slowed growth and can even kill the plant.

In hot conditions, pay particular attention to keeping plants well watered and healthy. In spaces that regularly get too hot, there are ways to create cooler microclimates. You can also choose plants better adapted to the heat and select containers that hold plenty of water.

In *Chapter 3 How to Design Your Container Garden*, 'Sun, wind and the "microclimate"', page 22, we looked at the importance of microclimate. The first step in managing heat in a space is to learn more about it. Look out for three different types of heat: direct heat from the sun, radiant heat that is reflected from surfaces like concrete or brick, and hot air, which can be the most damaging to plants. Try to observe:

▸ Patterns of sun and shade.
▸ How walls and concrete areas absorb heat in the sun and emit it later.
▸ How hot air flows through the space.

If heat is a major issue for you, borrowing or buying a cheap infrared temperature gun can be useful to help identify the coolest and hottest areas.

Extreme heat rarely poses a challenge in the cool North East of England, where I live. The tips here are mostly gleaned from experienced hot-climate growers I know, particularly Steve Willis in Australia. They will also be useful to anyone growing on a hot balcony or other hot space in a more temperate climate.

How to create cooler microclimates

When a growing space gets too hot, there are a few ways to cool it down, as outlined here.

Create shade
Special shade netting (or 'shade cloth') comes in various grades that reduce the sun's rays by anything from 20–80 per cent. Or you can improvise with something like a fine insect mesh (such as 'Enviromesh') or scaffold debris netting. If it's only needed occasionally, you can rig up temporary hoops in pots (plumber's piping works well here) to support the netting. Shade the plants on hot days and remove the cover at night and in cooler weather. Or fix up a more permanent frame over the patio or balcony to hold the netting.

Tall plants like fruit trees or climbers (for example, trellised beans, hops, grapes or hardy kiwi) can also be grown to create shade for more heat-sensitive plants such as lettuce and peas.

Elisabeth Spohr Canani, in Brazil, rigged up this netting to provide more shade for her rooftop veggies.

Use the cooling effect of water

A pond, basin pond or other water feature can be used to help moderate heat. Even saucers filled with water will make a difference. Or spray water with a hand pump onto shade netting or stone for a cooling effect.

Arrange plants and consider airflow

Moving objects around will change the microclimate – for example, by absorbing more sun or cutting it out completely. Try to arrange plants so that hot air can escape. Airflow can also be improved by using a solar-powered fan. Raising containers on small feet, away from direct contact with the concrete, will cut heat absorption considerably and create cooling airflow under the pot.

Use reflective containers and reservoirs

Avoid dark-coloured containers that absorb heat, particularly black (paint existing containers in a reflective colour if needed). Containers with water reservoirs will provide a more consistent and reliable source of water (cover the overflow and intake with mesh if mosquitoes are a problem).

Crops for hot spaces

Temperate crops like peas and leafy crops such as lettuce do not tolerate heat so well. Better choices for salad crops are Malabar spinach, New Zealand spinach, summer purslane, and amaranth. Other leafy crops that grow well in warmer spaces are 'Cavolo Nero' kale, chard and 'Giant of Italy' parsley.

In hot regions, look for varieties that are well adapted to local conditions. Local seed merchants who save their own seed are a good place to start and will usually be able to offer helpful advice. Saving your own seed and swapping seeds locally is another way to get varieties adapted to local conditions.

Managing in a heatwave

As our weather changes, we all need to be prepared for occasional heatwaves, wherever we live. In heatwaves, plants have less chance to adapt to hot conditions.

The steps outlined previously will also all help in heatwaves. In particular, keep plants well watered, put a few plates filled with water around your containers to evaporate heat, and move plants to a shadier space, if possible. Rig up some improvised shade netting if it looks as if plants need it.

After a heatwave, plants will often be stressed. Help them recover by feeding with liquid seaweed. Avoid removing any scorched or damaged leaves until after temperatures have returned to normal.

Eating the harvests

Part of the magic of homegrown ingredients is that they can make simple cooking taste delicious. You don't have to be a keen cook or follow complicated recipes to eat great food.

However, if you've never had a constant supply of herbs, cooked with chard or managed a glut of runner beans, it can be hard to know what to do with them all.

Here are a few simple ways to create delicious meals using common homegrown ingredients.

Seven easy ways to use herbs

Herbs grown in containers at home might have more potential to transform your food than anything else. With a few well-established pots, you'll be able to eat herbs with almost every meal. If you're not sure how to use them, these quick and easy ideas will help transform simple food into gourmet dishes.

Sprinkled in salads

Salads can taste amazing with a few herbs. It's so easy just to sprinkle in a few herbs and we rarely eat a salad without them. Lots of herbs work well. The best include oregano, mint, parsley, chives, garlic chives, basil, tarragon, chervil, dill, fennel, lovage (in small quantities), sorrel and, for spicy salads, Vietnamese coriander. Add one herb or try different combinations. Add a small sprinkling or, if you have enough, large handfuls. It's fun to experiment. Herbs can also be crushed in a pestle and mortar to flavour salad dressings.

In soups

Herbs can lift simple soups to another level. Scots lovage, thyme, sage and bay are brilliant for giving depth of flavour (add at the beginning with onion and garlic), while basil, coriander, chives, chervil and parsley make pretty and tasty garnishes. Since starting to grow herbs, we now have soup flavoured with fresh herbs for lunch nearly every day. It tastes delicious and is a great way to eat more veg.

With eggs

This is another example of how herbs can transform something simple into a restaurant-quality dish. Simply sprinkle sorrel, chives, parsley, dill, chervil or tarragon – or a mix of two or three of these – into an omelette. Or try 'oeufs en cocotte' – eggs baked in ramekins in the oven with any of these and a little butter or olive oil. Yum.

With grains

Rice, quinoa, bulgar wheat and other grains become a tasty snack or meal with the addition of herbs such as dill, mint, coriander and parsley and a good salad dressing. Simply chop them up and add whole handfuls if you have them.

Pestos

The classic pesto is basil and pine nuts, but pestos can also be made using many other combinations of herbs and nuts. You can use pesto on pasta, potatoes and roasted vegetables, as a garnish on soups, or on fish and meat dishes. The basic pesto recipe is herbs, nuts, oil and garlic, to which other ingredients like cheese or chilli can be added. Pestos will keep for several days at least in the fridge and are a useful way to use any herb gluts. Good combinations include mint and almonds, coriander and cashew nuts, parsley and walnuts, and nasturtiums and pumpkin seeds. You'll find many more pesto recipes online.

Cocktails

Mint, rosemary, basil, coriander and lavender can be used to create vibrant cocktails, both non-alcoholic and alcoholic, including the classic mojito. Perfect for a summer's evening on your balcony or roof terrace. A popular one in our household is cucumber and lime with ginger, homegrown mint and a little sugar or honey, all whizzed up in a blender.

Teas

Instead of reaching for another herbal teabag, why not pick a few fresh herb leaves from a window box? They taste excellent, look far prettier and save money and waste. Herbs that are good for tea include lemon verbena, mint (try chocolate mint or Moroccan mint), lemon balm, camomile and blackcurrant sage.

Salads

There is so much potential with homegrown salad, but simple, easy salad recipes are often overlooked by recipe books (perhaps because most people don't have fresh leaves growing on their doorstep). Here are some ideas to experiment with:

▶ Grow a wide variety of leaves (seed packs with mixed salad leaves are a good way to try this) and some microgreens to find those you love.

Some herbs from my containers that we enjoy in salad: oregano, purple basil, tarragon, fennel, chives, parsley and mint. Any of these will add lovely shards of flavour.

Lemon verbena makes one of the best herbal teas – you need just a few leaves for a cupful.

A variety of homegrown leaves, herbs and edible flowers make it easy to create pretty salads bursting with flavour.

- To eke out harvests, focus on growing flavour and buying lettuces for bulk. For example, just a few homegrown pea shoots and mint leaves will transform a simple shop-bought lettuce into a tasty salad.
- Grow lots of soft herbs, as they are wonderful in salads – see 'Seven easy ways to use herbs', page 244.
- Grow some edible flowers to add colour and flavour. My favourites include nasturtium, chives (break up the flowers), viola, pot marigold petals, rocket and society garlic.
- Grow your own bean sprouts to supplement the green leaves. These are useful for bulking up salads in winter when growth outside is slow.

To keep salads interesting and maximise their flavour, try adding one or more of the following ingredients:

A little finely sliced red onion, shallot or spring onion
Seeds or nuts for a crunchy texture and flavour – for example, toasted sesame, pumpkin or sunflower seeds or chopped almonds, hazelnuts or walnuts
Crushed garlic, garlic chives or society garlic flowers
Finely chopped chilli
Dried fruit like barberries or sour cherries (lovely, sweet-sour flavour)

Salad dressings

When the first new salad leaves are picked each spring, it's hard to beat a squeeze of fresh lemon, a dash of olive oil and a sprinkling of salt as a dressing. However, learning to make a few different dressings can enhance your enjoyment of salad through the year.

This is a wonderful recipe from Anna Hedworth at Newcastle's Cook House, and it is very popular in our home: mix 3 tablespoons of white wine vinegar, 2 teaspoons of Dijon mustard, 2 tablespoons of maple syrup, 100ml (3½fl oz) of olive oil and a pinch of salt. Very moreish and delicious.

For a more Asian flavour, we love this sesame oil dressing. It goes well with almost any salad but particularly shredded kale, cabbage, grated carrot or mixed mustards: 2 tablespoons of soy sauce, 2 tablespoons of rice wine vinegar (or substitute white wine vinegar or lime juice), 2 tablespoons of toasted sesame oil, 2 tablespoons of sunflower oil and 1 teaspoon of sugar or honey. For more depth of flavour, add a teaspoon of miso paste, too.

Another staple dressing recipe we enjoy is: 2 tablespoons of lemon juice, 4 tablespoons of rapeseed oil, ½ teaspoon of Dijon mustard, ½ garlic clove (crushed) and 1 teaspoon of honey.

For a lemony kick, this dressing with sumac is wonderful with rocket, mustard or other green leaves. Finely chop half an onion or a shallot and marinate it in the dressing for an hour, if time permits: 1 teaspoon of ground sumac, 2 tablespoons of olive oil, 1 tablespoon of sherry vinegar and 1 teaspoon of sugar. Add the salad leaves just before serving.

As they have so much flavour, home-grown leaves can also be enjoyed without any dressing at all. Do try it.

Soups

It's not uncommon to harvest bits and pieces that are too small to do much with, but I often add these to mixed veg soups.

Miso soup with fresh vegetables is a quick, easy and tasty soup option. Simply boil up a mix of vegetables in water – for example, potato, carrot, spring onions and kale, adding those that take longest to cook first. When just cooked (ideally still slightly firm to bite), remove from the heat and stir in some miso soup paste from a jar or sachet. That's it – ready to eat.

Preserving and storing a surplus

Even a small space can sometimes produce a surplus of herbs, tomatoes, chillies or runner beans. These can easily be preserved to enjoy at other times of the year.

Herbs

Herbs are easy to dry: simply tie in a bunch, hang in a dry place for a couple of weeks and then store in an airtight glass jar. Use in cooking or to make tea.

Alternatively, mix chopped herbs with olive oil and freeze in cubes to use whenever you need them. Or make them into a herb pesto that will keep for a week or two in the fridge.

Tomatoes

Green tomatoes will keep and ripen in a drawer for several weeks, sometimes even into January. Keep checking them and remove any that are going bad. When we get a surplus of tomatoes, I make a large pot of tomato sauce, divide it into portions and freeze it. Homegrown tomato sauce in mid-winter always feels like a treat and reminds me of summer.

Make pickles

Useful for green tomatoes, chillies and gluts of runner beans. Piccalilli is a good one for using a mix of surplus ingredients – for example, nasturtium seeds, courgettes and runner beans.

Homemade piccalilli makes good use of runner beans, nasturtium seeds and green tomatoes, among other things.

Build up your recipe repertoire

Start to collect recipes that make the best of your new homegrown ingredients. I have a book where I keep a list of my favourite recipes for each vegetable we grow and I refer to it whenever I need inspiration for what to do with a surplus of courgettes or beans.

Online recipes are an amazing resource for discovering new ways to use your home-grown veg. I'll often search for things like 'Asian cucumber salad' or 'courgette curry'.

Growing in rented or temporary accommodation

Containers can offer a great way to benefit from growing in rented and short-term accommodation, but this sometimes comes with added challenges.

Temporary and short-term gardens

Living in a home for a limited or uncertain amount of time can make it harder to invest time and money in lots of pots. However, small container gardens are still worthwhile. Even just a few herbs will add greenery, attract pollinating insects and provide delicious fresh leaves on a regular basis. Add a couple of cherry tomatoes, a few trays of microgreens, a chilli plant, a container of strawberries and a pot of runner beans and you'll have a nice variety in just a dozen or so pots. It's also possible to create a larger container garden at low cost as we've seen, but don't underestimate the work involved in dismantling one on moving.

Favourite plants can also come with you when you move. My apple, rhubarb, lemon verbena and bay tree have moved with me at least three times. Choose lightweight pots or pots with carry handles.

For very short-term gardens, growing microgreens in seed trays or potting up supermarket herbs in larger pots are good options. They are cheap to set up and produce quick results. They will still give growing pleasure and a good supply of tasty leaves.

Rules, restrictions and landlords

The rules around growing in rented accommodation vary hugely, as do landlords in how approachable, amenable and flexible they are. Sadly, rental properties sometimes have rules and restrictions around growing and some landlords even ban plants in pots completely.

When negotiating, try to understand their concerns (the mess of growing or water damage are common ones) and think of ways to reassure them. Plants in pots, if looked after, can actually improve the look of a home. Enlightened landlords will see this. I had one landlord who, after discovering my blog, made an unsolicited visit to tell me I could do whatever I wanted growing-wise at the property. Unfortunately, I don't expect all landlords are as friendly and amenable as this.

Rental agreements commonly don't allow drilling into walls. However, shelves can be freestanding and growing ladders can simply lean against a wall, held in place by the weight of the pots. Other tenancy agreements require that drilled holes are made good at the end of the tenancy. This does not have to be difficult – filler can be painted over or mixed with a scraping of brick dust to match the wall.

Growing in rented property is easier if the landlord has few causes for complaint. A tidy, attractive container garden will usually garner less attention than a messy or potentially dangerous one. Try to keep neighbours onside, too. Complaints from neighbours – for example, about dirty-water drips – might compel landlords to ask for the garden's removal.

Theft and vandalism

A common concern is that food and plant pots will be stolen, particularly from growing spaces easily accessible to passers-by. Some people are understandably put off growing because of this.

It's sadly true that theft and vandalism do happen. But, in my experience, occurrences are less frequent than often imagined. More commonly, people are surprised by the positive response their growing gets from the community. It's usually worth giving it a go with an open mind and you may be pleasantly surprised.

If theft does prove a problem, a few things can help reduce the risk. Using recycled pots like old tins makes them less desirable. Larger pots are heavier and more difficult to shift. And it's wise to put highly tempting crops like strawberries out of sight and reach if possible.

Anecdotally, the risk of theft also seems to reduce as more people in an area start to grow. Anything you can do to encourage others on your street or housing block to grow will help. A community of growers can also offer support if someone has a problem. When someone reports a plant theft on our local growing Facebook page in Newcastle upon Tyne, they get sympathy and support – and often receive replacement plants as gifts in a few days.

Food growing in public spaces is also a bit like an informal neighbourhood watch. The more of us who spend time on the street growing, the more eyes there are on what is going on.

Keeping tidy and organised (gardening with less mess)

It's often glossed over that growing in a flat or other small space can be a messy business. But there's no hiding from the fact that soil and carpets don't mix.

Keeping tidy and organised can be an ongoing challenge for you and those who live with you. The living-room table might double up as a potting bench, the window-sills as seedling nurseries and a kitchen cupboard as the toolshed.

There is no right or wrong level of tidiness, just what you're comfortable with. But, if you're looking for ways to keep tidier, here are some ideas.

Sowing, planting and raising seedlings inside

When filling pots, compost can easily escape over the sides onto the kitchen table, patio or a favourite carpet. A plastic sheet, tray, old washing-up bowl or dedicated potting tray will help catch the soil, and help when clearing up.

Some composts are cleaner and nicer to work with indoors than others. Coir (coconut fibre) smells nice and is easier to clean up than green or soil-based composts. Composted wood composts can be nice to work with, too. Coir Jiffy plugs (widely available online) are a neat, tidy solution for the indoor sowing of tomatoes and chillies.

Many of us find that in late spring, our homes become overrun with pots of seedlings that drip water and spill compost. Keeping the pots on plastic trays helps to catch water drips and soil spills, and makes it quicker and easier to move multiple pots around for hardening off.

Arranging pots and keeping the growing space tidy

Pots tend to multiply and can be hard to arrange neatly as they do. 'I find that pots spread out all over the patio and make it look untidy. My solution is to group them on shelves or other structures (usually home-made) like growing ladders or even bread crates,' explained Thérèse Jaifar, a longtime member of the Vertical Veg community. Old pallets are also useful in larger spaces for grouping plants together.

In early summer, crops like potatoes and courgettes can grow large and sprawl. Trim back some of their leaves, so they don't overshadow other plants too much. Removing older, dying leaves from plants like chard and kale reduces the spread of disease and looks better. Sprawling crops like potatoes can also be kept compact by boxing them in with string tied to canes in each corner of the pot.

Storage

In small growing spaces, finding a place to tidy away tools, seeds, bottles of fertiliser and bags of compost can be tricky.

Canes and sticks, which are prone to falling over and getting in the way, can be kept tidily and securely in a length of old plastic drainpipe or tubing (often found in skips). Seed collections (which are prone to growing out of control – be warned!) can be stored in boxes with dividers to keep them organised. Transparent plastic storage boxes can be useful for fertiliser, string and other bits and pieces, and then tucked under beds or on top of wardrobes.

Another solution is to keep your gardening equipment to a minimum. Most gardening jobs can be done with just your hands or existing kitchen tools like scissors (see 'The cost of growing', page 227). Try to avoid getting specialist tools unless you really need them.

In small spaces, it's always worth looking for solutions that fulfil more than one function. For example, a wooden box can be used as a balcony bench as well as useful storage. Growing ladders will increase growing space as well as provide useful storage behind them. Sometimes it's also possible to create new storage space under shelves, as we saw in *Chapter 3 How to Design Your Container Garden*, 'What about storage space?', page 25.

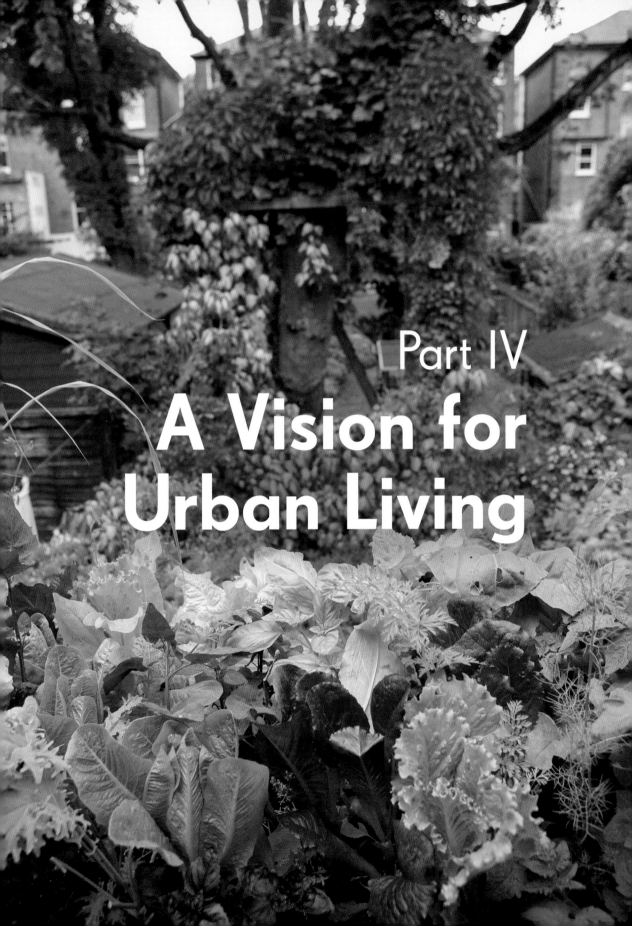

Part IV
A Vision for Urban Living

Chapter 12

More Reasons to Grow at Home

– for better eating, better lives and better cities

There are few better reasons to grow than for simple joy and fulfilment. It's hard to tire of the magic of watching seeds emerge, the smell of freshly picked mint or the excitement of plucking the first home-grown tomatoes of the year.

But there are also other, wide-ranging benefits of growing food at home in containers. Each of us has different motivations and interests, but whether you are inspired to eat more healthily, to support wildlife, to meet more people in your neighbourhood, to create beauty, to recycle more, to save money, to get more politically active or simply to eat more delicious food, I hope you will find practical ideas to help you get even more out of your growing over the following pages.

Grow for community (and friends)

Community growing projects are well documented and championed for their ability to bring people together. Growing on your own at home is less obviously community orientated, but nonetheless the community benefits are significant.

I don't want to overlook the fact that some of us, including myself occasionally, grow for solitude and use it as a time for quiet reflection. But growing at home can offer meaningful, joyful opportunities to connect with others of all ages and from all backgrounds in the local area. Here are some ways this can happen.

Grow in a publicly visible space

A front yard, or any space where passers-by can see you gardening, is a recipe for spontaneous conversations and meetings.

The street where I lived in London wasn't unfriendly. But people living there had busy lives, passing each other fleetingly as they moved in and out over the threshold of their homes. After ten years in the same flat, I had only met and chatted to my downstairs neighbours and the tenants next door. That all changed when I started growing. While I was watering and tending plants outside the front door, people stopped to talk. Not only did the vegetables and fruit arouse curiosity, but I was also more visible outside my home – and my activities provided openings for conversation. The builders working next door visited every day to inspect how much the squash had grown and my neighbours introduced themselves and told us how to cook the squash leaves – which I didn't even know were edible. Other people stopped to ask for growing advice and some, I learned, even made a regular detour in their route just to walk past our vegetables. It helped me to feel part of the wider community in which I lived for the first time.

My story is far from unique. Many others who grow have similar experiences. Here, in Newcastle upon Tyne, I've been involved in a

This squash plant aroused a lot of interest – and many people expressed surprise that no one had stolen it.

project supporting people to grow food at the front of their home. We regularly hear how growing helps people to meet and chat to their neighbours. Now, I sometimes joke that the three best ways to meet new people in a city are to have a baby, get a dog or grow plants at the front of your home.

Any food growing will pique the curiosity of passers-by, even just a pot of tomatoes, but you can also have fun nurturing this interest by growing eye-catching or exotic crops like purple peas or purple beans, phallic-looking tromba squash (or indeed any large squash), or alien-looking achocha. Large, visible plant labels can provide information to those curious about what you are growing, but too shy to ask. I've also seen pots decorated with signs sharing philosophical thoughts, political statements, vegetable jokes or puns as well as container gardens incorporating statues, sculptures and structures, from elegant abstract shapes woven out of willow to Darth Vader scarecrows. All acknowledge and welcome the engagement of those passing by.

Join seed, plant and food swaps

Edible gardening is generous in the opportunities it offers to bring family, friends and the wider community together to swap and share throughout the year: seeds in early spring, plants in late spring, produce in summer and autumn, and gardening advice and recipes all year round.

At its simplest, it's rewarding to share homegrown food with friends, even if this is just a small detail like homegrown mint in tea or cocktails or pea shoots in a salad. After I helped Hannah set up her first container garden on her London balcony, she was bursting with excitement to have friends round for supper to share her first harvests. Surplus pickings – a bag of fresh salad with edible flowers, a bouquet of herbs or a string of heritage chillies – also make a lovely present for friends or neighbours. Anything homegrown, particularly in the heart of the city, is special and warmly appreciated.

Local seed swaps are an enjoyable way to acquire new seeds and to get caught up in

Allan Rowell, in Sunderland, Tyne and Wear, puts up signs so passers-by can see what he's growing.

After first starting in Darja's small flat, *Zelemenjava* is now a national plant, seed and produce-swapping initiative, with events taking place in cities across Slovenia.

balcony in Slovenia, she found that her small flat was overflowing with seedlings, so she invited friends round to swap them. It was so successful, and so many people wanted to come, that she organised the next one in a larger venue. From this small beginning, the event grew and now takes place in cities across Slovenia, three times a year. People who do not have surplus seeds or plants can bring something else to swap, like home bakes or surplus cookery books. The only rule is that money can't change hands. There is a guide on how to organise a swap, written by Darja Fišer, on the Vertical Veg website and a link to more information on their *Zelemenjava* (Slovenian for greening) website.

Acts of kindness

Acts of kindness can change how people feel about their community and, as Klaus says in Sergio Pablos's film of the same name: 'A true act of selflessness always sparks another.'

A simple and easy idea that always goes down well is to put a sign in a pot or two inviting people to help themselves or to put out ready harvested bags or bunches. I often put out mint or apples – and sometimes we get thank you cards through the door in return.

It's possible to take this up a level. As a fun, engaging community event, Andy Jones in Newcastle upon Tyne volunteered to organise what he called 'Random Acts of Gardening Kindness'. After choosing a street at random, a few of us knocked on doors, offering free plants. Even though we were complete strangers, the overwhelming response was warm and enthusiastic. We all enjoyed meeting and chatting to families and talking about plants as we potted them up together on the doorstep. It wasn't difficult to organise: enthusiastic growers often have surplus pots and plants, so we collected these up, bought a few bags of compost and borrowed a wheelbarrow to carry everything in.

the buzz of spring. As you collect your seeds you can chat to other growers and pick up local growing advice. Look for seed swaps in your local area and bear in mind that often you don't need any seeds to swap yourself to join in. If you can't find one, you could organise your own swap among friends, at work or at a local community venue, just as Darja Fišer did (see her story, that follows).

Local plant swaps or community plant sales in late spring are an institution in many places and offer the chance to pick up herb, tomato and other vegetable plants. Perfect if you haven't had time to sow seeds yourself or if any of yours have failed to germinate. You can also mingle with other growers and usually there is a stall for a cup of tea and a piece of cake. Not all plant swaps are well advertised, so a bit of detective work may be needed to find one.

Darja Fišer's story of plant swapping is inspiring. In her first year of growing on her

Inspire and Support Others to Grow

If the growing bug catches you, there are many ways to share your enthusiasm with others. This can be anything from helping friends and neighbours informally to more organised buddy schemes, running simple stalls at community events or helping to deliver community planting sessions or workshops. You don't need a lot of growing experience yourself. Simple advice like what kind of compost or size of pots to use, and how much sun different crops need, can help beginners a lot. Enthusiasm goes a long way and teaching is a good way to learn yourself.

An easy and enjoyable way to engage others is to take a table at a neighbour-hood fair, fete or local school. Choose a simple growing activity for the stall: sowing pea shoots in yoghurt pots is a popular one or planting up supermarket herbs in larger pots. Most people love getting their hands into compost. You might also bring photos of your urban garden to show what is possible in the area, as well as plants in containers or trays of pea shoots or other microgreens for people to taste.

A planting session on your street or in your block of flats is a good way to bring people together and to share experience. In Newcastle upon Tyne, on the streets in the Wingrove area, we have seasonal planting sessions run by a community group and open to all. At these sessions, we introduce ourselves, then do a planting demonstration, followed by questions and knowledge sharing, and then everyone pots up their own plant to take home. To reduce costs, we use recycled pots and many of the plants we give away are grown by volunteers – and we ask for donations from participants to help us buy compost.

Workshops are a good excuse to bring people in the neighbourhood together. I've delivered workshops in blocks of flats where people started swapping plants and doing each other's holiday watering as well as sharing experiences of growing on their balconies. I've also run workshops through a local community organisation in London, each one hosted by a different person in their flat. This was a relaxed and informal way to meet others and to learn by seeing each other's growing.

A street workshop organised by Greening Wingrove and Vertical Veg in Newcastle upon Tyne. Holding a workshop directly on the street makes it easier for more people to join in and creates a space where they can make new connections.

Loneliness, isolation and segregation

These are major issues in many modern cities, but growing at home in the city has great potential to bring more of us together. Food is central to all our lives and growing can appeal across every culture and generation. Almost everyone will have a useful experience and knowledge to share, either of growing or cooking plants. Learning about different cuisines (and eating together) can also be a pleasurable way to bring different communities together.

Urban food-growing projects, whether in allotments, community gardens or supporting people to grow at home, give a wide range of people the opportunity to get together, reduce isolation, and strengthen local communities.

Grow for health

We all know that we should probably eat more fresh fruit and veg, but good-quality, organic produce is often expensive. Many of us struggle to find time to go food shopping more than once a week and locally grown fresh produce is often hard to find. What better alternative than to grow some veg and fruit at home? This will give you a regular supply of fresh, affordable and nutritious vegetables and fruit whenever you want it. With just a little outdoor space, it's possible to eat some homegrown food every day for most of the year. Not only will you know exactly what has gone into it (such as no pesticides), growing your own at home can also contribute to a better diet in several ways.

Grow highly nutritious crops

While any fresh fruit or veg is of benefit, many of the crops best suited to small spaces, such as salads, herbs and soft fruit, are also high in the minerals and trace elements needed for a healthy diet. Here are some that are particularly high in vitamins, minerals or fibre and which also grow well in containers:

Blueberries, blackberries and raspberries are full of Vitamin C and other antioxidants, and good sources of fibre.

Chard is very rich in minerals (including magnesium, iron, manganese and copper), Vitamins K, A and C, and also antioxidants.

Jerusalem artichokes are high in iron and potassium, one of the best sources of dietary fibre and an excellent 'prebiotic' (good for the beneficial microbes in your gut).

Kale is high in minerals, fibre, antioxidants and Vitamins C and K, as well as lutein (which is important for eye health).

Microgreens – peashoots are a good source of Vitamins A and C and protein. Most other microgreens, like broccoli and sunflower, are highly nutritious, too.

Eat more fruit and veg

Studies show that people who grow veg tend to eat more veg – it's easier to eat more fruit and veg if it is readily available, affordable and tastes delicious. Speaking from personal experience, my average fruit and veg consumption has roughly doubled from three or four portions to six or eight a day since I started growing at home in 2009. Fresh herbs, delicious salad leaves and berries on the doorstep have made this change easy.

New research is finding that the smell and feel of vegetables and fruit is also an important influence on what we eat. In the modern supermarket, most vegetables are either wrapped in plastic or processed and sealed in tins. We cannot touch or feel the furriness of broad bean pods, the soft bristles of courgettes or the waxy squeakiness of pea

Berries grow well in containers and are rich in Vitamin C and antioxidants. Here's a bowl of blueberries, blackberries and purple raspberries picked from my front yard in July.

With leaves growing on the doorstep, we eat fresh salad nearly every day. This salad is full of winter leaves, picked in mid-January.

More Reasons to Grow at Home | 259

pods. Nor do we get to smell the earth when digging up potatoes, the tomato leaves when picking tomatoes or the scent of herbs as we brush past them. All this makes food a more rounded, sensory experience when we grow it ourselves – and a more alluring and exciting prospect that can subtly nudge us towards healthier eating.

Eat a more diverse diet

Most nutritionists agree that eating a diverse variety of fruit and vegetables is a good thing and there is no shortage of edible plants on earth. Plants for the Future, an organisation compiling a database of edible plants, suggests there are over 20,000. Our hunter-gatherer

New Zealand spinach is one of the many leaves we grow that isn't widely available in shops. It's easy to grow and tastes good both cooked and in salads.

ancestors ate far more broadly than we do. But modern supermarkets stock only a tiny fraction of these edible plants and just 20 plants account for 90 per cent of what we eat, according to Plants for the Future.

As home growers, however, we have the seeds of hundreds, even thousands, of unusual and exotic varieties just a mouse click away. There are hundreds of different salad leaves alone. At home, I grow 20–30 types of leaves each year, including sorrel, New Zealand spinach, orach, land cress, tatsoi, winter and summer purslane, sun-flower shoots, nasturtium and mustards as well as other leaves that never make it to the supermarket shelves.

Edible flowers are almost impossible to buy, but they are rich in phytonutrients – including antioxidants, antibacterials and antivirals – which have wide-ranging health benefits. Edible flowers that are easy to grow in containers include nasturtiums, calen-dula, violas and most herb flowers like chives and rosemary.

Home growers also have access to numerous heritage varieties of chillies, tomatoes, French beans, kale and squash that never appear in the shops and which often taste better than commercial varieties. There are also unusual vegetables, fruits and herbs, like achocha, Chilean guavas and lovage, all described in this book, that you will probably only be able to eat if you grow them yourself. And home growers also get to eat things like radish, beetroot and turnip leaves that do not last long enough to make it into the shops as well as courgette flowers.

Eat fresher food

Rather than eating bags of wilting salad leaves picked several days ago, it's easy to enjoy homegrown leaves just minutes after picking if they are growing on your window-sill. Once picked, a plant starts to lose its

Nasturtiums, the queen of edible flowers, are almost impossible to buy.

nutritional value immediately. This is because it continues to use up nutrients but cannot replace them. Leafy greens lose nutrients particularly quickly. One recent study, published in the journal *Food Chemistry* in 2017, found that spinach leaves lost 35–86 per cent of their Vitamin C after ten days, even when refrigerated (nutrients are lost even faster in warmer temperatures).

Freshly picked leaves are also bursting with flavour, which usually indicates a high nutrient content.

Nutrient density

The nutritional quality or 'nutrient density' of crops depends on the quality of the soil they are grown in and whether plants have access to the full range of minerals they need. For example, spinach is theoretically high in iron, but the actual amount of iron it contains varies depending on how it is grown. Studies show that the nutritional quality of cereals and vegetables in the shops has been decreasing due to modern cultivars (chosen for yield and longevity rather than nutritional content), modern farming practices and eroding soils.

By growing at home, we can benefit nutritionally by eating fresher food and we can also try to grow more nutrient-dense food. We can do this by ensuring we meet all our plants' mineral and biological needs – for example, by applying good-quality worm compost and feeding with liquid seaweed and other good-quality natural feeds. If you have a keen interest in the nutritional value of the vegetables you grow, a simple tool called a refractometer (inexpensive but functional models are available on eBay) can be used to measure their Brix value. Brix gives a good approximation of their nutrient density and there are tables that enable you to compare the results.

At the time of writing, it is hard to find reliable studies on how to grow nutrient-dense food in containers. But, as we learn more about the importance of nutrition to our health and well-being, I hope there will be many more. It's a fascinating area for future research and experimentation.

Grow to reduce the grocery bill

Growing your own food can work out either more or less expensive than the shops, depending on what you grow and how you grow it. But as a general rule, good-quality, fresh, 'organic' ingredients can be grown at a fraction of the price of similar quality produce in the shops. This is particularly true of perishable items such as soft fruit, salads and herbs. On the other hand, it is harder (although not impossible) to grow staple veg like carrots and potatoes for less than budget supermarket prices.

The costs of building and running a container garden vary hugely. I estimate that my growing, roughly, costs me about 20 per cent of the value of the produce I grow, depending on the year – not including my time.

Which crops save the most money?

The crops that save the most money will vary, depending on what is available in the local shops (anything unusual is normally priced at a premium). Usually, the biggest savings can be made by growing the ingredients that will transform staple food into special meals – for example, the less-common herbs and salad leaves, microgreens, edible flowers, heritage tomatoes or unusual fruit or veg.

Chefs pay a lot of money for small bags of gourmet microgreens that can be grown at home for pennies. This is a tray of orach 'Scarlet Emperor' microgreens, grown from home-saved seeds.

Our rented backyard in Newcastle upon Tyne shortly after moving in was quiet, lifeless and a bit depressing.

However, once our backyard was filled with plants, sparrows came to collect greenfly for their young, blackbirds stole the tomato labels to add to their nest, and the hum of bees filled the air.

However, if growing a large volume of food is your main priority, you might make other choices – see *Chapter 7 How to Grow More Food in a Small Space*, 'High-yielding, high-value and fast-growing crops', page 137, for crops that will provide a large amount of food.

Grow for and with nature

One of the miracles of growing food in containers is that wherever you put plants, wildlife soon follows. This makes it possible to live in the middle of the city *and* have a bird and insect theatre to entertain you every day.

As well as providing entertainment, fulfilment and learning (for your family or flatmates), doing things to support wildlife can help protect these precious and vulnerable life forms. Even though our individual spaces are small, between us we can provide valuable refuges for insect and bird populations.

Last but not least, the chance to be with nature is important for our own well-being as more and more research is finding. Growing gives us the chance to be with nature at home in the middle of the city, every day.

Find time to observe and learn about the little creatures that visit and they can be as fascinating as those on any safari. Watch a cunning wasp hunting out caterpillars or a hoverfly larva sucking up aphids, like a miniature prehistoric monster. Or marvel at the phenomenal feats that some of them perform. A common balcony visitor, the marmalade hoverfly, at just 1cm (½in) long,

A marmalade hoverfly on a pot marigold on my London balcony. That this tiny insect can migrate thousands of miles is one of the wonders of nature.

migrates thousands of miles each year, all the way from the Mediterranean across the English Channel to the UK. Once you know this, it's hard to look at one without feeling awe and admiration.

Grow plants to support beneficial insects

Many fruit and vegetable plants also benefit insects. Apple, blackberry and other fruit blossom provides valuable nectar early in the season; peas and beans produce high-protein pollen which is important for bee health; and globe artichoke flowers are adored by bees, as are most herb flowers, most noticeably chives in early spring and sage, thyme and rosemary in summer. The following flowers will also attract and support insects:

Bird's-foot-trefoil (*Lotus corniculatus*): A small plant with yellow flowers native to the UK. Flowers from May to September. Not edible.

Borage (*Borago officinalis*): The pretty, blue flowers refill with nectar every few minutes, making them a magnet for bees. Flowers from June to October.

California poppy (*Eschscholzia californica*): No edible parts but the bright orange flowers provide a lovely splash of colour and are popular with bees, bumblebees, hoverflies and butterflies for their pollen. Flowers from June to September.

Coriander (*Coriandrum sativum*): Hoverflies and other insects love the white flowers of coriander, which is a good reason to leave the plant when it bolts and then pick and eat the green seeds – delicious! Flowers from June to July.

Fennel (*Foeniculum vulgare*) and dill (*Anethum graveolens*): Both tall, pretty plants with attractive, fern-like leaves and yellow flowers that are

Borage is a magnet for bees – the flowers are also edible and so pretty.

popular with hoverflies. Flowers from August to October.

Phacelia: Fast-growing with mauve flowers and popular with bees and other pollinators. Flowers from June to September. Not edible.

Poached-egg plant (*Limnanthes douglasii*): Small, low-growing plant, useful for planting around the base of larger plants to add a bit of colour. Flowers from May to August. Not edible.

Pot marigold (*Calendula officinalis*): Bright orange edible flowers that attract hoverflies and other insects. Flowers from May to October.

Birdbaths

Birdbaths provide valuable drinking water in dry summers and freezing winters as well as the local bird-washing facility. They need to be 3–10cm (1¼–4in) deep, with shallow, sloping sides and a rough surface, so that birds don't slip. Put birdbaths somewhere that cats can't ambush visiting birds and keep them clean and hygienic. My family derives huge pleasure from watching the antics of birds as they queue up and wash. And bees use the birdbath to drink, too.

Basin ponds

Filled with rainwater and suitable plants, basin ponds can breed small organisms such as common water fleas (*Daphnia*), which will support other wildlife, including water beetles and pond skaters. If a platform and shallow area is created at one end of the pond, bees and other insects will come down to drink. On patios and at ground level they can even attract frogs. All you need to make a basin pond is an old washing-up bowl or basin, some gravel for the bottom, some stones arranged to make it easy for small animals to climb in and out of the pond, enough rainwater (avoid tap water) to fill it and a few small aquatic plants like arrowhead (*Sagittaria sagittifolia*), frogbit (*Limnobium laevigatum*) or lesser spearwort (*Ranunculus flammula*).

Bee hotels

There is a shortage of nesting places for some solitary bee species, so bee 'hotels' potentially

Wasps are much maligned, but they play a vital role in nature and are the gardener's friend, pollinating flowers and hunting bugs and caterpillars.

provide valuable extra nesting space. Sadly, some designs do more harm than good, attracting parasites and birds that eat the larvae, making them more of a bee graveyard than a hotel. However, bee hotels that are well designed and carefully looked after *can* provide a useful and safe nesting space. Just be sure to research and design your bee home carefully.

Grow for knockout home cooking

For those who enjoy food and good home cooking, the quality and flavour of homegrown food can be a revelation. A container garden also makes it easier and cheaper to cook more ambitious recipes. For example, the genius chef, Yotam Ottolenghi (Prince of Flavour!) is famous for long lists of ingredients, often citing two, three or more fresh herbs in one recipe and hard-to-find and expensive ingredients like sorrel and chard. Most of these are easy to grow in containers. Once you can pick them at home, it's quicker and easier to cook these creative dishes any night of the week, rather than just for special occasions.

For those who like different cuisines, fresh ingredients are often hard to buy or expensive – but many are not difficult to grow. For example, my neighbours are always happy if I bring them a bunch of kailaan or shungiku (two greens popular in Taiwanese cooking) that are easy to grow in pots, but not widely available in the shops.

Plants for a food-lover's garden

Most vegetables and fruits taste better when they are homegrown, but for those who want to grow an outdoor larder full of fantastic and unusual flavours, here are some of the less common plants that I'd highly recommend growing alongside your favourite herbs and vegetables.

Herbs

Chervil: Makes a nice alternative to parsley and has an aniseed twist.

Green shiso perilla: A beautiful aromatic herb and essential ingredient for Vietnamese summer rolls.

Lemon verbena: For delicious herbal tea or to make a syrup for desserts and baking.

Scots lovage: Adds warmth and base flavour to stocks and soups or can be shredded finely and added sparingly to salads. Pretty, edible flowers.

Sorrel: Brilliant with eggs and goes well with fish or use to add a lemony tang to salads.

Tarragon: Strongly flavoured, this herb sings of spring and summer and goes well with eggs, fish, chicken, mayonnaise, mushrooms, salads and baby vegetables.

Vietnamese coriander: For an authentic Southeast Asian flavour in soups and salads (tastes completely different to common coriander).

Winter savory: Known as the pulse and bean herb. Easy to grow and pretty.

Edible flowers

These flowers all have a good taste as well as looking pretty:

> Chives – and most other herb flowers: lavender, rosemary, sage
> Yellow cosmos (*Cosmos sulphureus*)
> Courgettes
> Nasturtiums
> Pot marigolds
> Society garlic
> Violas

Leaves

Agretti/salsola: Succulent leaf that's quite similar to samphire. Adds texture to salads or you can lightly sauté in olive oil.

Chard: Productive in containers and you get two crops in one – stalks with a celery-like texture and spinach-like leaves.

A fistful of flavour: a handful of freshly picked herbs. When they are on your doorstep, you can have fresh herbs in every meal.

Yellow cosmos (*Cosmos sulphureus*), the only variety of cosmos known to be edible.

It's hard to beat a freshly picked, homegrown salad for flavour.

Mustards: There are many varieties, including 'Red Giant', 'Green in the Snow' and tatsoi.

Nasturtium: For leaves and seeds as well as flowers – pretty and tasty in salads and makes a nice pesto.

New Zealand spinach: This has a nice texture and slightly salty flavour.

Orach 'Purple Emperor': The beautiful, vivid magenta leaves have a mild but good flavour.

Summer purslane: Makes a nice succulent addition to salads.

Winter purslane: This is a pretty winter salad leaf with a good mild flavour.

Microgreens

Nearly all microgreens are delicious but hard or expensive to buy. For cooks in particular, micro herbs such as basil and coriander add bright shards of flavour. And salad microgreens like pea shoots, sunflower shoots and rocket can transform a few lettuce leaves into a gourmet salad.

Vegetables for flavour

Chillies: Choose the right variety and home-grown chillies have infinitely more flavour than supermarket chillies. Tasty varieties include 'Alberto's Locoto' and 'Aji Lemon' (both hot); 'Jalapeño' (medium); and 'Ancho' and 'Padron' (both mild).

French beans: There are many heritage varieties with pretty colours and excellent flavour, including 'Blauhilde' and Major Cook's climbing bean.

Tomatoes: Not unusual, but essential! There are so many excellent varieties – good ones for flavour include 'Black Cherry', 'Sungold', 'Gardener's Delight' and 'Sweet Aperitif'.

Fruits

Chilean guava: Tastes like a strawberry-blueberry cross, and was reputedly Queen Victoria's favourite fruit.

Japanese wineberry: This is similar in taste to raspberries, but has a sweeter flavour.

For some simple ideas on using home-grown food to make delicious dishes, see *Chapter 11 Solutions to Common Challenges*, 'Eating the harvests', page 244.

Grow for beauty and fragrance

Large swathes of bare concrete in cities can feel cold and bleak, sucking the life out of communities. Plants, on the other hand, add warmth and colour, soften the edges and change the feel of the place. Walk down two streets that are identical in all respects, except in one the residents have filled the bare concrete outside their doors with plants and you'll notice a stark difference. As well as adding beauty, plants help a street feel more cared for, welcoming and alive.

In the UK, the 'veg plot' is traditionally a functional, regimented space, separate from the 'ornamental garden' and often hidden behind a hedge or wall. But for many of us, our patio, balcony or front yard is the only outside space we have, so we often want it to be edible *and* beautiful. In France, there is a tradition of 'potager gardens', where both vegetables and flowers are grown together.

Garden designer Jennifer Lauruol helped me put the following ideas together to help you design a beautiful, potager-inspired container garden:

▸ Try fitting in one or two larger plants – like a blueberry or apple tree. This gives structure and focus to a container garden.

▸ Create different levels by raising plants with taller pots, pallets, tables, ladders, bricks or empty upturned boxes. Mix up pretty climbers like runner beans, squash and peas with trailers such as nasturtiums, short plants such as lettuce and chicory, and tall plants, including tree spinach, orach 'Scarlet Emperor', sunflowers and *Verbena bonariensis* (not edible but pretty).

▸ Use the same colour or style of pot to help create the look of a designed garden. Or paint a jumble of recycled containers the same colour or range of colours to unify the scheme.

▸ Mix in a rose or two – these help disguise vegetable gardens and give you edible flowers and hips (choose a fragrant variety for the best flavour).

▸ Hide less attractive pots behind a façade. For example, put plastic crates behind wooden planks.

▸ Grow evergreens like bay and rosemary and winter crops such as kale to add interest to your pots all year round.

▸ Add colour with edible flowers like nasturtiums, violas and pot marigolds or brightly coloured leaves like orach 'Scarlet Emperor' or tree spinach.

▸ Grow vegetables with pretty leaves, such as rainbow chard and 'Cavolo Nero' or 'Red Russian' kale, or frond-like leaves like bulbing fennel. Or try large, stately vegetables like globe artichokes.

Californian poppies, nasturtiums, cosmos, *Verbena bonariensis* and pot marigolds add colour when mixed in with vegetables and also attract pollinating insects. The plants in the foreground are growing in ugly plastic crates, hidden behind a painted facade made from recycled pallets.

Fragrance

Smell is one of our most important and evocative senses, but it's easy to overlook the contribution that fragrance can make to a container garden. The smell of tomato leaves is unique and oddly compelling and even the smell of healthy compost can be comforting and good for the soul. More conventionally, lavender is calming and restorative, while lemon verbena is uplifting and sings of summer.

There are many wonderfully scented plants that you can grow to help you relax, get creative or simply feel more alive. Some of the most aromatic plants with edible parts that are well suited to containers include roses, lavender, rosemary, mint, lemon verbena, scented pelargoniums, anise hyssop, juniper and camomile. Other plants that are not edible, but have beautiful fragrances, include sweet peas (*Lathyrus odoratus*), jasmine (*Jasminum*) and honeysuckle (*Lonicera*).

Grow for greener lives, greener cities and our future

As well as visibly greening the street and supporting wildlife, growing enables us to recycle our veg peelings and food scraps, to cut food waste by only picking what we need, to reduce food miles, cold storage and plastic packaging, and to recycle rainwater. When we grow, we can also start to nurture a greater connection to other life on earth, develop a deeper understanding of how everything is dependent on everything else, and look to nurture diversity. We might also choose to spend more time gardening instead of indulging in less sustainable pursuits.

Recycle food waste

Millions of tonnes of food go to landfill from households each year (6.6 million tonnes from

Scented pelargoniums come in a range of strong and exotic fragrances – try 'Attar of Roses' and 'Prince of Orange'.

the UK alone in 2018, according to the sustainability charity, WRAP). Wormeries enable us to recycle food waste in small spaces *and* convert it into brilliant fertiliser to grow more food. Making compost can also help shift attitudes to food waste. Speaking from personal experience, I used to scrape peelings and coffee grounds into the bin without a second thought, but a wormery helped me see them as precious organic resources.

Reduce food miles and plastic packaging

By growing, we can swap French beans grown thousands of miles away in Kenya for those on our doorstep. We can exchange plastic bags of salad and plastic punnets of tomatoes or strawberries for leaves and fruit without any packaging. We can also pick what we need as we need it – and put an end to sad, limp salad leaves and herbs wilting at the back of the fridge. In 2013, the large UK supermarket Tesco revealed that an estimated 60 per cent of the leaves in their salad bags went to waste.

Collect and recycle water

Instead of watering your plants with water that has been cleaned, processed and piped long distances, it makes sense to install a water butt if it is safe and possible to do so. As well as saving energy, collecting water reduces water runoff in the city. An unpublished study by Dr Claire Walsh, School of Engineering, at Newcastle University in 2015 showed that water butts, if installed by enough homes, could contribute to reducing urban flood risk by capturing the peak flows from heavy rainfall events.

Reconnect with life and earth

Since humans started migrating to cities, we have become increasingly distanced and

Fruit and veg peelings as well as coffee grounds can be recycled in wormeries in small spaces – smaller size wormeries are available!

separated from other life forms on earth, isolated in our homes and workplaces, cocooned in our cars, buses and trains. Precious animals have become categorised as 'pests', 'vermin' or 'game' and resilient wild plants as 'weeds'. This separation often prevents us from seeing the interconnections in life, how all life forms are dependent on each other and how every animal and plant species has an important role to play.

It's clear that a shift in our attitude to other life and natural resources is essential for our future. Growing food offers those of us who live in a city the opportunity to interact more closely with plants and other life forms. We can witness the miracle of life's diversity on our doorstep and use growing to learn about some of the complex interactions that we depend on.

Some indigenous cultures have long referred to our planet as 'Mother Earth', born from the instinctive understanding that we are totally dependent on earth for life. Yet today, in the West, many of us feel uncomfortable using language like this – and perhaps this is one reason why we treat the planet as we do. And yet language is critical. Words we all use, like 'pests' and 'weeds', have a big impact on how we feel and act towards these precious life forms. It's worth spending a bit of time thinking about the language you want to use – it might make more difference than anything else in this book.

Use growing as a source of fulfilment

Many of the choices we make in life, whether to buy more stuff, go on foreign holidays or move to a larger house, are ultimately about searching for fulfilment. For many people, growing is a profoundly fulfilling activity which may ultimately replace other less sustainable lifestyle choices. Perhaps the investment of time, care and attention required by growing offers an opportunity to access more productive, positive and deeply pleasurable experiences than most purchases can ever provide.

Support diversity in every form

Humans have done a good job at destroying habitats and diversity. The paradox is that we are also uniquely placed to use our knowledge and resources to nurture life and diversity, and to restore the earth to rude health – if we choose to.

At a farming level, this possibility is beginning to become reality through the 'agroecology' movement. Agroecology is farming that works with nature, where the aim is to use land to support diverse wildlife and grow food to eat.

In our own small spaces, we can replicate the ideas of agroecology on a small scale. We can grow a diverse variety of crops, support small-scale seed producers, avoid pesticides and do what we can to encourage and support other life. We can also use our growing to reach out and connect with other people in our area and help build a stronger local community.

Grow as a political act

Growing at home is a peaceful activity that nurtures life and nourishes the soul. For many people, it will always primarily be a rewarding and rejuvenating hobby. For others, it is also a channel for political expression and activism. Or as Frances Moore Lappé, author of *Diet for a Small Planet*, once wrote: 'Every aspect of our lives is, in a sense, a vote for the kind of *world* we want to live in.'

The modern food system has succeeded in giving us an abundance of food (for those who can afford it), but at a cost to our health, our communities and our planet. It's

By growing vegetables and flowers in pots at home we can take a step closer to nature in our daily lives.

madness that vegetables and fruits are imported thousands of miles in refrigerated trucks, ships and planes to a place where they grow perfectly well. Or that food manufacturers and supermarkets are allowed to use alluring marketing to sell low-quality, salt- and sugar-rich, processed foods that have exacerbated obesity, robbed many of basic cooking skills and knowledge, and impaired the health of millions at huge social and financial cost. It's shortsighted for governments to champion large-scale industrial farming with its monocultures, pesticides and inhumane treatment of animals above small-scale, mixed farming that supports more livelihoods, provides higher-quality food and nurtures diversity and life. And the unequal distribution of land is simply unjust: in England, over half the land is owned by less than 1 per cent of the population, according to research by Guy Shrubsole – with the consequence that a

small number of powerful people have a vested interest in maintaining the status quo, and that it's harder for those who want to start small farms to acquire the land they need. People in the future – if there are any of us left – will wonder why on earth we allowed the perpetuation of such a wasteful and self-destructive set of systems.

Whatever your views, and whether you agree with some or any of this or not, there is no escaping the fact that food and food growing is deeply political. Even in the wealthiest countries, swathes of people live in 'food deserts', without easy access to fresh fruit and vegetables. How well each person eats is ultimately dependent on income and postcode. But shouldn't fresh, good-quality food be a basic human right, like water and shelter?

My family and I are lucky enough to live a very privileged existence; we never go short of food and we can more or less eat what we want. I am often guilty of taking this privilege for granted, and not acting on and fighting against the injustices – to nature, the earth and to people – that underpin our food system. I know that I can and should do more. I offer the following ideas as much for myself as for any reader who feels inspired to grow for political reasons.

While the problems created by our industrial food system are complex and difficult to unravel, growing at home offers us the chance to take practical action, to feel more empowered and to better understand the issues so that we can campaign more effectively for change. The more enlightened and engaged with these issues we are, the more difference we can make. Here are some of the ways we can do that:

Become less dependent on consumer culture

Lots of people are discovering that swapping and sharing in the community is a more rewarding way to grow –and live – than going shopping. During the first months of the Covid pandemic in 2020, a whole new culture of community sharing sprang up. Where I live in Newcastle upon Tyne, we had almost daily offers of plants, pots and other bits and pieces like wormeries and wood on our local Vertical Veg Facebook group. As you can see elsewhere in this book, it is possible to grow almost completely for free. Growing, wholly or partly outside consumer culture, can help us to learn that there is a different and, I believe, more rewarding way of doing things.

Reduce our reliance on the industrial food system

By growing some of our own food, we can take a first step in reducing our reliance on supermarkets. Even if we just cut down on buying expensive and wastefully packaged products like herbs and salad bagged in plastic, we take back a bit of control.

Support urban food-growing projects

The politics of food are most keenly felt in less well-off urban areas, where many people live in food deserts, with local food options reduced to takeaway meals or heavily processed food. The lack of access to fresh, affordable fruit and veg exacerbates the issues of health and well-being. In these areas, people also experience the highest barriers to starting to grow their own food: lack of time and cash, and often few role models to show what is possible. However, this doesn't mean that growing food in containers can't happen in these places. With a little knowledge and access to some compost, pots and seeds, anyone with a little outdoor space can learn to grow a supply of affordable, fresh and nutritious food – and benefit from the other emotional and well-being benefits of growing.

Urban food-growing projects often struggle for funding and need our help and financial support. We might volunteer to mentor new growers or help to run planting sessions. We can also try to persuade governments and local authorities that investing in urban food growing and training can deliver multiple benefits, as we have seen.

Get involved in the local food movement

There are many excellent organisations working to promote local food and a fairer food system. The Landworkers' Alliance and Via Campesina work with small-scale farmers and are campaigning for more sustainable food and food sovereignty. Food sovereignty is about putting producers and consumers at the centre of the food system, ensuring that producers get a fair deal and consumers get better access to good, affordable and culturally appropriate food.

Incredible Edible work to inspire and support communities to create more communal growing spaces. Open Kitchens use communities and restaurants to cook and deliver free meals.

There are also hundreds of other small, dedicated, community projects doing fantastic grassroots work with local people – for example, OrganicLea and Capital Growth in London, and Greening Wingrove, Scotswood Natural Community Garden and the Comfrey Project in Newcastle upon Tyne. Do check out what is happening in your area for more inspiration. Local growing projects are great places to connect with others who are inspired to create a more just world.

Grow for food security

The idea that food growing in small spaces could make any meaningful contribution to food security is usually overlooked or dismissed without further thought. But my experiments and rough calculations show that it is possible to grow in the region of 5–15 per cent by value of a household's food in a small space like a patio, balcony or front yard. This isn't insignificant.

True, small-space urban growing can never meet all – or even a major part – of our food needs. Most high-calorie cereal crops need more space than is easy to find in cities. However, small urban spaces are highly suitable for growing salad leaves, herbs and soft fruit. These are high in value *and* nutritional content. By growing these at home, more of us can supplement our diets with super-fresh, affordable and nutritious food. In the UK, for example, we have to import around half the food we need, which

makes us vulnerable to any disruptions, whether that be from trade disputes, climate disasters (such as damage to crops from bad storms and flooding, which are already on the rise), or other natural or manmade catastrophes. In times of food shortage, small-space growing has the potential to make a big difference to the quality of our diets, enabling governments to focus efforts on non-perishable staples like wheat and rice.

For the future, urban food growing – in small spaces at home, at community projects and in urban farms – also has the potential to change the way we structure our food system. We can make it more efficient and less wasteful by growing most of our perishable food, like soft fruit and salad, closer to where we need it. This would mean that the food we transport would be mainly non-perishable items like rice, pulses and cooking

Only a small space is needed to provide some fresh, highly nutritious food that can make a difference to the quality of our diets.

Front yard foraging: my daughter, with purple-stained fingers, enjoys snacking from the garden.

After moving to London from a home with a garden in Bangladesh, Helal Ahmed found joy in being able to grow with his daughter on his balcony in Somers Town, London.

oil, reducing the need for refrigerated storage and transport.

There are millions of us in cities with enough space to grow a little food at home. If we can support more people to grow, there is the potential to make a significant contribution to our food supply, as well as provide more nutritious food – and re-skill the population in the art of growing food.

In our uncertain future, farming and food growing is likely to become increasingly important. As farmer and writer Brenda Schoep says on her website: 'My grandfather used to say that once in your life you need a doctor, a lawyer, a policeman and a preacher but every day, three times a day, you need a farmer.' In an era of 'cheap', abundant food, it's easy to forget how reliant we are on those who grow food for us.

Grow for and with children

Most kids love getting their hands into the soil, sowing seeds and watching them come up. There is something totally different to the whole experience of picking, podding and eating a freshly grown pea than a bowl of boiled peas from the freezer. Or of getting purple-stained fingers after popping blackberries and raspberries straight into the mouth from the plant, instead of eating them from a plastic punnet. Living plants offer a fuller sensory experience that encourages greater experimentation. I've done workshops with children who don't normally eat much salad and watched them polish off whole trays of pea shoots and even strongly flavoured land cress. Children also love picking and scrunching fresh herbs, immersing themselves in the smells and concocting their own perfumes and magic potions.

Container growing at home offers those of us without gardens the opportunity to grow with our children, grandchildren and next-door neighbours. There is something a bit miraculous about being able to give children the chance to pick berries and leaves in the middle of the city.

If you are growing with kids, you'll want to grow things they like to eat. Tom Moggach, who runs the outdoor learning at Rhyl Primary School in London, helped compile this list of kids' favourites:

Sorrel – a popular plant that has a lemony kick.

Strawberries – alpine strawberries fruit over several months and make the perfect foraging snack.

Pea shoots and trays of other microgreens – everybody loves these.

Podded peas – make a nice alternative for the lunchbox.

Nasturtiums and other edible flowers – for the fun and novelty of eating flowers.

Potatoes – children love harvesting potatoes!

And anything else that captures kids' imaginations – for example, growing some of the ingredients for their favourite dish, maybe tomatoes and basil for a pizza. My daughter loves the Chilean guavas and the Japanese wineberries that we grow.

Other fun activities to do with kids in a small container garden include bug hunts, making herb potions and perfumes, setting up a wormery, making bamboo wigwams for runner beans, decorating signs and labels for plants, making an urban scarecrow, drying herbs to make tea, potpourri or lavender bags, making a basin pond, saving seeds (such as tomato, sunflower or nasturtium) or growing some microgreens or storecupboard seeds (for instance, coriander, mustard, fennel or chickpeas).

People who decide to grow food later in life are often heavily influenced by memories of growing as a child. It's another reason to give children the chance to grow.

Grow for well-being at work

A lot of workplaces have an empty rooftop, car park or other place where plants can be grown in containers. As well as looking good and creating relaxing and creative spaces, office container gardens can be used to bring employees together and provide salad ingredients for staff lunches and fresh herbal teas as well as healthy fruits and rejuvenating fragrances like lavender.

An office container garden can be designed to reflect the organisation and the interests of its employees. Some staff might be motivated by a recycled garden, others by a beautiful or fragrant garden. Design the garden to take into account the time and resources available. Even a few well-chosen pots can look good, create a talking point, and will not be too much work to maintain.

Herbs and fruit trees are relatively low-maintenance and offer beauty and fragrance as well as leaves to pick for fresh herb teas or fruits to snack on. Alternatively, for a quick, one-off growing project, a crop of microgreens can be grown in just two or three weeks and then shared in a communal meal. Or a variety of different chillies can be grown for an office chilli-tasting session.

It is also possible to reduce food waste in the office by composting it and then using it in the gardens.

Don't overlook the fact that container gardens do need regular attention. Any successful office garden needs one or two people to oversee it and a daily watering routine (or an automatic watering system). An afterwork or lunchtime gardening session once a week or month can be a nice way for people to get together and keep on top of the seasonal jobs at the same time.

Conclusion

Growing a Better Future

Growing food in small spaces at home has the potential to change lives and build communities and green cities. A bold assertion for something as gentle as growing in pots, some might think. But this is my personal experience, backed up by talking to and working with hundreds of people growing food in containers in the city. It's what inspires and excites me, and it's why I started Vertical Veg to support more people to grow.

Living in the city, the delicate and precious web of life is often invisible to us. Growing food at home and in our local communities can help to deal with the disconnection from nature – and our food supply – that many argue is at the root of our environmental crisis. It's all too easy to live only distantly aware of how the resilience of life on earth comes from both its abundance and its diversity – and how all life, even aphids and flies, are integral to a healthy planet. Growing our own food is no quick-fix solution to the scale of the environmental problems we face, but it does offer a window through which we can forge a closer connection with nature:

watching the miracle of seeds germinating, observing bees, hoverflies and wasps pollinating, and replicating the bacterial and fungal wonder of the forest floor in wormeries.

Growing and tasting food we've produced ourselves raises our awareness about the food we buy, prompting us to ask more questions about where and how it is grown. By increasing our broader awareness of where food comes from, the work that goes into producing it and the benefits of local, sustainable food systems, we can help ensure our choices are better informed.

Growing our own food can also offer one small part of the solution to the problem of urban food deserts, where access to fresh fruit and vegetables is non-existent or extremely limited. Growing fresh, affordable food in areas where it is hard or impossible to buy can enable communities to take back some control over the food they eat, creating a supply of good-quality, nutritious fruit and vegetables, irrespective of food prices in the shops or changes in household income.

Finally, food growing – whether at home or locally – can bring people of all ages and from all backgrounds together. It offers chances for the kinds of positive, informal everyday interaction that builds community as well as relationships between neighbours, to help address social isolation and to make a significant contribution to the rebuilding of connections between diverse groups in local communities.

Yet the barriers to growing at home are also greatest in the places where it could be of most benefit. Convenient, affordable places to buy compost and seeds rarely exist in areas where it is difficult or impossible to buy fresh produce. For those who have not grown before, the risk of investing money for an uncertain reward is often too high. Most

significantly, perhaps, vast swathes of the population simply do not have access to ground in which to grow. A 2020 survey of Ordnance Survey Map data highlighted that 20 per cent of households across the UK (in town and country) do not have a private garden. This figure rises when other markers of inequality are considered: 32 per cent of Asian households and 50 per cent of Black households do not have access to a garden of their own. This figure rises further in densely populated urban areas – in Somers Town, in the Borough of Camden, London, for example, 79 per cent of homes do not have a private garden. In central Newcastle upon Tyne, the figure is 58 per cent. This survey also revealed that people who are unemployed or in low-wage jobs are almost three times as likely as those in managerial or professional jobs to be without a garden.

In the future, the number of households without gardens is only likely to increase. Over half of the world's population lived in cities in 2018, and this is predicted to rise to over two-thirds by 2050, according to the UN. So, many more households will need to look to the small spaces that they do have if they wish to grow food at home. There is huge potential here: a small container garden on a patio, rooftop, balcony or windowsill can provide a restful oasis of green, a connection to the natural world, and fresh food, too.

Through my work with Vertical Veg, I've realised that many others have had the same experience. I've come across thousands of people who have discovered that growing food – even in just a few containers – can be transformative. Some use it as a route to support a plant-based diet or simply to eat more unprocessed food. Others get more involved in their local community, organising plant or seed swaps, helping out at or setting up community gardens, or running planting days and workshops. Some find that it improves their mental health and well-being

Interacting with plants in the city can be relaxing and healing as well as connect us with nature. Even a windowsill is large enough to grow a good crop of herbs like mint.

or increases their sense of belonging in the city, while other people get involved in the politics of food, campaigning for change or helping out at local initiatives like food banks.

It's also clear to me that many more people would like to grow food if they had the opportunity. My Facebook page, set up without previous experience of using the platform or a marketing budget, became more popular than several multi-million-pound national gardening charities in the UK, attracting over 200,000 'likes' from 2012–2016 when I ran it most actively. There are many other signs that the interest in growing our own food is increasing. During the 2020 Covid pandemic, seed retailers were reporting a threefold – even a tenfold – increase in sales of vegetable seeds. In a community project in 2021 in Newcastle upon Tyne, we knocked on several hundred doors of homes on two long streets that don't have gardens, offering people the chance to sow and grow a tray of microgreens. We were overwhelmed to find that between eight and nine out of every ten people who answered the door were keen to try and grow something, including a significant number who'd never grown anything in their life before.

Still, it's important not to underestimate the barriers and challenges that prevent people from moving from enthusiasm to the reality of a lush, productive container garden. Lack of time is clearly a major issue, as is the cost of compost and containers, or access to them. Lack of knowledge or experience and lack of visible role models are also significant hurdles, as are buildings that are designed without any viable growing space and landlords that ban growing on their property. But much can be done to help reduce these barriers and enable more people to get the materials they need to grow conveniently and affordably. More community growing projects could stock the basic needs for food growing – compost and seeds – and make them available at cost price or for

Mohammad Afzal Choudry and Mrs Nasim Afzal display their first crop of microgreens – when offered the chance, over 80 per cent of residents of two streets in Newcastle upon Tyne wanted to grow something.

containers to urban residents. Architects and town planners can also help by designing every home with space to grow food. Local and national governments can incentivise planning applications to incorporate well-designed food-growing elements: fitting balconies with containers and a water butt or hose for easy watering, for example.

More scientific research could be undertaken in this area, too. For example, we need to learn more about how to grow nutrient-dense food in containers, how to make and sustain healthy, productive and sustainable growing media that don't require regular replacement and how to enable more of our urban food waste to be recycled for food growing.

free to local residents. National and local governments could subsidise the cost of container gardens, particularly for those on low incomes in areas where allotments are in short supply, or make small grants available.

More could be done to raise awareness about how much food it is possible to grow in containers, how to design a low-maintenance container garden and how to use homegrown produce like herbs in everyday cooking, so that more people are aware of their potential.

Gardening programmes, magazines, charities, health organisations and the relevant local government departments can focus a more proportionate amount of their activity on the needs of all those who don't have a garden, and try to provide them with inspiring and reliable information about growing in containers.

Community growing projects and urban farmers could be supported to offer more workshops and training in food growing in

I've found that container growing at home offers maximum convenience, bringing nature and fresh food to the doorstep and windowsill, as well as a sense of deep personal fulfilment and pride. But most, if not all, of the arguments outlined here also apply to other urban food growing, including community growing projects, allotments and urban farms. Indeed, increasing the synergy between all forms of urban growing – through sharing skills, knowledge and resources – could make growing at home more accessible and viable for many.

Food is essential to human life, and I believe greater engagement with its production can help us address some of the problems which have become endemic to urban living. I believe that growing at home can be a catalyst to wider change. It has the potential to be a valuable stepping stone towards a more connected and sustainable future, full of happier and healthier people. Creating green oases in previously barren spaces has given me profound satisfaction and pleasure. I hope that it will give you great joy, too.

Acknowledgements

One of the great pleasures of working in the food-growing world is the kindness and generosity of other food growers. I have met so many people who have unhesitatingly shared their wisdom and experience. My growing – and this book – are informed by hundreds of these exchanges. Any errors and mistakes are, of course, entirely my own. There are too many people to thank everyone individually, but I'd particularly like to acknowledge the help of the following:

I learned the basics of how to grow – and how to teach growing – from Ru Leathland at OrganicLea. I learned about herbs from Lorraine Melton at Herbal Haven, chillies from Steve Waters at South Devon Chilli Farm, tomatoes from Nick Chenhall at Tomato Growing, unusual edible crops from Anton Rosenfeld and Sally Cunningham at Garden Organic, and Paul Barney at Edulis. Mark Diacono at Otter Farm expanded my knowledge of plants for flavour. Lewis McNeill of the Orchard Project and Niels Corfield shared invaluable tips on growing fruit, Tom Moggach on growing with kids.

Catherine Dawson at Melcourt and Ben Raskin of the Soil Association helped me understand more about compost and the different ingredients that are used to make it. Steve Willis in Australia, Elisabeth Spohr Canani in Brazil, and Abeer Baghdadi in Saudi Arabia shared their knowledge and experience of growing in the heat. Murhala Zigabe in the Democratic Republic of Congo inspired me with his ingenuity and productive container gardens created on almost zero budget.

Kate Bradbury shared her passion and expertise on wildlife in small spaces, Charles Dowding on winter growing (and much more), Peter Brinch on saving seeds and biodynamics, Hedvig Murray on permaculture, Jennifer Lauruol on designing a container garden, Woody and Ken at Bubble House and Rhonda Sherman on everything about worms and wormeries, Elizabeth Quinn on food and nutrition, and Julie Smith of Capital Growth on growing in windy places.

The Vertical Veg community of container growers from around the world has been an ongoing and invaluable source of inspiration and learning. Many individuals have also generously helped fund the running costs of Vertical Veg over the years. I'm particularly indebted to those who joined me early on in my container-growing journey, including Darja Fišer, Valerie Fairbank, Therese Jaiffer, Janne Toft Jensen, Rod Clayton, Rachel Brooks, Susan Seymour, Alok Shah, Sara Paasch Knudsen, Becca Clark and Abeer Baghdadi.

I'd also like to thank Willem Van Cotthem for all the work he does to raise the profile of container growing on his Container Gardening Facebook Group, the Real Farming Conference for tirelessly working to change how food is grown, and all the community growing projects up and down our lands that do so much to give more people the opportunity to grow and pick and taste real food in the city. And all those who I know, with my appalling memory, that I've forgotten to thank.

A lot of other people have helped behind the scenes. The brilliant photographer, Clare Bowes, took many wonderful photos to help lift this book. Andy Jones and Catherine Dawson read through various chapters and offered invaluable feedback – and my old friend, Pilgrim Beart, kindly read the entire manuscript and made lots of helpful suggestions. The good folk at Chelsea Green have all been a joy to work with, guiding and helping me through the whole, rather daunting, process of writing my first book. I'm particularly grateful to Muna Reyal for her calm, unflappable support, thoughtful suggestions and tireless work in the editing.

Above all, I want to thank my wife Helen for her unfailing encouragement and support while I've pursued this passion for growing in containers over the last decade. Vertical Veg and this book wouldn't be able to exist without her.

Further Reading

None of these books is specifically focused on container growing, but they all include a great deal of useful and relevant information.

General food-growing and gardening books

Two excellent general handbooks for growing vegetables:

Dowding, Charles. *Organic Gardening: The Natural No-Dig Way*. Green Books, 2013
Larkcom, Joy. *Grow Your Own Vegetables*. Frances Lincoln, 2013

For a reference book on all aspects of gardening – everything from design to seed saving – this answers many common questions:

Pears, Pauline. *HDRA Encyclopedia of Organic Gardening*. Dorling Kindersley, 2001

What to grow

For an overview of oriental vegetables, including mizuna and pak choi, many of which are ideally suited to containers and small spaces:

Larkcom, Joy, *Oriental Vegetables*. Frances Lincoln, London, 2007

For an excellent overview of all the different salad leaves and edible flowers:

Larkcom, Joy. *The Organic Salad Garden*. Frances Lincoln, 2003

For what to grow in winter, when to sow and how to look after them:

Dowding, Charles. *How to Grow Winter Vegetables*. Green Books, 2011

And for ideas on what to grow to create a beautiful edible garden:

Larkcom, Joy. *Creative Vegetable Gardening*. Hachette UK, 2017

Seed saving

Stickland, Sue, and Susanna Kendall. *Back Garden Seed Saving: Keeping Our Vegetable Heritage Alive*. Eco-Logic Books, 2008

Soil life, wormeries and fertilisers

For a handy, short introductory book to wormeries:

Pilkington, George. *Composting with Worms – Why Waste Your Waste*. Eco-Logic Books/Worldly Good, 2005

For a more comprehensive and advanced look at wormeries:

Sherman, Rhonda. *The Worm Farmer's Handbook: Mid-to Large-Scale Vermi-composting for Farms, Businesses, Municipalities, Schools, and Institutions.* Chelsea Green Publishing, 2018

For a fascinating look at a wide range of homemade fertilisers and how to make them:

Palmer, Nigel. *The Regenerative Grower's Guide to Garden Amendments: Using Locally Sourced Materials to Make Mineral and Biological Extracts and Ferments.* Chelsea Green Publishing, 2020

For an introduction to soil life and how it contributes to a healthy garden:

Miessler, Diane. *Grow Your Soil!: Harness the Power of the Soil Food Web to Create Your Best Garden Ever.* Storey Publishing, 2020

For a more in-depth look at the soil food web and how it relates to growing:

Lowenfels, Jeff, and Wayne Lewis. *Teaming with Microbes: The Organic Gardener's Guide to the Soil Food Web.* Timber Press, 2010.

For details on how healthy plants become more resistant to pests, see John Kempf's Plant Health Pyramid:

www.advancingecoag.com/plant
-health-pyramid

For an interesting look at nutrient-dense food and ideas on how to grow it:

Solomon, Steve, and Erica Reinheimer. *The Intelligent Gardener: Growing Nutrient-Dense Food.* New Society Publishers, 2012

Wildlife

Kate Bradbury helps us to see garden wildlife with fresh eyes and offers practical ideas for gardening with wildlife:

Bradbury, Kate. *Wildlife Gardening: For Everyone and Everything.* Bloomsbury Publishing, 2019

Growing more food in a small space

A detailed look at a wide range of techniques for growing more food in small spaces:

Hunt, Marjorie B., and Brenda Bortz. *High-Yield Gardening: How to Get More from Your Garden Space and More from Your Gardening Season.* Rodale, 1986

For a free, downloadable guide to rooftop gardening, including detailed instructions on making containers with reservoirs and a gravity fed automatic water system:

Germain, Amélie, Benjamin Grégoire, Ismaël Hautecoeur, Rotem Ayalon, and André Bergeron. *Guide to Setting Up Your Own Edible Rooftop Garden.* Alternatives and the Rooftop Gardens Project, 2008. http://archives2019 .rooftopgardens.alternatives.ca//sites /rooftopgardens.alternatives.ca/files /ready_to_grow.pdf.pdf.

For some historical perspective on urban food growing, this fascinating book shares how vegetables were grown intensively in Paris before the railways changed everything:

Aquatias, P. *Intensive Culture of Vegetables on the French System.* Applewood Books, 2009 (first published in 1913)

Ben Hartman runs a small farm but a lot of his 'lean farm' ideas can be applied by anyone serious about trying to grow more food in a small space:

Hartman, Ben. *The Lean Farm Guide to Growing Vegetables: More In-Depth Lean*

Techniques for Efficient Organic Production. Chelsea Green Publishing, 2017

Learning from Indigenous cultures

Prior to the Industrial Revolution, humans pioneered growing across all continents for thousands of years, usually in far greater harmony with the earth. There is much we can learn from our ancestors. See for example:

Kimmerer, Robin Wall. *Braiding Sweetgrass: Indigenous Wisdom, Scientific Knowledge and the Teachings of Plants.* Milkweed Editions, 2015

Pascoe, Bruce. *Dark Emu: Aboriginal Australia and the Birth of Agriculture.* Magabala Books, 2018

Urban traffic pollution

Ercilla-Montserrat, M., P. Muñoz, J.I. Montero, X. Gabarrell, and J. Rieradevall, 2018. *A study on air quality and heavy metals content of urban food produced in a Mediterranean city (Barcelona).* Journal of Cleaner Production, 195, pp.385–395.

Säumel, Ina, Iryna Kotsyuk, Marie Hölscher, Claudia Lenkereit, Frauke Weber and Ingo Kowarik. "How healthy is urban horticulture in high traffic areas? Trace metal concentrations in vegetable crops from plantings within inner city neighbourhoods in Berlin, Germany." Environmental Pollution 165, 2012

Other

Dewhirst, Rebecca A., Graham JJ Clarkson, Steve D. Rothwell, and Stephen C. Fry. "Novel insights into ascorbate retention and degradation during the washing and post-harvest storage of spinach and other salad leaves." *Food chemistry* 233 (2017): 237–246.

Lappé, Frances Moore. *Diet for a small planet: The book that started a revolution in the way Americans eat.* Ballantine Books, 2021.

Shrubsole, Guy. *Who Owns England?: How We Lost Our Green and Pleasant Land and How To Take It Back.* William Collins, 2019.

Growing websites

Vertical Veg: Verticalveg.org.uk (my website) for container growing tips, podcasts, videos and monthly seasonal tips. There is also a Vertical Veg Community you can join on Facebook.

Charles Dowding: charlesdowding.co.uk is a treasure trove of information on vegetable growing – see his excellent YouTube channel, too.

Garden Organic and the RHS: gardenorganic.org.uk and rhs.org.uk are two useful sources of general and reliable gardening information as well as advice on plant-specific pests and diseases.

Malawi-Chitukuko: malawidevelopment.wordpress.com for lots of interesting experiments and case studies on growing food in pots.

Support the movement

Via Campesina and the Landworkers' Alliance: viacampesina.org and landworkersalliance.org.uk are two organisations working to create a better food and land-use system for everyone.

Other useful websites

Capital Growth: capitalgrowth.org has the useful 'Harvest-ometer' online tool as well as info on London growing. See also their parent organisation, Sustain (sustainweb.org), the alliance for better food and farming.

Growing Real Food for Nutrition (GRFFN): grffn.org is a project dedicated to growing good-quality food that is both more nutritious and pest-resistant.

Open-Pollinated Seeds: open-pollinated-seeds.org.uk for useful information on seeds and seed saving.

Plants for a Future (PFAF): pfaf.org is a database of over 7,000 edible plants.

Some useful suppliers (for UK growers)

Compost: melcourt.co.uk for excellent peat-free compost; fertilefibre.com for coir bricks.

Fertilisers: fertilefibre.com for vegan fertiliser; Biocanna and BioBizz for good-quality organic liquid feeds; Sea Nymph for liquid seaweed feeds.

Good-quality seeds for the home grower: seedcooperative.org.uk; realseeds.co.uk; tamarorganics.co.uk; southdevonchillifarm.co.uk.

Plants: for an excellent choice of herb plants, try herbalhaven.com and poyntzfieldherbs.co.uk; for good-quality fruit bushes and trees suitable for containers, see kenmuir.co.uk.

Seeds in bulk for microgreens: hodme-dods.co.uk (for peas and fava beans for shoots); skysprouts.co.uk (for radish, rocket, broccoli and sunflower seeds); cn-seeds.co.uk (brilliant selection but high minimum order).

Tools: implementations.co.uk for copper trowels; greenhousesensation.co.uk for Quadgrow self-watering planters; haws.co.uk for watering cans with good-quality brass roses.

Worms: bubblehouseworms.com for worms bred in the UK.

Glossary of Gardening Terms

I've tried, where possible, to avoid gardening jargon. But the following words are widely used by growers and are useful for you to know.

Anaerobic An absence of oxygen. Water-logged soil is depleted of the air that plants need to breathe.

Annual A plant that flowers, seeds and dies in its first year.

Biennial A plant that lives for two years, usually flowering and seeding in its second year.

Bokashi A form of composting, invented in Japan, that ferments food waste in a bin by using bacteria (Effective Microorganisms) which are added in a special bran.

Bolting When a plant, for example, lettuce or chard, flowers before it should. It's usually a sign that a plant is stressed.

Checked growth When a plant starts growing vigorously but then stalls. It is caused by stress – for example, a hot or cold snap.

Cloche A plastic or glass cover to protect plants from weather – purchased or homemade from hoops and polythene.

Foliar feed Dilute fertiliser sprayed on the leaves of plants.

Hardening off The process of putting young plants outside for a few hours each day to help them acclimatise to wind and temperature fluctuations.

Hardy A plant that can tolerate frost (unlike tender plants which cannot) – some plants are hardier and can survive colder temperatures than others.

Hybrid The offspring of two plants of different varieties. Different vegetable varieties can be crossed, with human intervention, to create new, often more vigorous, varieties, labelled on seed packs as 'F1 Hybrids'.

Mulch A layer of paper, wood chip, stones, compost, leaves, straw or even plastic, added to the top of the soil. Mulches help to retain water and some also feed plants.

Open-pollinated Plants that are pollinated by natural mechanisms (insects, wind or birds). Most heritage and heirloom varieties are open-pollinated.

Perennial A plant that lives for more than two years. Perennials include globe artichokes, sorrel, most fruits and many herbs.

Propagate To breed a plant. Plants are most commonly propagated from seed, cuttings (many herbs), tubers (like potatoes) or by dividing the plant (some herbs).

Propagator/heated propagator A tray, often with a transparent Perspex lid, that helps provide the right conditions for seeds and cuttings. Heated propagators maintain a constant temperature to improve germination. Often used for chillies, tomatoes and cuttings.

Protection A cloche or fleece material to keep plants warm and protect them from wind.

Subtropical crop Crops from the subtropics, such as tomatoes, potatoes and chillies.

Temperate crop Crops that originate from temperate zones, such as peas, lettuce and mustards, which usually grow best in cooler weather.

Tender Plants such as basil or chillies that will be damaged or killed by frost and therefore cannot be moved outside until all threat of frost has passed.

Topdressing A topdressing is a way of feeding plants by sprinkling a small amount of fertiliser onto the top of the soil.

Transplant To move a small plant, usually a seedling, into a larger pot.

Plant List

This list provides UK and US common names, and the botanical name, for the main vegetables, herbs and fruit featured in the book.

Achocha/fat baby (*Cyclanthera brachystachya*)

African kale (*Brassica oleracea* Acephala Group)

Agretti (*Salsola soda*)

Alpine strawberry (*Fragaria vesca*)

Amaranth (*Amaranthus*)

Anise hyssop (*Agastache foeniculum*)

Apple (*Malus domestica*)

Asparagus kale (*Brassica oleracea* Acephala Group)

Aubergine/eggplant (*Solanum melongena*)

Basil (*Ocimum basilicum*)

Bay (*Laurus nobilis*)

Bean sprout/mung bean (*Vigna radiata*)

Beetroot/beet (*Beta vulgaris*)

Beet spinach (*Beta vulgaris* subsp. *cicla* var. *cicla*)

Blackberry (*Rubus fruticosus*)

Blackcurrant sage (*Salvia microphylla* var. *microphylla*)

Black mustard (*Brassica nigra*)

Blueberry (*Vaccinium corymbosum*)

Borage (*Borago officinalis*)

Broad/fava bean (*Vicia faba*)

Broad-leaved sorrel (*Rumex acetosa*)

Broccoli (*Brassica oleracea* Italica Group)

Brussels sprouts (*Brassica oleracea* Gemmifera Group)

Buckler-leaf sorrel (*Rumex scutatus*)

Buckwheat (*Fagopyrum esculentum*)

Bush basil (*Ocimum minimum*)

Cabbage (*Brassica oleracea* Capitata Group)

Carrot (*Daucus carota*)

Cauliflower (*Brassica oleracea* Botrytis Group)

Celeriac (*Apium graveolens* var. *rapaceum*)

Celery (*Apium graveolens* var. *dulce*)

Chard (*Beta vulgaris* subsp. *cicla* var. *flavescens*)

Chervil (*Anthriscus cerefolium*)

Chia (*Salvia hispanica*)

Chickpea (*Cicer arietinum*)

Chicory (*Cichorium intybus*)

Chilean guava (*Ugni molinae*)

Chilli pepper (*Capsicum annuum* var. *annuum* Longum Group; 'Alberto's Locoto' is a cultivar of *Capsicum pubescens*)

Chinese artichoke (*Stachys affinis*)

Chinese cabbage (*Brassica rapa* Pekinensis Group)

Chives (*Allium schoenoprasum*)

Chocolate peppermint (*Mentha × piperita* f. *citrata* 'Chocolate')

Choy sum (*Brassica rapa* var. *parachinensis*)

Coriander/cilantro (*Coriandrum sativum*)

Courgette/zucchini (*Cucurbita pepo*)

Cranberry (*Vaccinium macrocarpon*)

Cucumber (*Cucumis sativus*)

Curly-leaved parsley (*Petroselinum crispum*)

Daubenton's kale (*Brassica oleracea* var. *ramosa*)

Daylilies (*Hemerocallis*)

Dill (*Anethum graveolens*)

Endive (*Cichorium endivia*)

Fava/field bean/small broad bean (*Vicia faba*)

Fennel (*Foeniculum vulgare*)

Fenugreek (*Trigonella foenum-graecum*)

Fig (*Ficus carica*)

Florence fennel (*Foeniculum vulgare* var. *azoricum*)

Flat-leaved parsley (*Petroselinum crispum* var. *neapolitanum*)

French/green bean (*Phaseolus vulgaris*)

French marigold (*Tagetes patula*)

Garden mint/spearmint (*Mentha spicata*)

Garlic (*Allium sativum*)

Garlic chives (*Allium tuberosum*)

German camomile (*Matricaria recutita*)

Ginger (*Zingiber officinale*)

Globe artichoke (*Cynara cardunculus* Scolymus Group)

Golden oregano (*Origanum vulgare* 'Aureum')

Gooseberry (*Ribes uva-crispa*)

Grape (*Vitis vinifera*)

Greek oregano (*Origanum vulgare* subsp. *hirtum*)

Haloon (*Lepidium sativum*)

Hardy kiwi (*Actinidia arguta*)

Honeyberry (*Lonicera caerulea* var. *kamtschatica*)

Hooker's onion (*Allium hookeri*)

Hops (*Humulus lupulus*)

Japanese wineberry (*Rubus phoenicolasius*)

Jerusalem artichoke (*Helianthus tuberosus*)

Kailaan/Chinese broccoli (*Brassica oleracea* Alboglabra Group)

Kale (*Brassica oleracea* Acephala Group)

Lamb's lettuce/corn salad/mache (*Valerianella locusta*)

Land cress/American cress (*Barbarea verna*)

Lavender (*Lavandula* species)

Leek (*Allium porrum*)

Lemon balm (*Melissa officinalis*)

Lemon grass (*Cymbopogon citratus*)

Lemon thyme (*Thymus citriodorus*)

Lemon verbena (*Aloysia citrodora*)

Lettuce (*Lactuca sativa*)

Lovage (*Levisticum officinale*)

Malabar spinach (*Basella alba*)

Mangetout/snow pea (*Pisum sativum* var. *macrocarpon*)

Marjoram (*Origanum majorana*)

Mashua (*Tropaeolum tuberosum*)

Mibuna (*Brassica rapa* var. *japonica*)

Mint (*Mentha*)

Minutina/Erba Stella/buck's-horn plantain (*Plantago coronopus*)

Mizuna (*Brassica rapa* subsp. *nipposinica* var. *laciniata*)

Mooli/daikon (*Raphanus sativus* 'Longipinnatus')

Moroccan mint (*Mentha spicata* var. *crispa* 'Moroccan')

Mouse melon (*Melothria scabra*)

Mustard (*Brassica juncea*)

Myrtle (*Myrtus communis*)

Nasturtium (*Tropaeolum majus*)

New Zealand spinach (*Tetragonia tetragonoides*)

Oca/New Zealand oca (*Oxalis tuberosa*)

Onion (*Allium cepa*)

Orach (*Atriplex hortensis*)

Oregano (*Origanum vulgare*)

Oyster plant (*Mertensia maritima*)

Pak choi/bok choi (*Brassica rapa* Chinensis Group)

Parsnip (*Pastinaca sativa*)

Pea (*Pisum sativum*)

Peppermint (*Mentha* × *piperita*)

Potato (*Solanum tuberosum*)

Potato bean/American groundnut (*Apios americana*)

Pot marigold (*Calendula officinalis*)

Pumpkin/squash (*Cucurbita maxima*)

Purple basil (*Ocimum basilicum* var. *purpurascens*)

Radish (*Raphanus sativus*)

Raspberry (*Rubus idaeus*)

Redcurrant (*Ribes rubrum*)
Rhubarb (*Rheum × hybridum*)
Rosemary (*Rosmarinus officinalis*)
Runner bean (*Phaseolus coccineus*)
Sage (*Salvia officinalis*)
Salad burnet (*Sanguisorba minor*)
Salad rocket/arugula (*Eruca vesicaria*
    subsp. *sativa*)
Scots lovage (*Ligusticum scoticum*)
Shallot (*Allium cepa* Aggregatum Group)
Shiso perilla (*Perilla frutescens*)
Shungiku/chopsuey greens
    (*Glebionis coronaria*)
Sichuan pepper (*Zanthoxylum piperitum*)
Society garlic (*Tulbaghia violacea*) – in the
    text I also mention *Tulbaghia* 'Fairy Star'
    which is a distinct variety (and I prefer
    to *violacea*).
Sour cherry/morellow cherry (*Prunus cerasus*)
Spinach (*Spinacia oleracea*)
Spring onion/scallion (*Allium cepa*)
Squash (*Cucurbita* species)
Strawberry (*Fragaria × ananassa*)
Sugar snap pea (*Pisum sativum*)
Summer purslane (*Portulaca oleracea*)
Summer savory (*Satureja hortensis*)
Sunflower (*Helianthus annuus*)
Sutherland kale (*Brassica napus*)
Swede/rutabaga (*Brassica napus*
    Napobrassica Group)
Sweet/bell pepper (*Capsicum annuum*
    var. *annuum* Grossum Group)
Sweet cherry (*Prunus avium*)
Sweetcorn (*Zea mays*)
Tarragon (*Artemisia dracunculus*)
Tatsoi (*Brassica rapa* var. *rosularis*)
Texel greens/Ethiopian cabbage
    (*Brassica carinata*)
Thai basil (*Ocimum basilicum* 'Horapha')

Thyme (*Thymus vulgaris*)
Tomatillo (*Physalis ixocarpa*)
Tomato (*Solanum lycopersium*)
Tree spinach (*Chenopodium giganteum*)
Tromboncino squash (*Cucurbita moschata*
    'Tromboncino')
Turnip (*Brassica rapa* Rapifera Group)
Vietnamese coriander (*Persicaria odorata*)
Wasabi (*Eutrema japonicum*)
Wild garlic/ramsons (*Allium ursinum*)
Wild rocket (*Diplotaxis tenuifolia*)
Winter purslane (*Claytonia perfoliata*)
Winter savory (*Satureja montana*)
Yacón (*Smallanthus sonchifolius*)

Months and seasons

Although seasons are used in general throughout the book, we refer to months of the year in some of the cultivation tables and in sections describing in detail how to grow various vegetables, herbs and fruit. These months relate to gardens in the Northern Hemisphere. For gardeners in the Southern Hemisphere, please use the following seasonal equivalents:

January	Mid-winter
February	Late winter
March	Early spring
April	Mid-spring
May	Late spring
June	Early summer
July	Mid-summer
August	Late summer
September	Early autumn
October	Mid-autumn
November	Late autumn
December	Early winter

Image Credits

Index

Page numbers in *italic* indicate tables and illustrations.

About the Author

Clare Bowes

Mark Ridsdill Smith founded Vertical Veg in 2009, after discovering how much food he could grow on the balcony of his flat. His website and Facebook page inspire and support people to grow food in small, urban spaces and Mark has run workshops across the UK, including for Garden Organic and Capital Growth.

Mark has shared his growing experience on BBC Radio 4's *Gardeners' Question Time*, Alan Titchmarsh's *Love Your Garden* on ITV and BBC1's *Countryfile*. He has also written a series of 15 articles for the Guardian's Live Better Campaign and a feature for *Which? Gardening*.